My Indian Jatra

Half a Century Life in India

By

Frances Major

ISBN: 1-4140-3650-7 (e-book)
ISBN: 1-4140-3649-3 (Paperback)

Library of Congress Control Number: 2003098716

This book is printed on acid free paper.

Printed in the United States of America.
Bloomington, IN

1stBooks - rev. 01/21/04

Table of Contents

Dedication

In memory of my parents

Waymon and Etta Major

They provided a home filled with love
and taught me Christian values which are:
love God with all your heart and your neighbor as you self,
find and follow God's plan for your life,
God supplies all the needs of those who follow Him.

The genesis of this book was my attempt to share my life with them.

Preface

Jatra is a word common to all the Indian Languages. It is used when a person makes a journey to worship at holy places. It is sometimes translated as pilgrimage. In South India the Christans have a huge jatra where several thousand go out into the jungle and camp for several days. They spend the days singing, praying and listening to sermons. The event is referred to as Jungle Camp Meetings in the English language.

Following God's call throughout my life has been a spiritual journey for me. The Journey continues in retirement. The book describes my sojourn in and for India. Thus I name these pages MY INDIAN JATRA

Most of the pages are taken directly from letters I wrote to family, friends and supporters with editing as necessary. During my first term, 1946 -1951, there were many exciting historical events such as India's gaining of independence from Great Britain, the creation of the new nation of Pakistan, the assassination of Mahatma Gandhi and the framing of the new constitution for India. About half of the pages of the book were written about those events and my own experiences during that period.

I lived in Calcutta all of the first term and I describe the events that happened in that area of India. The various regions experienced the political events differently. For instance the Muslim — Hindu riots were very serious in Bengal prior to Independence. In northern India the riots took place after freedom came. Religious festivals vary widely in different areas of India.

I am indebted to Ms Doris Hess for the many hours she contributed to reading and correcting the manuscript and for her helpful suggestions.

Foreword

The reader of this book is in for a treat. It affords an unusual glimpse of the life and work of a missionary. It is a missionary journey led by a rare and gifted guide. One who has spent forty two years of Christian service in India has a story to tell and here it is told very well indeed. Anyone who has been a missionary himself and has known hundreds of others who have filled this role, I feel in a position to commend to others this book which deserves a wide reading. It has been my privilege to have known Frances Major for more than half a century and have long observed her work both at close range and from afar.

Frances has had a very clear call to mission service and has fulfilled it with unwavering devotion. She has always displayed simplicity of faith; she has shown this by practicing it. She understands the meaning of the holy life and for decades has striven to live this vocation. It should be encouraging to admirers of Mother Teressa that a Protestant missionary —a Methodist- who lived in the same city at about the same time also was committed to a life of deep devotion and service, especially to the poor. She worked with other Christians of similar commitment. Mrs. Ada Lee (six of her seven children were wiped out in a landslide disaster in Darjeeling in a single night in 1899); Walter and Mabelle Griffiths (likewise heroic champions of the poor — widows and orphans in Calcutta); and a host of other uncelebrated saints of God.

Most of this volume has been generated from letters written by the author to family and friends over several decades. Thus there is a freshness and immediacy about the narrative. Frances is a keen observer; little of significance escaped her sharp eyes. The reader is there, present to the sights and sounds and smells of a teeming Asian metropolis or remote tribal village. She recounts the story of food riots, the coming of Indian Independence, the birth of free India, the genesis of Pakistan, the assassination of Gandhi, the death of Jinnah, the visits to Calcutta of Nehru, of leading churchmen, the Assembly of The World Council of Churches in Delhi. Always in remarkably vivid phrase she portrays the passing scene upon which she makes insightful comments. Mostly, she shows us people, mostly people in need. But also some captives of greed, the sick, the persecuted, the hungry, the forgotten ones of earth; and always we find her serving the least ones in the name of Christ.

While never neglecting the sordidness with which she was surrounded, she has an eye for beauty as well, so we find ourselves awed by the spectacular and overwhelming grandeur of snow covered Mt. Kanchinjanga as viewed from Darjeeling, palm-studded Bengal beaches, the Taj Mahal — resplendent on a full-moon night.

A thoughtful Christian must often wonder <u>what do missionaries do</u>? Again Frances Major pulls back the curtain so that we may see. Of course, she worked in many places — in metropolises like Calcutta and Bombay, but the rural scene and in villages as well. She was a teacher, preacher, foster-mother of orphans, headmistress, evangelist, high school principal, district evangelist, founder of night schools and community centers, finally Treasurer of Methodist Women's work throughout much of India. Through it all she tried — as missionaries are wont to do — to care for the "whole person," to address the need at hand, to do the necessary deed. It is, in fact, hard to describe what missionaries do: perhaps it is best simply to follow them around for a day or two and see! You can do that here.

Frances clearly loves India and her people. She loves Bengal. She loves Calcutta (and wore a badge which said so), while most visitors have seen only its sordid side. She likes to live close to the people in slums in <u>chawls</u> (Bombay/Mumbai) in <u>bustees</u> (Calcutta/Kolkata), but was no less at home among the most needy in India's countless villages. Of course, she knew loneliness, suffered repeated illness, was sometimes under threat, the target of thieves. She does not emphasize these things. Rather, she keeps the focus off herself and concentrates on the plight of others. From time to time she went on furlough to the United States but says almost nothing about these visits. Instead, she seemed eager to get back to India —

where her heart was, where her people were. As I read this book, I experienced a growing pride in the mission of the Church, in rediscovery of what it is to be a faithful missionary, a fresh summons to be a better missionary myself.

James K. Mathews
Bishop, United Methodist Church, (ret)

Chapter 1

THE JATRA BEGINS

One day as I straightened my back and looked back across the cotton fields, I saw my father coming toward me. In spite of his past year of accidents and hospitalization, he still bore himself in an erect proud manner, and he still worked as hard as ever. It was to save him that I insisted upon helping in the cotton fields during this waiting period.

I waved as father waved at me and he kept waving. Soon I could hear what he was saying. "Frances, it's a telegram from the Mission Board". With trembling fingers I read the telegram. "Can book passage for you on S. S. Vulcania leaving October 4. Wire acceptance" October 4 that was just ten days away!

I dropped my cotton picking bag and left the cotton fields to begin my journey to Calcutta, India. The Voice, the Presence that I had discovered between the cotton rows was my companion as I began the final preparation for my journey. I moved as one in an ecstatic dream. I was realizing the fulfillment of a dream - yes, but more than a dream the fulfillment of the call that I had heard several years before. Reports of riots in Calcutta could not dampen my ecstasy.

1

One week later my father took me to the railway station in Greenville, South Carolina where I boarded the train bound for New York. During the journey I had time to review my life and the events leading up to this moment.

I was baptized at an early age at Shiloh Methodist Church, Piedmont, South Carolina. At that time it was a small rural church on a three point charge. Along with my parents, members of that church nurtured me. As there was "preaching" at Shiloh every other Sunday, my father and I often attended the services at the Piedmont Wesleyan Methodist Church. In the summer we attended the Wesleyan Camp Meetings. Often I responded to altar calls in the Wesleyan services. At some point I found the assurance that I was saved. Then I sought for a holy or sanctified life as preached by the Wesleyans. I knew I had to be totally committed to God. I tried to consecrate my life completely to God. The Wesleyans introduced me to missionaries and the challenge of answering God's call.

For my high school education I transferred from Rock Hill to Piedmont High School. My father sent us to Piedmont as Rock Hill High School was not accredited at that time. My father started college but had to drop out for financial reasons. He wanted all his children to attend college. Piedmont High School was four miles from our home. There were no school buses. Father took us to school in the morning, but we usually had to walk home.

Sometimes I would take a break by stopping at the Rampey home on King's Street in Piedmont. Aunt Marion was father's sister. She had thirteen children. The Majors and Rampeys spent many happy times together. I considered Aunt Marion a saint. When I stopped by her house she gave me a snack and discussed spiritual matters with me. At that period she was a great influence in my life. I loved to hear her shout "Glory, Glory to God" as she floated around the church in a spiritual trance. It was like beautiful music. Through her shouting I felt the awesome presence of God.

When I graduated from high school I knew I must go to college, but how? My father struggled to feed and clothe his eleven children. To pay for his tuition fees, my oldest brother, William, walked with a cow the thirteen miles from our home to Central Wesleyan College in Central, S. C. The two brothers in between were very poor students, and there was no mention of their college education. How was father to find the funds to pay my tuition and boarding fees? Perhaps my love affair with a neighbor's son gave him added incentive to get me away. So he sold some land. And I happily enrolled in Central Wesleyan College. The president of the college married my first cousin, Helen Rampey. They took good care of me. The college was much more economical than many other colleges that had offered me some scholarship.

My first year at Central was a very happy one. The student body was predominantly Christian. It was a place with likeminded students. The second year began with a nagging question that would not go away. Was God really calling me to be a missionary in India? Surely not! I was an ordinary student with no gift of singing or speaking like many others of my classmates. Like Moses and others I argued with God about it. Then when the call would not go away and I felt surely it was the voice of God speaking, I found that I was not as totally committed as I thought or professed. With others I sang "I'll Go Where You Want Me to Go". In the second week of January, 1939 I could not concentrate on anything else. I finally came to a point when I could say "yes" and mean it. And in a praise service I testified that I had said yes to a call to India. That brought much peace for awhile.

In March and April of that year Satan tempted me by trying to convince me that this whole Christian experience was bogus. It all centered around my economic plight. At home on the farm there was a terrible fire that killed more than half the dairy cows and all the hay stored in the barn. When I asked for money for the commencement activities and for new clothes my mother wrote that it was impossible to provide. I could not go on the trip with my classmates. I was very depressed. I had always known poverty. But somehow my parents had found a way to provide. When my shoes wore out and there was no money for new ones, I wore my mother's shoes. We lived on milk until the cows went dry due to a drought. Then we ate black-eyed peas Now there was no money and no substitute. My faith was severely tested. But in a wonderful way God let me know that He was real. My classmates came to my rescue. Out of their meager resources they provided for my needs.

I graduated from Central Wesleyan Junior College with a diploma and a teacher's certificate in South Carolina. But I could not find a job. I was driven by my call and put more trust in God than I had previously. Christmas came and I had no job and was dependent upon my parents. At that point I was willing to take any job and was making applications in a variety of places.

My parents and my brother, William, decided that I should join him in the Kentucky Mountain Holiness Association. William, while working in a camp meeting in Michigan, had met Dr. Lela G. McConnell who had founded this mission in the hills of Kentucky. She invited him to teach in the newly started bible school. He accepted and taught there one year. While he was home in Piedmont during the summer of 1939 a flash flood destroyed the buildings and killed some of the staff of the bible school. That fall William went back to the mission and taught in the high school. My brother Paul went with him to attend the high school. Paul, though older than I, had fallen behind me in the grades and had a hard time with school work. Later he was diagnosed with dyslexia.

In January, 1940 I began my journey with the Kentucky Mountain Holiness Association. I was appointed to be a companion with one of the women working with a church on Devils' Creek. I worked with her for six months and learned about the loneliness, isolation and other hardships of this home mission work. It was a marvelous initiation into mission as "faith work." We lived on what God provided. We had all the necessities but not everything we wanted.

During the summer I moved to headquarters where I began working to earn my study in the Kentucky Mountain Bible School. It was a three-year course but I was given one year credit for my study in Central Wesleyan College. My study at the Kentucky Mountain Bible Institute was a time of spiritual growth. I learned to trust God as I studied the Bible in depth and had training including practical experience in Christian leadership. God re-affirmed my call to be a missionary in India. I graduated from Kentucky Mountain Bible Institute in the spring of 1942. What next?

I needed a degree. The best place for me was Marion College, Marion, Indiana which was the Wesleyan degree college where most of the students from Central Wesleyan sought to complete their degree studies. So Marion was my goal. But I had no secure financial provision. In the summer of 1942 I spent time at home with my parents. Waymon, a younger brother, joined the Navy and William volunteered for the air force. Others were subject to the draft. I felt it would be easy to find a job to earn my way through the rest of my education. I wrote to Marion College and sought permission to come a week early in order to spend time looking for a job.

In early September I boarded a greyhound bus in Greenville, SC. In spite of my profession of faith in God to supply all my needs I was a scared little girl on that long trip. My brother had been with me before. Now I was alone. No, not really alone; God was with me. In Indianapolis I changed buses. I sat on the front seat right behind the driver. I talked to the driver and asked him questions about Marion. When he found out I was going to Marion College. He said: "I go right by there. If you want I can stop and let you out there." Giving a silent thank you to God, I said: "thank you for such a favor." When we got there, he stopped, unloaded my small trunk from under the bus, and took it to the girls' dorm. Real service with a smile! Mrs. Charles (Leora) Devol, Dean of Women, welcomed me. As I was early she not only showed me to my room but prepared my breakfast, then the noon meal and the supper. I had expected to scrounge on my own. Mrs. Devol spent a lot of time talking to me during the day, finding out all about me and my ambitions. God was in those conversations. At the end of the day she said: "I am looking for an assistant. I believe you could be my assistant, would you be willing to accept that job?" Wow! That surely was exceedingly abundantly above all I could ask or think. Without much hesitation, I said yes. The job took care of my room, board and tuition. From that time forward it was much easier to trust God to supply my needs.

Mrs. DeVol was a Friends missionary to China. At the time her husband was a prisoner of the Chinese and she did not know where he was. Being a part of her life was further training for my missionary calling. Even when all physical needs are securely met there are many other ways we have to learn to trust God.

I graduated from Marion College, now, Indiana Wesleyan, on June 5, 1944 with a B. S. in education and on August 11, 1944 with a B. A. degree.

I received a teaching appointment to Warren High School, Warren, Indiana. During the year I had appendicitis and had to have surgery. I rejoined my duties of teaching too early and suffered with health problems. I enjoyed the students. But felt my year there was a failure. At the end of the year I refused to promote one of the basketball players who was a good player but a poor student. As a result of that and other things I was not invited back.

So at the end of my first year of teaching (May 1945) I felt like a complete failure. I spent the summer in South Carolina on our farm. Farm work was nothing new for me. My father was not well and needed farm help. Between rows of cotton I talked to God as I had done in earlier years. Miss Lela G. McConnell invited me to teach in the Mt. Carmel High School. Once again God took care of me. I had a wonderful year of teaching in the midst of loving praying saints. In the fall of 1945 they often prayed for me.

We spent Christmas at my home in Piedmont. My brother Paul drove us back. He parked the car, we walked across the swinging bridge and up the hill. I saw Miss McConnell standing at her office window waving at me and shouting something. When I was within hearing distance I understood she had a letter for me. I went straight to her office and read a letter from Dr. Warren McIntyre of Asbury College regarding the need of someone to teach English as a second language to orphan children rescued from starvation by the Lee Memorial Mission in Calcutta, India. Miss McConnell asserted: "Frances, this is for you. This is the answer to our prayers."

I replied to that letter from Dr. McIntyre. By return post he sent me the address of Rev. Walter G. Griffiths, Lee Memorial Mission, 13 Wellington Square, Calcutta, India. I sent my application to him.

9

On Feb 4, 1946 I received the following reply from Dr. Walter G. Griffiths, Lee Memorial Mission, 13 Wellington Square, Calcutta 13, India:

"Your welcome letter of January 9th reached us a few days ago. It was especially welcome as we have been praying that God would send us some help and we believe that this is a token from Him. While there has not yet been an opportunity to consult our trustees, nevertheless, I feel I should write you this exploratory letter and tell you something about the work. Under separate cover (by sea mail) we are sending you some leaflets which will explain more fully what our main kinds of work are. An illustrated booklet is in the press and ought to be available in a week or ten days. These things should help you to think and pray about this matter. In the meantime I shall take the matter up with the trustees who are the ones to whom I must refer such matters.

The story of the Lee Memorial is told briefly in the enclosed leaflet. We are a semi-independent and interdenominational mission, yet linked to the Methodist Church in India. The Lees were Methodists and from the beginning have cooperated with the church on the field although the financial support for the work has come from many different sources and not from the Methodist Board. In the future the Board may cooperate more fully, as they have already begun to contribute a salary, but our plan at present is to keep the interdenominational aspect. We are evangelical and conservative in outlook and from your letter we should judge the same of you. We do not believe that modernism, so-called, has any message for India.

Mrs. Griffiths and I are the only Americans on a staff of some 60 workers. We are overloaded. Our furlough is due in a year from now. Mrs. Griffiths is principal of our schools and has charge of the hostels and a hundred other things as well. There is no end of opportunity in this needy city to do the will of God and render loving service in the name of Christ. From what you write you would seem to be prepared for work such as this Mission is doing. If God should send you it would mean that your main task during the first year would be the study of Bengali. Your Wesleyan background and experience would be welcome here and this emphasis is needed. Only a deep religious experience will hold one through the many adjustments and problems of a missionary life. For this life, while wonderfully rewarding when in the will of God, is not easy and to come to India means to take up one's cross and follow Him. Those who have come prepared for this, and for anything He sends have been of inestimable blessing to this land and its people. You would love our teachers and girls. How much we need one to work with them and pray with them — leading them on to higher things. There is so much to do and from your letter it appears that your background is consistent with the task here. You would live at Wellington Square with us for the present. Many other missionaries who pass through

11

Calcutta come and go and during the past five years we have averaged 25 per day at our table. During the last weeks we've had 50 and above — folks waiting to get boats to U. S. A. and China. We meet hundreds of grand folks. You would love it."

Missionaries of the Lee Memorial have been receiving Rs 150 per month, the equivalent of $50. Living in a family as we do, we pay Rs.60 per month for board and room. Vacations are given each year. As the work is self-supporting, missionaries are asked to do all they can in securing friends to help support the work. Further matters along this line can be discussed later.

The history of the Mission follows.

David H. Lee worked with the William Taylor evangelistic campaigns in India and pastored English speaking congregations. Ada Jones came to India with the Woman's Union Mission in Calcutta. She learned Bengali and was transferred to work with Bengali women in Benaras. Her life was endangered because of her attempt to rescue some of the women who had been forced into prostitution. As a result her mission officials urged her to leave Benaras. She married David Lee and served with him in Bangalore, India until his health broke. He returned to the United States to recover his health. Reaching America, Mr. Lee's health improved and he joined the East Ohio Conference of the Methodist Episcopal Church and served several charges.

During the following years in America the Lee's hearts were in India and it was their constant prayer that they might return. They applied to the Board of Foreign Missions of the Methodist Episcopal Church, but the Board felt unable to send them as by that time they had six children in their family, and Mr. and Mrs. Lee were over age. Nevertheless in a wonderful way God opened the door for their return and they landed in Calcutta in 1894. Bishop James M. Thoburn welcomed them and appointed them to Calcutta. At that time Dr. Frank Warne was the pastor of Thoburn Church and with his help and advice they found a suitable location in Calcutta and began to devote themselves to the service of underprivileged Bengali women and children. At that time work among women was not popular.

A seventh child joined the family. Six of the children attended a school in Darjeeling, in the heart of the Himalaya Mountains. On September 24, 1899 in the landslide at Darjeeling, God called upon them to return to Him six of the children He had given them. Their story has been told around the world. A detailed history of the Mission along with Mrs. Lee's account of the tragedy has been printed in India and is available from the Mission.

Dr. and Mrs. Lee proved the power of the Gospel to sustain and empower in the darkest of human experiences. Believing friends the world over, hearing of their tragic loss and glorious faith, rallied to their support. Gifts received made possible the continuation of the work and a beautiful three storied building was completed in 1909.

Dr. Lee went to be with his Lord and loved ones on June 28, 1924. Mrs. Lee carried on as head of the work until 1940. In March, 1940 Walter and Mabelle Griffith joined Mrs. Lee. Walter became Superintendent and Mrs. Lee became Superintendent Emeritus and continued to live in retirement in one of the units until God called her to His House of Light on June 11, 1948.

Soon after the Griffiths assumed responsibility for the work the second world war found the Japanese at the door of India. The area was bombed. All schools had to be evacuated from the city. While the Indian staff evacuated the boarding students to the mission station in Pakaur, Santal Parganas, Bihar, the Griffith stayed behind in Calcutta. They housed and hosted many missionaries who were evacuated from China, Burma, Malaysia and other countries. They entertained hundreds of U. S. military personnel.

In 1943-44 there was the great Bengal Famine. The staff of Lee Memorial opened and carried on a relief hospital in cooperation with the Bengal State Government. Records show that 522 starving and dying children were picked up from the streets of Calcutta. In addition, Dr. Griffiths was secretary and treasurer of the ecumenical Famine Relief Committee.

On the closing of the relief hospital all the children were taken care of. Many were returned to relatives. Some became wards of the Lee Memorial Mission. And I responded to the call to come and teach them English.

According to Walter Griffiths' notes the following events were taking place as I prepared to go to Calcutta.

"February riots...Anti-foreign and anti-Christian. Thoburn Methodist Church entered by the mob and badly damaged, and burned inside...The Lee Memorial freshly color-washed and decorated was untouched, and we give thanks to God. Before it was realized what was happening some of our missionary guests were insulted and hit by stones on the streets...These days we see many missionaries leaving India and a few, comparatively, arriving. One day we fed 68 missionary guests. Mrs. Lee's 90th birthday. The Sunday Evenings At Home fade out in May. No more G. I.s. We have missed them. So have the children at Elliott Road where they had a regular service for the kiddies every Sunday afternoon. Dear little children they need all the love we can give them and we are so short handed. God be praised for the new missionary who is coming this fall, please God.

She is Miss Frances Major of Piedmont, South Carolina. How thankful we are, too, that the Archibalds have agreed to come this fall to carry on that we may be home for a few months on furlough... Word comes that they have sailed! We are assured that their coming is in the will of God. So you may see the Griffiths trio in 1947...A madness sweeps over Calcutta with the Muslim/Hindu riots beginning August 16th and 15,000 to 20,000 are killed or injured. A paper calls it "The Great Calcutta Killing." Mobs, bent on murder loot and arson surge around our buildings but God spared our large family... How India needs Christ. We must live and proclaim the Gospel before it is too late..."

In April, 1946 the trustees accepted my application and appointed me to work in the Lee Memorial Mission. After giving that news Walter Griffith continued with his instructions.

"May I suggest that you get in touch with the present secretary for India, Dr. T. S. Donohugh, 150 Fifth Ave, New York 11, NY and tell him that I have asked you to do so and ask him to get you the first sailing to India possible after the 15th September and at the same time set in motion the passport formalities. The later are sometimes rather complicated, but I do not know how matters stand at the present time. I shall get Bishop Rockey to enclose a statement to the effect that you have been appointed to the Lee Memorial and that he on behalf of the trustees will guarantee your support while in India, and in possible repatriation. The formality is part of the situation.

"You have received the copy of our illustrated booklet by this time. For the present you will be living at 13 Wellington Square and will have a room on third floor overlooking the park. We have a lovely fellowship here and meet many people who pass through. The days will be full for there is no end of the doing of the Master's will in this place of need.

"May God lead you in the final decision and if His call is yours, give you also an indubitable sense of His presence and of His thrusting you forth into the Harvest Field of Bengal at this particular time".

I followed Dr. Griffiths instructions in his letter and wrote to the Methodist Board of Missions. They treated me like one of their own and took care of all formalities and arranged my travel. As it was war time they explained that they could not give much advance notice of sailings. They instructed me to be ready for a short notice. Again I returned to my home. While I waited I helped my father by picking cotton until the telegram arrived informing me of a sailing date.

I arrived at Penn Station early in the morning. With the instructions I had been given I was able to collect my two small trunks and find my way to the Board of Mission office of the Methodist Church, 150 fifth Avenue, New York. On arrival there I was taken care of by the staff and eleven Methodist Missionaries sailing on the same boat.

Frances Major on board the ship

We boarded the S. S. Vulcania at pier 84 in New York in the morning of October 4 between 9 a. m. and 12 noon. Later the ship pulled out of the harbor. We stood on the deck watching the shore line disappear. Irene Wells was the only other new Methodist missionary and we stuck together most of the trip. She was headed for Kanpur, India.

Among the missionary group we have a great variety of churches and boards. There are four young people who are going to Calcutta and they are going to stay at the Lee Memorial. They are under the Mennonite Central Committee and will be doing relief work. There are also several other people going to Calcutta - a large group of the Assembly of God.

Each morning at nine we have prayer meeting. After prayer meeting we have an hour of language study. The language study is mostly a basis for any language in India. I will be learning a little of a language but I thought I could use it some day even if it was not the language of my area.

On October 13th between 10 and 2 we went through the Strait of Gibraltar. By the moonlight we could see the outline of both Africa and Europe. We could also tell the shape of the Rock but that was about all.

Yesterday afternoon we came in sight of Portugal. We saw whales. I got an excellent view of one. The weather has been fine but cool most of the way. Everything has been excellent, and I am enjoying it.

Our first stop was in Naples. We were busy sightseeing every minute. I will never forget those two days in Italy. There were many pleasant things as well as unpleasant ones. There is still much to remind us of war. The sightseeing excursions were very profitable. On the first day we visited the ruins of Pompeii. The ancient city was destroyed in 79 A.D. by a volcano and was excavated in the 17th century. Some excavation is still going on. These ruins were very much like history and geography books picture them.

On the second day we spent the entire day on the isle of Capri. It was the most like a fairyland of anything I have ever seen. It was two hours from Naples on a small ferry. Our first stop was at the Blue Grotto. As we approached it looked like a very small tunnel. We got off the ferry four at a time and got into a small canoe. We lay on our backs while the boatman pulled us in by a chain. On the inside was a very beautiful array of all the shades of blue. It is indescribable. From there we got back on the ferry and went to the regular docks. We traveled up the rocky mountain island on a fernicular. (I would call it an elevated subway) When we got to the top we found a regular town. We went to a hotel and had a lovely dinner. After dinner we got into sky view buses and continued to climb up the rest of the rocky island. We were carried to the home or castle of Dr. Munthe. He has written a book about the island, and his home, "San Michele." The scenery from his home was certainly beautiful. His home is very unique and original. It took him 20 years to build it. After we left the castle we went back to the town, bargained for a souvenir or two, and then came back to Naples to hear again the cry for cigarettes.

We left Naples on October 16th and traveled down the coast of Italy. We passed very close to Stomboli (active volcano). We went through the Straits of Messina around 4:30 p. m. We could see very clearly both Italy and Sicily. Yesterday it looked as though we might have a storm but today the sky is clearer and we are sailing on calmly.

We stopped outside of the Alexandria harbor as princesses and other important people disembarked and after that docked in a big harbor. Egypt is much different from Italy in most every way. There is a feeling of security and you can tell the government means more. Coming down on the train to Cairo we saw many different African scenes - camels, water buffaloes, irrigation canals, mud huts, goats, sailboats on the Nile river, cotton fields with people picking and oxen threshing grain.

Everything for the 120 of us is taken care of by a travel agent. They pay every bill, hotel, tip, meals and train. We get the one statement and pay them. They are really nice. They go shopping with us, and drive away peddlers.

Because we could not get our baggage transferred our original passage booking was canceled. On the Empress of Scotland we left Egypt on October 26th. We are due to arrive in Bombay early Saturday, November 2nd. We have slowed down because of headwinds so we may be late. This ship is larger and nicer than the Vulcania. I am in a cabin with eleven other people but we have a little more room than we did on the other ship. There is no class since it is still war time. That makes it very nice because we have the same conveniences as high military officers and English government officials. Most of the passengers are English families. There are a few Indian troops.

We got on the ship at Port Said and sailed about 10 a. m. We sailed down the Suez Canal and into the Red Sea. The canal in the desert is about as impressive as anything I have ever seen. The Red Sea was very calm but hot. Until today we hardly realized we were traveling because the ocean was so calm. I would have been a very poor sailor to get sick on this trip.

We have been kept informed of the news of the world and have heard reports of the riots in Calcutta. Griffiths wrote that if there was any danger whatsoever we would not go to Calcutta. The English tell us that since the riots the Indians are very happy to have the Americans and English around. They are looking to them for protection.

Our ship arrived in sight of Bombay at sunrise. We didn't get into the harbor until around 11 and off the boat at 1 p. m. Our trunks have not been unloaded yet. We are hoping they will come soon, otherwise we will have to come back Monday. No train reservations in sight yet. I had mail from Calcutta here. Trains are going through to Calcutta. We can get into the city provided we can get on a train.

On Monday, Nov. 4, at 1:30 p.m. we received a telephone call telling us to be at the station in 45 minutes. We rushed around and made it in plenty of time. I don't know what happened but we certainly received the best accommodation possible on the train here. In India you travel by classes. We came second class. There is not much difference between first and second. In both classes there is a place to sleep but it is different from the Pullmans in the States. On this train in second class there were compartments with four places to sleep. Our group of five had two compartments. On the first night we shared it with some other missionaries who were traveling a lower class because they could not get reservations in second class. The second night some Indian men occupied the extra berths.

Our train was due to arrive in Calcutta at 9:30 a.m. However we lost about four hours getting the engine repaired. Being late was a good thing. The Griffiths did not receive my telegram until 9:30 saying that I was coming. If our train had been on time I would not have been met. All the way through everything has worked out for our good.

The Lee Memorial Headquarters Building built 1907

Chapter 2

THE FIRST PEAK

On Nov. 6 at 1:30 p.m. as the train pulled into Howrah station near Calcutta five excited Americans anxiously stretched their necks and tried to identify two Americans on the platform of the station. Having never seen Mr. Griffiths I was jittery but as the train stopped I recognized him. There was no question because he was so much like his picture. The instant I recognized him he also recognized me. I felt as though I was coming home after a long absence. Yes, this is my home.

Mr. Griffiths guided me through the crowds of people who were jabbering in several different languages; claimed my baggage, hailed a taxi and rushed me to the Girls' School and my new home. Even though they had known the exact time of my arrival only a few hours they had a royal welcome awaiting me. At the gate of the compound Mr. Griffiths turned me over to Mrs. Griffiths and before I knew what was happening I was being showered with flowers. They had made garlands and they placed them on me until I was literally covered with flowers. During all of this they were singing to me in their language. It was a real joy to view the faces of those with whom I will be working. Their bright shining faces are a happy contrast to the sad faces on the streets. Christianity makes a real difference and it is very noticeable in this great city.

Later in the day I went across the city to another part of our Mission. There I was greeted first by dear Mrs. Lee now in her 91st year. As I sat in her presence I knew that I was in the presence of a real saint of God, one who had suffered much and one who had accomplished great things for the Kingdom of God. As she prayed with me I realized in a greater way why I was here. God answered her prayers. From Mrs. Lee's room I went down to see the small children. A group of the smaller ones rushed up and took hold of me and many of them insisted upon kissing me. They are precious children and very happy in the mission home. Just a few months ago these same children were rescued from starvation. Again the contrast of these children with those of the streets was very gratifying. Oh, that we could reach more of them!

I am sure that I have come to a place where there is great need. The two missionaries in charge are very, very tired. The many tasks that they have performed during these past few years would have been impossible by human strength alone. God has richly blest them and is rewarding them in many ways.

As I view the task ahead of me I feel weak and helpless but the Voice of God speaks to me from Isaiah 41:10 saying: "Fear thou not; for I am with thee: be not dismayed; for I am thy God: I will strengthen thee; yea, I will help thee; yea, I will uphold thee with the right hand of my righteousness." I know He has helped me in the past so I can rely upon Him for the future.

My first task is to learn to talk with these people. Tomorrow I begin my language study. It is a great handicap for me to be unable to talk to the people.

Calcutta is getting back to normal if that is possible. Ever since the day before I arrived trams have been running. More and more people are out again. Yesterday many of the children came back to school for the first time since the "Great Calcutta Killing."

The trouble seems to be spreading North. It will take a long time for Calcutta to recover from the riots. Many innocent people are suffering.

Life at Lee Memorial is very interesting. Now that our ice man is out of jail we are having ice cream every night. It is very good. We had English ice cream on the Empress. I didn't like it. I imagine I will gain weight if I continue to eat as I am now. I'll try to give you just a little about my daily schedule. At 6:30 a. m. I get up and take a shower, make my bed. At 7 a.m. we have tea in our rooms. This consists of two cups of tea, two slices of bread, butter and a banana. After tea I have been doing odd jobs- washing, ironing, unpacking, writing letters. At 9:45 or 10 we have breakfast. This is a big meal with cereal, vegetables, bacon and eggs. After that meal I intend to study until lunch time at 2:30 p.m. Lunch, or tiffin, is a small meal with curry or spaghetti and bread, butter and jam. After lunch I study or do odd jobs. At 4 p.m. I have my language lesson. This will last until about 6. At 7 p.m. we have dinner- a regular three course meal with ice cream as dessert. After dinner we have a short service with our missionary guests. After prayers we visit with them until bedtime - anywhere between 9 and 10:30. I rest some time during the day, either before or after lunch.

I had my first language lesson on Monday. Yesterday, Tuesday, I had a class in girl guiding which is practically the same as girl scouts. In two weeks, I will be tested on what I have learned. That will be the first task that Mrs. Griffiths will turn over to me.

Our guests now include an Australian family waiting to get to Australia; about six Norwegians- some coming and others going back to Norway; and one each of a Methodist, Presbyterian and Baptist missionary family. All are waiting to go to the States. Nine Mennonite relief workers are in and out. This is their headquarters but they work over a wide area giving relief where there is need. Our regular family includes Dr. and Mrs. W. G. Griffiths, Miss Doris Welles and myself. Miss Welles is a Methodist missionary. She stays here and carries on her work in the surrounding villages. I haven't learned just where the work of the Lee Memorial ends and that of the Methodist begins. In fact there is no dividing line.

On Sunday I attended a Bengali service. I understood about five words of all that was spoken. Nevertheless I enjoyed it. The pastor is a converted Hindu. In the evening at 5:30 p.m. I went to Thoburn Church. Repairs have been finished and there is no sign of damage except for the battered face of Bishop Thoburn on his memorial plaque. Thoburn Church is about one block from here. An Englishman is the present pastor. Those who attend are mostly Anglo-Indians and Europeans. The Calcutta Girls School for those seeking English education is also a block and a half from here. It is also Methodist. All of our school work here at the Lee Memorial is in

Bengali. All of our teachers are native Bengalis and most of them trained here.

On Monday I went to the hospital along with Miss Welles and one of our boys, age 11. We took Reuben to be examined. We are afraid it is TB. The hospital is a government hospital and staffed by Indian doctors. It seems to be very efficient although slow. I didn't see any wards, neither was I in the emergency room, but I saw plenty. However, we don't have to go to the hospital to see human wrecks. We go around them on the sidewalks.

Calcutta has most everything I will ever need but prices are very much inflated. Nylon hose are about $4 in our money. Other things are much higher. With a small salary you can see that a missionary could not buy very much at such terrible prices. Dr. Griffiths had to pay a big sum to get our jeep repaired.

Today I am going to the American Consul to register with them. I need my birth certificate but I suppose it will be months before I get it. Ocean mail is not coming in very well now. Letters being received are dated middle of September. If we could send our mail through Canada as many do, it would be much faster and not so expensive. I may try to arrange it.

As the people begin to move around more and more freely there are more noises. Today, Calcutta is much nosier than it was two weeks ago. There are many more people on the streets. The trams run later and begin earlier. Every available standing place and hanging place is taken up in the trams. It is a very interesting sight to see how many people hang onto the steps and the railing around the side, and then people at home think buses and street cars are crowded! I have traveled the trams and buses some. No matter how crowded I always get a seat and so does every other lady. Few women travel and when they do, they sit. This is a man's country. Many women are still in purdah although many others move about freely. I have seen a few women covered thoroughly with peepholes to look through. The Anglo Indian women try to be Europeans. It is very interesting to sit and watch the things that go on in this corner of Wellington Square and Dharamtala Street.

In front of my present room is the water fountain. Practically any time of the day I look some one is there - taking a bath or washing their rickshaw, buggy or something else. In form the people are very clean. They go through the motion of keeping clean more than any other people on earth and yet are so very dirty. It is because the water is so dirty and they use no soap. Another interesting thing that goes on at the watering place is the washing of ashes. Every day at least three people spend hours washing off charcoal ashes. They wash, scrape, and when they are through they have small pieces of charcoal that will burn. This they sell and make an anna or two to live on. An anna is worth two cents. A little further in this corner of Wellington Square a mother and daughter go through the garbage cans and wastepaper baskets. They comb through everything.

On the other side of Dharamtala street are many shops. Some of them are not open. There is a barber shop on the sidewalk where the men get shaved and their hair cut. There is also a mechanic shop. I don't know what many others are. On the roof of the shops under tin coverings some Anglo Indians live. We look down into their home and see them washing dishes and doing other household chores. They do a lot of screaming and yelling. In front of our building is the Wellington Square Park. It is a playground and many boys get their physical culture there. They play many interesting games. In the park are palm and coconut trees, cows and water buffaloes.

Yesterday afternoon the Archibalds arrived. They got tired of waiting for the boat to come on to Calcutta so came by train. They are also very nice people. They are equal to the Griffiths. Everywhere I have gone in the city Dr. Griffiths has been with me. It does me a lot of good to see the respect and honor that is given to him by British, American and Indian officials. It is not a respect they naturally give a missionary. I saw many things to the contrary before I got here. Dr. Griffiths has won their admiration through his service to the world in the last seven years. The Griffiths dearly love children and the children are crazy about them. They have no children of their own. They have one adopted Anglo Indian daughter and treat many others as their own children. At present they have a Brahmin boy that two American officers turned over to them. They picked him up on the streets when he was begging and took him to their camp. They tried every available means of getting him to America but failed so they turned him over to the Griffiths. Brahmin is the very highest class or caste. We do not know all his background but we are sure some relative was trying to get rid of him so he would not get his inheritance. He is a very lovely boy. I judge about nine or ten in age. Every child in our custody has a very interesting history. We have about 200 besides the ones who come into the day school.

Today our missionary group will be the smallest it has been since I have been here. Some of the same ones are still here. The Australian family has no hopes of getting away soon.

The weather has turned much cooler and a coat feels good I am sleeping under two blankets at night. However the temperature is in the sixties and seventies.

Last week from Monday until Saturday noon I stayed in this building and stuck to my language study. Staying in this building is not like being closed up in an American building. The building is built for a warm climate. We have verandahs on each side of the rooms and a lovely open flat roof so I can be in the open air and still be in this building.

On Saturday and Sunday I did enough going to make up for the rest of the week. Saturday afternoon Dr. Griffiths and I went "jeeping" with five teachers. First we went to the United Mission High School where nine Lee Memorial girls are in school. After a visit with the girls and the Australian missionary in charge we drove through some other parts of Calcutta. We saw the Victoria Memorial which is perhaps the most elaborate building in India.

On Sunday afternoon Dr. Griffiths and I, with some workers, went south of Calcutta to three of the villages where we have preachers, Bible women, colporteurs and teachers. We had a service in one of the villages. Three persons were baptized. I enjoyed Sunday afternoon very much since it was my first close up view of the villages. Calcutta is too modern in some respects to get a real view of Indian life. We were the only white face or person in western dress out in the villages. Not only did I see the villages but I had a nice long walk up a trail between villages. I also had a typical Indian meal after the service. We had tea and fried rice mixed with fresh coconut. The rice tasted much like our puffed rice and was very delicious with the coconut. Early in the afternoon I drank dab jal (green coconut juice).

As yet I have not seen all the work that is carrie
Memorial. We have our hands in many things. Much of it needs
much closer supervision than it is getting at the present but two
people have not been able to do everything. The Indians are carrying
on the best they know how and are successful in many places. There
is still so much to be done.

I still sit and listen to Bengali and act as though I know what is
being said. I recognize a few words and phrases occasionally. This
week I am taking in some kindergarten classes. Then I have the
children read to me. It is helping me to get the sounds and to see how
they work their tongues.

This school year is drawing to a close. Final examination of
Normal Training School begins tomorrow. Government inspectors
supervise these. Last year our school won most of the honors. The
program this year has been very much upset due to frequent outbreak
of violence between the Hindus and Muslims. We have managed as
well or better than most schools.

We will observe Thanksgiving on Thursday. It hardly seems
possible that it is only a month until Christmas. I have been here
three weeks and time is flying by. I have not received any mail from
the United States. I hope it starts coming soon. I had a letter or two
from people in India so that helps out. Two months is a long time to

go without hearing from home. Ocean mail ought to get better now that the maritime strikes are over.

We get very little news of what is going on in the United States. We learned of the coal strike though and heard very indefinite reports of a sudden drop in the price of cotton. One news article predicted that wheat in the States would also go down since the bumper crop was being kept there because of the maritime strike. It is predicted that it would be disastrous to American farmers. England has an extensive program of raising grain and cotton in India, Australia and Egypt. All we read is in condemnation of U. S. for not getting food to the needy parts of the world. India now has a bumper crop of grain so the food situation should be greatly relieved. However they tell us that the terrible famine days of 1943 and 1944 were entirely manmade. Rice rotted while people died on the streets. Rice is very high now. Many people have lost every thing because of riots. The riots are horrible for the Indian people. The atrocities committed equal any of those during the war. On Sept. 30 the International issue of "Life" had only one page of pictures. I suppose the one at home had more. According to what people tell me it certainly could not be exaggerated. Terrible things have happened in Bihar since I have been in India. Whole villages, homes and people were literally destroyed. Europeans, including Americans and Anglo-Indians move around freely but a Hindu will not go near a Mohammedan section and vice versa. There are neutral areas but much of Calcutta is either Hindu or Muslim. It affects us in that we try to get a taxi or other conveyance to take us some place and they refuse because they might get out of their territory. They will not go to our Elliott Road section because they have to go through both areas. Luckily there are a few Sikhs that will go anyplace. Sunday evening Mrs. Griffiths had a hard time getting back here from Elliott Road. We were out and the trams were not running.

This morning I took a long walk through some of the streets of Calcutta. I went through a bazaar (merchants) section and also past some of the big English shops. It was surprising the things that I saw. I wasn't interested in buying anything so didn't price them. I had to pay $1.45 to get a suit cleaned and then it wasn't clean.

Tomorrow and Friday we are expecting a lot of people. Many children of missionaries will stop over here on their way to their parents. Woodstock School (American) has just closed this year. Eleanor Griffiths will be among the group. I am anxious to meet her. She will be here until they go to California.

What is missionary life like? I am describing this day's activities. Each day is different and today was interesting for several reasons. So far there has not been a dull moment, and I don't see how there could be.

About 5:45 a. m., I was suddenly awakened by the cracking and breaking of wood. At first it sounded like some one destroying a house, but as I became wider awake, I realized it was the soldiers in the 'mat' below my room cutting wood to use in their open fire while they prepared breakfast. As I lay in bed and listened to the cracking of the wood my mind recalled more of the details of this particular road. Just one week ago I saw the same soldiers take the sticks away from the men on the street to prevent violence. Some of those sticks had been for a show. After the noise of the cutting of the wood came noises of the streets. The trams and buses started running. Loud conversations in shops across the street were audible. Vendors of all kinds passed up and down the street selling all kinds of things. Sleep was impossible so about 6:15 I crawled out. It was rather cool, but I had my usual cold shower and then did a small washing. At seven o'clock Miss Welles (my roommate) and I had our morning tea. We lingered over the tea cups, read our devotional books and prayed together until about eight. Afterwards I stepped out onto the verandah to learn my new Bengali words. As I studied I saw many of the usual street scenes. The same American army convoy passed going to their work, that of locating bodies buried here to send back to relatives in America. The oxcarts, rickshaws, phaetons, jeeps, and taxies were on the street. A variety of people were going up and down the streets. Even if there were many distractions I learned a few new words.

At nine I got ready to leave because I was to spend most of the day at Duff's School. I had an early breakfast at nine, then collected my lunch and a book to study. We packed ten girls into our jeep then Dr. Griffiths and I crawled in to make a total of twelve. Yes, a jeep can be used for everything and we use ours for a bus. Those ten girls were to be the first load to Duff's School. They were middle school graduates. At the close of the school year in December the government gives examination to those completing some department. They have three hour examinations in each subject. They usually meet at a center. Our group went to Duff's School along with two other schools. I went along to be an invigilator - one who watches. The school system here is very similar to that in England.

After weaving through the vehicles, people and animals on the streets we reached the school and went immediately to the room for examination. The first one for today was English. It was the most interesting one for me because I could read what they were writing. It was a consolation to see them struggle with our English. Now I know they should be more sympathetic with me as I learn their language. They noticed that I was studying a first grade Bengali reader. As they noticed they smiled sympathetically. They had many difficulties with our English and their mistakes were interesting. For example in describing the scenery one girl wrote, "Many little green grasses are there." I never dreamed there could be so many differences in the way people talk. Their language is just the opposite of ours in so many ways.

At one o'clock they finished their English examination and had an hour for tiffin (lunch). I had my light lunch with the Scotch lady in charge of the school. The mission is under the Church of Scotland. In our work we contact many missionaries from other countries. The sewing examination began at two. The girls had to knit a very small sock, cross stitch their initials and cut out and make a small blouse without any pattern. It is amazing what some of those small girls can do.

As I watched the girls work I could not help but think of the future of the 18 girls from our school taking that examination. About half of them are Hindus. The other half are our girls. They have no parents. The destiny of the Hindu girls is decided by their parents but we decide the future of the others. Those who make good enough grades are sent to high school. At present we do not have a high school in the mission. We send our girls to United Mission High School where we pay fees. We are asking the Lord to supply the scholarships for the ones who need to go on to high school. There are some lovely girls in the group.

At 4:30 the sewing examination was completed and the first load packed into the jeep. I waited with the second load. When Dr.

Griffiths returned the girls begged for a round about trip home. He kindly consented so we drove through the north part of the city and saw the masses of people on the streets. At that time of the day everything seemed to be covered with people. They literally fill the buses and trams on the inside and outside. We went through some bazaar sections where the shops or stores are right in the open on the sidewalk. As a special treat he took us to the Jain Temple, one of the famous religious temples in India. It has a lovely compound with several buildings. Everywhere on the walks and in the gardens there were beautiful designs done in ivory. The whole sight was very dazzling. We went to the main temple. As we reached the steps we took off our shoes and then went inside. It was just getting dusk so they turned on the lights for us. Gems of all colors and sizes sparkled at us. There were a few images. A man who knew a little English pointed out some of the prized diamonds to me. I overheard them ask our girls questions about me. You see I understand a little of their language. It was a rich display of gems. These temples are one of the tragedies of India. Just outside the temple compound gate was a display of the poverty of India. The contrast is staggering.

We arrived home around six p.m. and got ready for dinner at seven. In the meantime we reported on the days activities to other teachers and to Mrs. Griffiths. Then we had dinner of soup, cauliflower, potatoes, mutton and ice cream. After dinner we went to the living room and had worship with our missionary family. Dr.

Griffiths led tonight and as usual his prayer was very refreshing. Afterwards we visited with missionaries present. They include four American children and their chaperon going from school to their parents in Burma; four Burma Baptist missionaries doing Christmas shopping and taking care of other business, and three Mennonite relief workers who board with us all the time.

The bugle has just sounded so the soldiers living in the first floor classrooms have gone to bed. They have lived there since "The Great Calcutta Killings" to keep the peace in this area. The curfew has started, the streets are quiet and so I must also crawl in.

The cool weather began the middle of December. They tell me it will stay this way for about three more weeks and then it will get hot again. It is always warm in the sun if the wind doesn't hit you. Calcutta is peaceful. The curfew has lifted. One company of soldiers moved out but another group moved in so we still have them around. We are getting anxious for them to get out of our way.

On Monday I moved from third floor to fourth floor. I am now in a small room by myself. I will move again when the Griffiths go. There are three rooms on this floor. The rest is open roof (or terrace). I like it up here. I'd like it better if the soldiers would move the wireless station. Most eastern countries have flat open roofs on their buildings. It is quiet on the roof and our building is as high or higher than any in this area. Now I can study and look out over the city. I am also away from the noisy corner of Wellington Square and Dharamtala Street.

Nehru visited Calcutta on Monday. He stayed with Dr. Roy who lives on the other side of the square. The square or park was filled with people trying to get a glimpse of him. I didn't make an effort to see him. I suppose I should have because he is a world figure. It was his sister, Mrs. Pandit, who defended India at the United Nations Conference.

On Sunday the Archibalds and I had dinner with Mr. Mondol, the head of Collins Institute, a boy's school operated by the Methodist Church. Mr. Mondol is an Indian but was in the United States for several years. His brother is one of the Bishops. In a speech to some of the Indian preachers Bishop Mondol told them that Americans didn't get sick much and about all they had were colds and operations. When you hear about all the things that people have in this country you don't wonder at him saying that. They tell me that missionaries usually have a certain run of diseases during the first year. I'm putting mine off. Others around me do not fare as well as I have so far. However Mrs. Griffiths says there is only one thing that I have to have and it won't hurt me. It is a kind of fever caused by a mosquito that bites in the afternoon. She thinks sleeping under a mosquito net is adequate protection against malaria. We don't go out in dark places at night.

Last week the school year closed. Our students made excellent records. One of our students received the highest scholarship award of the Bengal Province. Two others also received recognition in the province. These were the results of the 1945 examination. We learn the results of the 1946 examinations sometime next year.

Our children in other schools also made excellent records. The boys in another mission boy's school took several of the honors. One boy stood first in a very large class. He was a Mohammedan beggar boy. Dr. Griffiths took a liking to him when he saw him begging in a train depot and took him to the mission. Several of the boys stood second and fourth in their classes.

Of the nine girls in the United Missionary High School all except one were in the upper ranks taking 1st, 2nd and 3rd places in their classes. The most outstanding, who is a junior in high school, was a temple baby. Several years ago 14 babies were rescued from a temple and brought to Mrs. Lee. Their mothers served the priest in the temple.

After their schools closed the children came home. They will be here about two weeks. Everyone with us now is entirely dependent upon us. In other words they are our children. The boarding students who had parents or relatives went to them for the vacation. Our vacation family is just about 100. They range from age three or four to college students. Of the children who went home many of them are partially supported by us. Some of them are given free boarding; others pay a very small fee that doesn't cover expenses. It takes Rs15 ($5) per person a month for boarding alone. In prewar years it was about 1/3 of that. Rice and fish are very high now. In the closing days of school I learned much about our school I didn't know before. There is so much to learn about the work of the Lee Memorial. It seems as though we lend a helping hand to everything. Last week Dr. Griffiths went with a Burmese student to the police to try to help him get a passport to go to America to school. Not knowing who Dr. Griffiths was the police said to the Burmese: "There is only one man in the city that can help you and that is Dr. Griffiths of the Lee Memorial." That particular official had had many letters and telephone conversations with Dr. Griffiths but had not met him in person.

Christmas Eve was a lovely cool evening. The stars shone brightly in the moonless sky. Our missionary family listened to records of all the Christmas carols and put the finishing touches on the Christmas gifts for the children in our care. We thought and talked of our Christmases at home but the feeling of homesickness was not intense as we were in a nice homelike atmosphere.

Late in the evening we retired still thinking of home. During the night our sleep was interrupted several times by carolers. Many of the tunes were familiar but all the words were strange. It was good to hear the songs of Christians and as I listened I had a much more comfortable feeling than I had when just a few weeks before "Pakistan! Muslim League" rang through the air with piercing shrillness from the same streets.

Before dawn we were up. The morning was very cool and as we looked out into the misty darkness we could almost imagine there was snow but as we looked at the thermometer we discovered it was only 55 degrees. The bells on the horses pulling the garies (buggies) added to the Christmas feeling. Throughout our building there was an air of excitement. At eight the small children came from our Mission home in another part of the city. They greeted us with their smiling faces and eager eyes. Each was given a new pair of shoes and a new dress and then there was the excitement of getting ready for the Christmas service at 9. The small girls were very much pleased with their red dresses but to them the pocket was the greatest treat. They liked their new white shoes but they looked very awkward in them. Many had never worn shoes before. We put red bows in their hair. They were precious. Finally all were ready and we lined them up, two by two, and marched to the Central Methodist Church about four blocks away. As my co-workers were busy with other tasks, it was my duty to take them there and back. As we passed down the narrow street many people on the streets stopped to look at us. They stood in their doorways and watched us. The poor old widows who were digging in the filthy garbage pile stopped their search long enough to watch us go by. The small children playing on the streets in their grayish black rags looked on with their sad eyes. As we marched I viewed our hundred children with pride but at the same time my heart went out to those who were looking on. We were just a very small group in a very large city.

The small church very similar to an American rural church was decorated for the occasion. Streamers of red and green crepe paper were draped across the ceiling. Potted palms were placed around the pulpit. People kept coming throughout the preliminary service until practically every seat was taken. They sang several songs to the tune of "O come All ye Faithful," "Hark the Herald Angels Sing" and others. I had a book and could pronounce the words even though I didn't know what they meant. I sang wholeheartedly. I believe the pastor preached a very good Christmas sermon. I understood a few sentences. His theme seemed to be "Accepting the Christ of Christmas." It was a very timely message as so many Christians are called that because their parents were Christians. They, too, need to accept the Christ of Christmas as well as the people around us of other religions. After the service we returned to our home on Wellington Square.

At high noon I had Christmas dinner with our missionary family. Our guests for the day were: Rev. and Mrs. Atkinson, the British pastor of Thoburn Methodist Church, Miss Redinger, director of Calcutta Girls School, two Norwegian ladies of the Scandinavian Alliance Mission, Miss Amstutz, a Mennonite relief worker, Rev. Nickels Roy, a Christian member of the Indian Constituent Assembly, a preacher in Assam and Kumudini, one of our college students.

Mrs. Lee, now almost 91, sat at the head of the table. Before the meal she led us in prayer. We enjoyed the meal. Four nations were represented at the table but there was a wonderful sense of unity. We had a typical American Christmas dinner with goose instead of turkey.

At two o'clock we gathered in our hall and Mrs. Lee gave out the Christmas presents to the children. Each child received a gift of small toys and useful articles from the Mission. Each child's name was called and as they walked to the front to receive their gifts there was a great big smile on their faces. It gave me an opportunity to fit their names to their faces. There are still many that I cannot call by name. Dr. Griffiths sat by me and told me interesting things about each as their names were called. There was little De- Leep and his sister Reba, both were famine children and very sick of starvation when they were rescued by our workers. In the group there were about 14 who had been rescued during the recent famine days (1943-1944) Little Premie now three was brought to us when she was a week old. The eight small girls sat in a row together. They were a lovely sight in their red dresses and white shoes and all looked very fat and healthy. Then there was the beggar girl who has been with us a very short time. An English soldier brought her here. Next came some of the boys. Among them were the two little boys who had been found as beggars. They are both very bright - one stood first in a large class and the other took three classes this year in order to be in class with boys his age. Among the high school girls several had been rescued from a temple and brought to Mrs. Lee several years ago. Among them are some jewels. The backgrounds of some are a mystery. Others were left without parents and brought here by relatives. A few were children of prostitute mothers.

As I looked at them there was a great feeling of satisfaction. I cannot describe the feeling of my heart. It certainly repays for any so-called sacrifice that I have to make. I'm so glad that I came and if I can help one poor unfortunate child I will be well repaid. As I watched them play with their new gifts I remembered other children I had seen a few days ago who were begging. The face of the little boy who had followed me around the day before begging for an anna (two cents) kept coming before me. How I long to rescue more of these children. There is so much to be done. My heart is filled with a prayer for each one. I asked God to make them flaming evangels for Him - ones to go out and preach full salvation in this needy province.

After all had received their gifts they were dismissed and went to the play ground. They had a great time for the next few hours. The boys spun their tops and the girls jumped rope. I visited with some of them. I practiced all the Bengali I knew and they helped me along.

Late in the evening I put on my new sari and got ready for an Indian meal with all the children. It was the first time I had dressed in a sari so they were pleased. At 7:30 we ate with them. We sat on the floor and ate rice and curry with our fingers. Their food is delicious. Fish is their favorite meat and they use plenty of it.

After supper we had a candlelight service with singing of more Christmas carols, scripture reading and prayers. The Lord's presence was very near and even though I could not understand their prayers there was a prayer in my heart that God would continue to preserve this Mission. I thanked Him again for the miraculous way He founded and preserved this institution. My heart took fresh hope for the future. This is our Father's world and He is the ruler yet. He will lead us through the uncertain future.

After the candle lighting service we lingered talking to our co-workers and learning more about what God has done here. It was with much hesitation that I pulled myself away and came to my room. I went to bed with a great feeling of satisfaction and sleep came easily. It had been a glorious day and one of much peace in my heart.

One day last week I took a very long walk through the city. The high point of interest was the "New Market." In one sense you could compare it with Marshall Fields store of Chicago, but Marshall Fields would not like the comparison. Marshall Fields is that great big store that covers a block. New Market is a large shopping place. It is mostly under one roof. In it you can buy everything from precious diamonds to monkeys. I'm sure there is nothing else like it in the world. It is made up of lots of small shops. They display their wares in bazaar fashion and if you want to shop you must bargain the prices down. It is very nice to go into a place where they actually want to sell you something. I certainly was amazed at the things I saw there. I believe they had anything in the world a person could ever dream of wanting. There are lots of American made goods. Plenty of Lux soap for washing and bathing. As I would walk through the owners of shops would yell out: "Meme Sahib, come in and see what we have, just look." If they had American made goods they would point them out. I don't know how they always know the Americans but they do. The place was crowded with all types of people: rich, poor, beggars, foreigners and all.

Some officers of the Thomas Sims Lee (freighter boat) have had meals with us. Two Norwegian ladies are waiting for a boat. The Mennonites had their jeep stolen.

During Christmas week I attended two weddings:- One here and one at Elliott road. One of our teachers was married in the Central Methodist Church. At Elliott road one of the girls was married. The wedding ceremony used is very similar to those at home. It is the arrangement of the marriages that is different. Mrs. Griffiths arranges most of the marriages for the girls under her care. Fathers of grooms to be come seeking a wife. Then Mrs. Griffiths chooses a girl. Unlike some Hindus she gets the girl's consent. She always allows the girl to talk to the boy and see if she wants to marry him. Probably that one talk is the only courtship they have. Yesterday an arrangement was made in about 15 minutes. The man came here presented a letter of recommendation to Mrs. Griffiths. She brought the girl out to see him. The girl looked at him and said "yes." They will be married in about six weeks. However the wedding this morning was different because the teacher knew the boy she was marrying. In fact she arranged the wedding herself.

In their weddings they stick to a few of the old customs. Yesterday each of the girls being married today had what is called "Gae Holud" ceremony. It was a very simple ceremony where each member of the family smeared a little holud on the bride to be and then fed her a little bit of food. The holud is a preparation made from mustard. It is supposed to make the girl very beautiful and fair. The interesting thing about the ceremony is that after you have put some on the bride then the person you touch next is supposed to be the next one to get married.

People are very color conscious. The thing that the groom wants most is a fair skin bride. The blacker girls have a hard time getting a husband. It is a real disgrace if you are not married. Here in Calcutta it is not so bad but they tell me that in the villages a single missionary has to overcome that obstacle. Many of the missionaries tell the people they are young yet and have plenty of time to get married and that they probably will later. Mrs. Archibald has proven it to them. She was a single missionary in the Lee Memorial for several years before marrying Mr. Archibald.

The soldiers moved out about five days before Christmas so we have the whole place to ourselves now. A company had been living in the ground floor of the school building since the "Great Calcutta Killing". We were glad they left before Christmas. Last Saturday evening I went to St. John's Cathedral and heard their choir perform the Messiah beautifully. The participants were English and Anglo-Indian.

On Monday the Griffiths, Ram and I went to the botanical gardens for a picnic. It was Eleanor's 14th birthday so we celebrated in that way. It was a nice quiet place and very beautiful scenery. It was a real treat to be out of the noise and smoke. The gardens have many interesting trees and flowers. The water lilies were especially beautiful. The most interesting thing was the great banyan tree. It covers more ground than any other tree in the world. It is about 180 years old. The Banyan tree is a holy tree to the Hindus. Roots from the branches go down to earth and start another trunk. I think there were about 800 trunks, all started from the same tree.

Another interesting thing about the day was the drive out there. Calcutta is a very large city — the fifth largest in the world. I haven't seen all of it yet. We drove along the Hooghly River (branch of the Ganges) and saw where the boats dock. We drove through some of the dirtiest parts of the city. As you walk or drive along you can see people doing everything that man does. Nothing is private. The day I came they told me Calcutta was not normal because there were not many people on the streets. I thought there were plenty. It looked like any busy shopping day just before Christmas in any American city. But now that Calcutta is more normal I can see what they meant. Now there are people everywhere. There are multitudes of them. Where they live I don't know. Many of them live right on the streets. Even on our picnic in a nice quiet place there were a few people squatting around watching all our moves. The men especially have a way of squatting with their knees up. They stay that way for hours. On the streets you see mostly men. There are probably as many men as there are women so you can see what a mass of people there must be in the city.

During the Christmas week we have had a distinguished Indian politician with us. He is not only a politician but also a very splendid preacher - a real Christian. He is a member of the Constituent Assembly and came from the session to here. They discussed the type of government India would have after Independence from the British. He is highly respected by other Indian politicians. Nehru stays in his home. In one large mass meeting in which Nehru spoke our guest opened the meeting with prayer in the name of Christ. He is very optimistic about the situation in India. There are certainly two sides to the story and there are many bright points. India can be an independent country without too much civil strife is the belief of many. News commentators in America seem to be able to make conclusions much better than commentators in India. To make such statements that I have read in a recent TIME magazine is certainly unjust and not altogether true. I don't think any one can predict India's future. There is a bright side as well as a dark side. The chief trouble is ignorance. In the educated classes we find men taking sensible attitudes.

It is amazing the way Russia has a hold in this country. Recently in looking over books in a book store I was horrified at Russian propaganda. Most of the books there were by Russian authors and they were all presenting communism in a fascinating way and, at the same time belittling the work of foreigners - British officials and missionaries. The hardest thing for us to take is not the presence of the books but that the Christians accept them wholeheartedly and we are helpless in trying to disprove them. In fact we dare not try. Unfortunately many of those who are called Christian need more help than the Hindus and Muslims. I am reporting the dark side with the bright side. It has been interesting to note how much scripture is quoted by the politicians. Many of Gandhi's speeches are practically all scripture. The man already referred to (Christian politician) thinks that India will turn to Christianity in a great way. Sometimes it looks to me as if they were just taking the principles of Christianity and embracing them along with the rest of their Hindu code.

Lee Memorial girls eat their rice meal

Chapter 3

EXPLORING THE TRAILS

The Griffiths are busy turning over duties and the Archibalds are busy assuming the responsibility. The Griffiths are actually booked on a boat and it will not be too long until they leave. How I hate to see them go because we will certainly miss them. They are planning to visit my family.

On Monday Nehru was in the city again. I went across the park and stood by the driveway of the house where he stays. I got a very close up view of him as he drove in. Later he came out on the verandah and waved to the mob of people around the house. When he drove in we were at the back gate and very few people were back there. I'm hoping Gandhi will come to town so I can see him. He also comes to the same house across the park in front of our mission. We are located in the center of the city. I didn't realize that until I began to study a map. We are almost in the dead center.

Tonight after our dinner of fried chicken, vegetables, mince pie and ice cream we saw movie films of Australia. During Christmas we had very few guests. Now we are getting a full house again. We have more Baptist missionaries from Assam. Their work in Assam is so far from civilization that they have to come here and stock up on supplies. The same is true of the Scandinavian Alliance missionaries on this side of India.

School opened on Jan 10, 1947 for another term. We have Bible class at 10 and regular classes begin at 10:30. We have many children this year and of all religions. All our classes are full and many have been turned away and yet they come and plead. One man on learning that the class in which he wanted to place his daughter was already full said put her in a lower class. Unfortunately the next lower class was also full. It is a great responsibility to have so many from the other religions coming to us daily. Many of them also attend the Bible classes.

In the kindergarten there are about 50 children. It is very interesting to observe them at their work and play. The type of dress of the children varies greatly. Today one small boy who looks to be about four or five had on a bright pink satin pajama and shirt. A few of these small children wear the sari or the dhoti but most of them wear dresses. Some of the girls are from families who are refugees. Many of the others did not go to school last year because of the disturbed conditions in the city. Here in our school Muslims, Hindus, Jains, Buddhists, Christians and others are studying and playing together. Some of the parents are very poor, some of the children have no parents. Others come from wealthy parents. We strive to give all the same treatment. When we realize that we live in a land of caste systems, and a land torn with bloodshed, we praise God that it is possible to carry on our school with such lovely feeling among all the students. In the city all around us we continue to see evidences of peace and goodwill all about us. Can these people who fought each other so long and endured the misery and suffering of those terrible "Killings" turn to them again? We continue to hope that the peace in this city will be for a long duration.

Today has been a full day. I got up cleaned my clothes. Then started my language lesson at eight o'clock. I studied for seven hours, and then I played with the girls for about two hours. We played checkers, ping pong and badminton. After that I took a bath and ironed some of my clothes. After dinner tonight I played Chinese checkers with Miss Welles and the three Mennonite relief workers. At present we do not have any outside guests, just the seven regular ones.

The past two days have not been as warm as the last week when it got up to 90 degrees. The wind keeps things cool. On Thursday, Friday and Saturday of last week I attended the Bengal Teachers Conference. It was interesting to meet people of other Christian mission schools as well as those from Hindu, Muslim and Brahmo schools. Most used Bengali so I did not understand everything.

The tram strike continues. The trams have not run in a long time; the buses struck for one day only. When I go out I take the rickshaws - a two wheel cart pulled by a man. They are much better than trying to get into a crowded bus.

On Sunday night, out in the park, they had some public boxing matches. I watched some of them from our grandstand seats on our porch. I saw two men get knocked out. In the far end of the park they have it all boarded off. It looks like they are going to have something very private and special. They have even put a top on the area so we will not be able to see very much of whatever goes on there.

One night last week the baby of the beggar family, that sleeps on the sidewalk in front of our building, cried all night. It sounded pathetic. Our helpers said it was because the husband beat the mother.

On Sunday I went to Elliott Road. I had not been there in a long time. It was good to see the children again. They wanted to sing to me in English. I was surprised at the number of English choruses they know. The American solders taught them. On the way over and back we passed through some excitement. The Muslims were having some protest meetings on the activities in the Punjab. It looked as though they might get out of control but they did not. They went all over the city in big trucks yelling "Zindabad" meaning revolution. Something is going on all the time. If it is not one thing, it is another.

Since the middle of February the weather has changed. A few days ago we had a thunderstorm. Since then it has been very cloudy and unpleasantly cool. Last night blaring loud speakers interrupted our sleep again. It didn't bother me as much as the others who live here. An All India Labor Congress has been in session out in the park. I think it closes today. They had representatives from many places. It seems to be a communist meeting

The boat the Griffiths left on was the last one to leave before a dock workers' strike. The departure of many people is delayed. In the last week we have had many guests. A man from the Methodist Board of Education is still with us. These days we are getting a lot of world travelers. A young man who claimed to be traveling for the Baptist Church suddenly disappeared without paying his bills.

Spring came in March. All the trees have new leaves on them. It was interesting to see the old leaves fall off as the new leaves come out. It looked like fall and spring at the same time. Last Sunday afternoon we went riding. We went to the Lakes and saw much of the beautiful scenery. Many of the trees are blooming now. There are many new bird nests in the trees. The children have been pointing them out to me. There are some small birds in them. This afternoon while at Elliott road the children and I saw a wild parrot. They were very excited and told me all about how he could talk. I have learned to understand much of their language but there is still much that I do not understand. Lately I have been spending more time listening and talking to the children.

This week we have several boys and girls who are waiting to go to the American School located in North India. They are all children of missionaries in Assam and Burma. One little boy from Burma missed the boat he was supposed to come on so he came on an airplane. They put him in care of the pilot and he sat in the co-pilot's seat. The pilot let him drive the plane. He certainly had a grand time. He was so excited when he got here that he could not be still.

Today the children sang their English choruses for me. They want me to teach them some new ones but they know most of the ones I know. Today we tried to teach them "Jesus Loves the Little Children." They liked it very much. We translated some of them and they sing them in both languages. They sing "Jesus Loves Me" and "I am so Happy" in both languages

On March 7th the Hindus had a special festival. They celebrated it by throwing color all over each other. Now every one looks like they have fallen into someone's dye. Their clothes and hair are spotted with many colors. It will take days for it to wear off. The colors are red, green, yellow and blue. I saw a small baby with hair a raspberry color. We did not go out anywhere that day because we did not want our clothes and hair ruined.

On March 19 I received the Griffiths account of their Piedmont and Westminister visits with members of my family. They raved and raved about the good milk. They described every thing so well and with much detail. It made me feel as though I had been there.

It is much cooler now. In fact it has been very pleasant for the last week or more. Tonight it is trying to rain but is not succeeding. The trams are supposed to start running tomorrow. Some think it will cause trouble because the dispute is not settled. I'm not going to ride on them for the first day or so. There was a little trouble of riot nature on Sunday but the police got things under control immediately

This afternoon we took a long walk. We walked to the Presidency Hospital to see a missionary who is a patient there. It is supposed be a European hospital but there were more Indians than Europeans in the wards we visited. We went through the grounds of the Victoria Memorial. They had lots of beautiful flowers in bloom. The walk took us through some nice, quiet clean places. I notice the noise more when I get out of it than I do while I am in it. If the trams do start running it will be noisier than ever. We've gone a long time without them.

I'm taking typhoid and cholera shots. I've already had one and I get another one. According to official reports around 150 died of cholera in the city last week. We felt an earthquake and are wondering where it was located. No one seems to know. The instruments here report it only 900 miles away.

We celebrated Mrs. Lee's 91st birthday on March 23rd. She came here in the morning and we had her birthday dinner and a program afterwards. She was feeling fine, the best I had ever seen her. One would never have guessed that she is 91.

On Monday I went to a tea at Lady Ezra's home It was my first visit with royalty. The home was as interesting as a zoo or museum. They had lots of peacocks and other birds. The occasion was a council meeting of the Girl Guides and I represented our school. I met many of the missionaries and other leaders of the city that I had not met before. The main kind of social occasion is a tea. They take various forms. Some turn out to be a feast and some just have tea. The one Monday had tea and a lot of fancy cookies.

Last Sunday was also Pakistan day. Everyone expected trouble but the Muslims celebrated it in a very civilized way and everything was peaceful. Yesterday was also very peaceful and quiet as for as we were concerned. About 1 p.m. we noticed a change in tones on the street. On looking out we discovered that shops were closing and people were moving about in a hurry. Shortly afterwards the buses stopped running. Fathers came and took their girls home from school early. On making inquiry we found that a few people had been stabbed and that some Hindus and Muslims were fighting in another part of the city. It was deathly quiet around here the rest of that day. Police, soldiers and the Red Cross workers passed frequently. It was very evident that no one wanted to fight. I think every one went to their homes and hid. Last night they had curfew and all was quiet with very dim lights. Today the shops are slowly reopening. Traffic is coming back to normal but people are still very cautious.

A general strike was set for tomorrow but on account of the trouble the union decided to postpone it. For once a union showed some consideration. If and when they do strike we will be without water, lights and transportation.

The daily routine of the boarders in the Lee Memorial mission begins at 5:30 a.m. All the girls get up, roll up their beds and stack them neatly at one end of the big halls. This only takes a very short time and they are ready for morning worship. After that is finished they drink a cup of tea and begin the day's work. They are busy cleaning, cooking and so on. After the morning chores the girls study or bathe. They take turns and some study while others bath. The bath is very important routine in the life of most all people but to the Bengali it is like a religious duty. Each day the girls take a complete bath in cold water and wash the clothes they wore the day before. A bath is not a real one to them unless their hair is also washed. They rub the entire body with coconut oil after the bath and washing of the clothes.

They eat breakfast at 9:30. They eat rice, dal, (lentils) and fish curry. Their kitchen and dining room is in the northeast corner of the compound on the first floor. Children have their own plates, usually of brass. They always sit on the floor in lines around the wall with their plates in front of them.

Before the girls finish eating the day scholars come from all directions. Widow women wearing plain white saris which also covers her head are hired by parents to accompany some of the girls from their homes to the school. Girls usually do not walk on the streets alone even though it may be a very short distance. Other children are accompanied by servant who carry their bag of books. Some fathers drive their children in cars. Those fathers will probably go on to their office from here. At ten o'clock the school bell rings. For the first half-hour the students will have Bible study. They have learned to sing many of our choruses and love to sing them as well as their Bengali tunes.

After the Bible class they begin their regular classes. I have a drill class with the girls in the afternoon. Today the girls do not want to play because they received cholera injections. We are afraid of a cholera epidemic in the city so we are giving the injections early this year. Last week they were vaccinated for smallpox and next week they will take typhoid injections. This is a part of the annual routine to keep the girls well and to escape epidemics that are prevalent.

There is very small playground between the two wings of the building. We have crowded a badminton court into it along with a place to play basketball and other games. On the first floor of one wing we have a large open hall which we use when it rains. Class work ends at 4 p.m. and the day scholars go home. At 4 p.m. the girls in boarding play. Badminton is one of the favorite games. It is almost as much fun as tennis and not nearly as strenuous. I often play with them in order to get daily exercise. After the playtime they eat their evening meal of rice and curry. After eating they will study for a time and then go to bed at 8:30.

My first five months were spent observing the activities of the mission and studying Bengali. The missions that worked through the Bengali language organized a language school for new missionaries in

Darjeeling, India. This language school was in session during the hot weather months of April, May and June.

I went to Darjeeling to the language school on April 1. Darjeeling is 7000 feet above sea level. I was the only American in boarding for a few days. We students are in the living room together, three Aussies and two Londoners. Some are writing letters and some are sitting before the fireplace talking. This really is a beautiful place. We see many lovely mountain ranges but it has been too misty to see the snow peaks. We cannot see Mt. Everest at this location. They say it is veiled in clouds much of the time. It's surprising the effect the altitude has on us. Coming from one foot below sea level to this is quite a change. I had specific instructions on how to act. I have followed them so have no ill effects.

The trip up from Calcutta was a unique experience. On account of the riots I did not connect with the group traveling to the language school. I came alone all the way. From Calcutta to Siliguri it was nighttime. At Siliguri I changed from the ordinary Indian train to what they call a miniature train or toy train. It was certainly a baby train and never exceeded 10 miles per hour.

Many times I looked down but could not see where we would land if the train slipped about three feet. I thought the U. S. hairpin curves were something but the loops here make them appear like nothing. I could usually see both ends of the train. I could see the man sitting on the front (cowcatcher) sprinkling sand on the rail. Sometimes the train made a complete circle, the engine going over a bridge it had just gone under. Some times the little train would puff away and I wondered if it would get up the hill. Then all of a sudden it started going backwards and I was afraid. It gained momentum as it went backward and then to my relief I discovered it was rolling up an incline backward. It coasted up to a good height and we could look down and see the tracks we had just rolled down backwards. What an odd sensation this gave me. But that is the way the train climbed up the steep mountains. Coming near the crest of a hill the train then rolled back until it went up to a different level.

Often the train stopped and filled up with water. Beggar children and others sold peanuts and bananas. We looked down on ranges of mountains and then lifted our eyes to the towering ranges above. There are several average sized towns on the way up. When we first entered the hill area it was jungles but it did not take us long to reach the tea gardens. All the space on the sides of the mountains is used for something. The terraced tea gardens are lovely. I look down on them from the window of my room. The people have a very different appearance than the people in Calcutta. They have Mongoloid features. It seems that the women do all the work. We see them going by with the great big baskets on their backs supported by a strap around their forehead. The children have red cheeks and round faces. I think they are beautiful. They look so healthy. The skin of the grown-ups looks so tough.

We have had two days of class work before Good Friday. On that day we went to Mt. Hermon for services. It is a school for English children. Our Methodist Board supports it. I find that my knowledge of Bengali compares favorably with that of those who have been in India about the same length of time.

It is very restful here. We have lots of flowers all over the place - roses, snap dragons, nasturtiums, sweet peas, and many other familiar and unfamiliar. The mountains are very lovely but we still have not seen the high ranges with the snow on them. The rainy season should start soon and clear the atmosphere so we can see them.

At 6:30 a. m. we have tea brought into our room, then we get up and if we do not have a private tutorial we study until breakfast at 8:45. Breakfast is a large meal. This morning we had oatmeal, liver, bacon, bread and toast, bananas, oranges and tea. After breakfast we have worship, Classes start at 9:45. At 10:45 we have 15 minute recess to drink our cocoa. We go back to classes and stay until tiffin time at 1 p. m. Then we usually play for about half hour and then go to our rooms and study. At 4 p.m. we come to the living room and tea is served with bread and jam. We continue studying until 6 p. m. Dinner is at 7:45. When we finish dinner we have worship again and sit around the fire - visiting, playing games, writing letters or anything else we want to do until bed time. We don't have classes on Saturdays so we do as we like.

Last Monday we hiked to Ghum about eight miles from here. We took our tea along and made it on top of one of the mountains. The name of the place should be 'gloom.' Last Monday it was covered with a cloud all the time we were there. Part of the time we could hardly see the person in front of us. So we had our tea in a cloud! Here we are eating some of the raw vegetables which we did not dare eat in Calcutta. We have lettuce and celery.

The temperature is pleasant. Last week in Calcutta it was 104 degrees and humidity 95 per cent so they are really steamy hot down there. I escaped the heat for this time. Riots are still going on.

I have been in India almost six months. Ever since I left home and went to college I have learned what things count most in life. A thousand times I have been thankful that I received the foundation for all important things at home. There are two things I consider essential for a happy life. The first is a faith in God and the second is the ability to get along with other people. My mother taught me both of these. I think the one common personality trait that she imparted to all of us from the oldest to the youngest is the ability to get along with other people. All of my siblings are different in other ways but I believe one can say without exception that we get along with the people we contact.

Long ago I learned how important it is to get along with others. Now I see its importance in a much greater way. There are many other things that mother taught me that I am thankful for - being satisfied with what we have, eating all types of food and how to work. I have been very happy and am still happy but everyday I see people unhappy because some little thing irritates them. I've thanked God many times that my mother did not give me any complexes in life.

Indian independence from Britain was assured many months ago. The negotiating committee is busy working out the details. The Muslims are demanding a separate country to be known as Pakistan. Gandhi and his associates have resisted this. Jinnah, the Muslim leader is adamant. Now it seems certain that the country of Pakistan will be created and it will be in two sections. Our province of Bengal will be divided into Pakistan and Hindustan. I am not sure I understand all the points of division but it is certain that Calcutta will be in Hindustan.

In the meantime the situation in Calcutta has not improved. The folk at Lee Memorial stay in because of curfew orders. One had a pass so he could go about. Sometimes the curfew is for a day and a half. In one area it was for two and a half days. Then, too, the weather has been very hot. It is hotter than for several years.

On last Saturday we went to Tiger Hill - elevation 8,500 feet. It was lovely scenery all around but we could not see Mt. Everest. We walked about 12 miles.

During a short break in May twelve of us took a 60 mile hike to Kalimpong Our seven coolies carried our beds and food. We climbed up to Ghum about 8,000 feet and then descended down to 5,300 feet and stayed in a "dak" bungalow. The view all along the road was wonderful and varied. From our bungalow we had a wonderful view of the snow ranges and other mountains. Early the next morning we got up and started down the mountain. It was real steep. We went down to the famous Teesta River where the elevation was about 700 feet. Then we went straight up again to a level of more than 4000 feet. In Kalimpong we went to a mission. The Church of Scotland (Presbyterian) has a very large orphanage with 540 unwanted children of mixed parentage. Many are war babies. They have an ideal location of 650 acres. From there we looked up to see the snows, over 20,000 feet, and then down to the river below, 700 feet - Spectacular!

We got up on Sunday morning and went to their church service. The children dressed in their different colors were a beautiful sight. They live in small groups in cottages and each cottage wears a different color. Their youngest child is three weeks old. Other than the orphanage they have a hospital, leper colony, services and schools for Nepalies, Tibetans and Indians. We thoroughly enjoyed our day there. Early the next morning we started back over the same route.

The day before we left for our trek we had a Bengali language examination. I made 84 and was third in our class of fourteen. Now we will start studying again and work hard until June 29th. We have more teachers and will be divided into smaller classes which means that our progress should be much faster. We will also have more private lessons.

Just a few minutes ago I watched the sun set over ranges of these Himalaya Mountains. In the background were the snow peaks, partly covered by frayed clouds of all colors. In the valley below was the lovely green of the tea gardens and scattered buildings about. This is a real paradise. I have never seen lovelier scenery and I never expect to. All kinds of flowers are blooming everywhere.

In our language school there are about thirty students - all new missionaries. We come from England, Scotland, Wales, Norway, Denmark, Australia, New Zealand and America. We also represent many missionary societies. We have a grand time of fellowship.

Darjeeling at this time of the year is a very interesting place. It is a summer resort. As we go through the streets we see a variety of people, the rich English lords and ladies and the rich Indians. Also the common ordinary folk The coolie women in Tibetan dress, the Catholic sisters and fathers in their habits, the Buddhists monks with their long hair, beards and very unusual dress and the Hindu ascetic. There is a religious group who try to dress as people did in Biblical times. Then we have the soldiers and the police in their bright dress.

All during the week and all day we study Bengali and I mean we really study. They tell us that Bengali is one of the harder languages. It is not hard for me - believe that? We are studying hard and are still looking forward to the day when we can speak fluently. By speaking very slowly and with much effort we can make ourselves understood and get all that we need but it is still a tremendous effort.

Since being here I have met many other missionaries. Mt. Hermon School is near here - one of the many American Methodist schools. It is for English speaking children but there are many children from Nepal and nearby countries. We are very near Tibet, Bhutan and Nepal. Nepal is a small country. It has always been called the country with closed doors because outside people are not allowed to enter it. Missionaries work on the border but have never been allowed inside the country. Recently Nepal has made trade agreements with the U. S. A. and it is believed it is opening its doors.

While here I have met several missionaries working among the Nepali people and hoping the way will open to get into the country.

The economic system of Bengal is already critical and dividing the province will make it worse. Many of my Language School friends are located in what will be Pakistan and their condition will probably be much worse than mine. The Muslims have never allowed missionaries to carry on their work unhindered.

Today (Saturday) we visited a tea plantation and factory. We saw all the processes of making tea. It rained and rained and we got wet. We still have some sunshine occasionally. The other night we saw the snow capped range of mountains in the moonlight. Beautiful!

This is the time of the year for mangoes and insects. The mango is a wonderful fruit. Until recently I ate an orange every day. Now we are eating mangoes and pineapples. It is impossible to get oranges now as they are out of season. We still have bananas. They last throughout the year.

I had always heard about the millions of insects in India. I had not noticed them until recently. There are so many kinds that bite and make you very uncomfortable. I have escaped most of them but I had one good dose of bites on my legs. The varieties are leeches, sand flies, ants, pipsy fly and others such as fleas and bedbugs. Then there are the kinds that destroy clothes, books and pictures. Oh yes, India is a land of snakes, too. I have seen a lot of baby ones lately but I haven't seen any large ones.

Early in June the monsoons began in Darjeeling. I had read a lot about monsoons before coming out and had heard a lot more since being here. We were given many instructions on what to do and what to expect. Thus far it has not been as we expected. The weather in the tropics also does funny things. It rained much in Darjeeling but there were also many lovely days.

Our last class was over at 12:45 on June 29th. By two o'clock six of us had our trunks and bedding rolls packed in a station wagon and were on our way down the mountain. We hired the station wagon in Darjeeling rather than taking the baby train down the mountain.

My traveling companions down the hill were a girl from London, another from Wales, Mr. and Mrs. Sen and their Nepali servant whom they recruited in Darjeeling. Mr. and Mrs. Sen are Bengalies who taught us at the Language school. They are not Christian but belong to a reformed Hindu group who have done away with the practices of worshipping idols. They worship one God and think Christ was a great teacher but nothing else. Their religion is called Brhmo Samaj. Mr. Sen is also a high government official and was a former inspector of schools. He is sympathetic toward mission work and gives very valuable help. They were pleasant traveling companions. Much of the way down the mountain it was rainy and foggy. When we were about half way the clouds lifted, and there ahead of us we saw the vast level area four thousand feet below. The rivers could be seen winding through the monotonous flat area. The sudden view was breath taking. By 5 p. m. we reached the foot of the mountains and unloaded our things and waited for the big train to take us on to Calcutta. The breeze felt as though it was coming from an oven when we got to Siliguri. We immediately began to feel sticky and have only been relieved of that feeling while standing under the shower.

The "Darjeeling Mail" soon came into the station. We chose the Inter Reservation. By getting the reservation we are assured of a place to sleep. We think it is more comfortable than first and second and there is a big difference in the price. The cars (bogies) were used as hospital bogies during the war. We always take our bedding rolls and place them on the wide bench like board. Since I had packed all the bedding in mine it was very comfortable. I went to sleep soon after the train started and slept until we were almost in Calcutta. My sleep was somewhat disturbed at times by tiny inhabitants. That is another thing we expect here.

It was almost ten before we reached the mission because it took us so long to get out of the railway station. We were very happy to get back and to be with the folk here and with the teachers. Mr.

Archibald is tired and has a very bad cold. Mrs. Lee is in very poor condition. She was very sick last night and it was thought she would not live. She is much stronger today. She has these bad attacks often.

Calcutta is in a very disturbed area. Many important steps have been taken and many more are to be made. We do not know just how we will be affected. A part of the province will be divided into what we call Pakistan. The British government is making hurried steps to give Independence and to leave India.

Recently, the policeman in charge of this area was killed. When they were having the funeral procession everything went out of control. Lots of people were killed and many more were injured. Last night others said they heard bombs, small home made ones which go off all night long. I slept through it all. These bombs do very little damage unless they are filled with acid. The favorite method of attack is to throw an acid bomb at a crowded bus or tram. The buses have not run by here for weeks and now the trams have stopped. Practically all the shops are closed and it is very quiet. I'm very careful to stay away from trouble and as long as they are not aimed at me I will be perfectly safe. It's these poor missionaries that will be in Pakistan that we worry about. We are already hearing things that indicate that they are not welcome there. Thus far, here in Hindustan (India), we have been assured that we are more than welcome to stay. They want our help. As long as they keep that attitude all will be well. However there is an agitation in some circles to make a law against proselytizing. Just how wide spread that is I do not know.

The weather here is UNBEARABLE. It had been lovely but it has not rained for several days and there is very little breeze. When we have no breeze I feel as though I am choking or smothering. The sky looks as though it is getting ready for a rain storm so we should have some relief soon. In Darjeeling I hated the rains but here I love them. You cannot imagine how refreshing they are. They take away all the heavy feeling and everything looks and feels so refreshed. India has had the least rainfall in ten years. I've decided the water has all gone to the Mississippi river. There has not been enough here to plant rice this season. If this situation continues it means another bad crop failure and famine. The Indians are just barely living now. We read of the need all over the world and the bumper crops in America. We've had first hand information from China recently and it is worse there than here.

Ram has broken his leg and is in the hospital with it strung up. I went to see him yesterday. He has developed fever also, maybe malaria. They were bringing in riot cases while we were there. Mrs. Lee is still very weak. I had a nice visit with her one day last week

Five small girls are still with us. I'm afraid they are getting spoiled here. I gave two a spanking the other day and it certainly did work. They are as sweet as they can be. They never get tired of looking at my fingers. One of them wanted to know if I could eat rice. They always eat with their hands. I guess they think I am greatly handicapped. I'm not doing much besides studying. There is not much school going on since the serious trouble. The day scholars cannot come but we try to carry on with the boarding students.

A lovely breeze has just started and it certainly feels wonderful!

We had a good Fourth. It was also a Muslim holiday. They celebrated much as we do on our Fourth. We saw lovely fireworks that day.

Recently at the docks here in Calcutta the two sergeants hired to watch the cargo were arrested for stealing. It seems to me that the policemen here run from trouble. I do not blame them as so many of them have been killed. Two came into our building the other day and asked Mr. Archibald if he heard the firing out in the Square. He said he did. Then they wanted to know why he didn't go out and see who it was. And so life goes on while I sit here under a fan and study, sleep, eat and walk up and down steps. There are too many people here for it to get boring and plenty to see from my box office seat, the verandah in front of my room.

The other day I had to do some shopping. The buses were not running. The trams had just stopped because of the danger in this area. There were a few taxies, rickshaws and horse gharries on the street. An order had just been issued that no jeep or other vehicle could be driven unless it was painted red, white or pink. Ours was in the process of being painted pink but the shopping was urgent. I went out on the street and tried to get a conveyance but all refused to take me where I wanted to go. I finally walked. In the bazaar I found prices very high. Some more than double what they should be. One man explained that they had to ask more because of the risk they were taking. I have learned to bargain so I bargained the prices down somewhat but not as low as I thought they should be. I was determined to get a conveyance to bring me home so began looking. Many were anxious for customers but when I gave my address they looked frightened and made the "cut-throat" sign. Not one would give me a ride. Finally I got a rickshaw to give me a ride part of the way. Later in the day I tried to use the telephone. When I picked up the receiver I could talk to many people but could not get the operator to dial the number I wanted. After long patient waiting and trying I was able to get connected to the right number. The telephone operators are afraid to go to work and thus we have extremely poor service. The same is true of the post office and dozens of other services.

Most of us do not realize the vastness of this country. It is huge and has many types of people. Life in other parts varies greatly. We live in the center of this large city. Calcutta has been classed as the fifth largest city of the world and the second largest of the British Empire. We find just about everything here that is found in any large port city. Just this week our large daily paper described the life of 10,000 Chinese that live in this city. There are many ethnic groups including a very large European population and a still larger Anglo-Indian group. Most of these groups can be numbered but there is a vast Indian population that amazes us when we think of the number of human beings that are crowded into this small area.

We have many types of transportation. Calcutta has a fine tramway system. The nice clean modern trams are a real comfort. One can go a long way for about two cents. I especially enjoy the trams: maybe it is because we don't get the privilege to ride on them very often. When I first came there was a strike that lasted for months. Now they do not run some days because of the riots. Unfortunately those who want to make trouble like to shoot or throw a bomb into a crowded tram. We also have buses that are just as cheap and convenient as the trams but not quite as comfortable. Some of the buses are double-deckers. Both the buses and trams are filled to capacity. It is a real sight to see a full bus. They hang on the fenders and usually there are two rows on the back bumper. How they stay on is a mystery to me. We have plenty of taxies driven by

Sikhs, a small religious group. We know them here by the turbans they wear on their heads. The taxies range from real old rattletraps to the latest model of Fords and Chevrolets from the USA. Then we have the gharries. Gharries are buggies and in some parts they call them victorias.

But the method that was the strangest to me was the rickshaw. They are a two-wheeled cart like thing pulled by a man. We find them very convenient to use when the trams are on strike and the buses full. The men seem to pull them with ease. We practically always use them when we go to market. Out in the villages they are often pulled by some one on a bicycle. All these modes of transportation are affected by the division of India. The pullers or drivers always tell us whether they belong to Pakistan or India. There are many types of cars and army vehicles on the streets. These have taken on new color recently since the Government ordered all to be painted red, white and pink.

Food and other commodities are transported in all ways from coolies carrying the baskets on their heads to slow carts pulled by oxen. As we travel we see large groups slowly winding their way along and getting in the way of all other traffic and causing traffic jams.

On Sunday July 20th we had five and one-half inches of rain. The streets were flooded because the drains could not carry the water off fast enough. We did not get out all day. We had services here because we could not go to the church. That rain brought us relief from the heat but the relief has about worn off. The atmosphere is very damp. Living in this monsoon season brings new experiences. I find that practically every thing I have is getting very moldy. We have to watch everything very closely lest it be completely ruined. Things that I use everyday, like my Bible, get moldy. This is the time of the year we do not want many belongings to take care of. I have succeeded in keeping things from the mold but some insects ate holes in two of my garments recently. I have taken care of them by giving them a good dose of ddt.

People here are eagerly looking forward to August 15. That is the day the British hand over government to the Indian people. We are hearing much about plans of celebration. In the recent weeks the Muslims have been demanding that they be given Calcutta. We are afraid that this might cause more trouble.

I teach a class three times a week and do many other small odd jobs. Mrs. Lee seems stronger now. One of our boys broke his leg and has to be in the hospital for some time. Another very small boy had to go to the hospital for another sickness. There is always something in our large group in this land of diseases.

They are unloading flour here from the USA and are we happy about it! I am not half as happy as many people because I've not actually gone without bread. Our bakery has been able to supply our ration all along. But many people here had to go without. We have heard the 'no bread' song many times. This should bring some relief.

Chapter 4

INDIA TAKES A NEW WAY

The unbelievable has happened! And it is nothing short of a miracle. Gandhi and all the leaders are saying it is a miracle. On August 15th as Independence was declared, Muslims and Hindus embraced each other and started yelling "We are one." The communal trouble that broke out in all its fury one year ago tomorrow has come to a sudden stop. Three days ago it was very bad and the situation looked hopeless. Men, children and even women are thronging the streets. Christians, Sikhs, Muslims, Hindus, Chinese and the white people are all joining in the celebration. A few moments ago I saw one of the American army trucks go by. It was loaded with people all yelling "Jai Hind" - Victory to India!

Last night at about seven they started yelling, parading, shooting of guns and bursting of large crackers. It had a much different tone than that which we heard days before. All night long it went on and is continuing to increase in volume now at 12 noon. There are many types of procession and parades. Now in front of me the communists are carrying their flag with the Indian National flag. We marched our girls to church for a short service and then back here to a flag raising ceremony.

The buses are not collecting fares and the trams are giving theirs to charity. They are all crowded to capacity, fuller than I have ever seen them before with everyone yelling to the top of their voices. Everything is decorated with green, white and orange and the flags are innumerable. Small schoolboys go by with their spotless white suits and white Gandhi caps. Gandhi himself came to Calcutta this week to try to restore peace. He toured our area. The situation was so bad he decided to stay and moved into a small hut near the property that used to be our boys' school. He is spending the day by fasting.

As we see the scenes today and read the Independence speeches of both new countries we are very encouraged. Maybe India will show the world what she can do. Pakistan realizes that she must cooperate with her Indian neighbor in order to exist.

Park in front of Lee Memorial where students gathered.

The air of festivity continued for about two weeks. This morning on the park in front of our building thousands, probably 50,000 students from all groups, gathered and began their parade to show the good feeling that existed among them. Then they were to give money to relieve thousands who have been made homeless in the eastern part of our Province that is now East Pakistan. It was an impressive sight to see the throng of students rejoicing in a very orderly way. The youth here as in other countries are the ones who get the most excited. They have often been the leaders of the trouble but today they are a united group. All religions were represented as they paraded the streets. Gandhi is in the city and speaks to large groups every day ranging from 50,000 to 200,000. I went to one of his meetings and saw him. He is probably influencing more people than any other one man in the world. He has constantly stood for nonviolence in a country that has been torn by war for years. He is very happy over the change in Calcutta. He says he is seeing one of the dreams of his life come true. In this time of crisis India has some great men in charge. In spite of all that has been said to the contrary there is hope that India will become a strong, independent, and peaceful nation. I am glad that I have come to India at this time. I am ready for any thing that comes. Her problems are my problems.

In the joy of excitement the people seem to have forgotten many of their struggles. Everyone knows that there are many problems facing the new government but the masses of the people think this new government will be able to do anything to meet their need. In a few short weeks we are told the supply of rice which is the main food will soon give out. I pray that with this fresh enthusiasm the new Government will be able to do something to prevent the people from starving to death. This approaching food crisis will bring new burdens and responsibilities to our mission. The scarcity of some foods will make those available much higher.

The monsoons are bringing us much rain now. With the rains come some forms of sickness. Many people about us are sick. I, myself, did not escape. I was sick for about a week with the flu. I am much better now and have just started studying again. Aside from being sick I have found many other duties to keep from studying the language. I was busy helping plan Independence Day programs. Next week we are to be presented to the Governor of the state along with other Girl Guides (Girl Scouts) of the city. Our group has one of the main parts on the program so I will be helping in that. We have been told that our new Governor is a very wonderful man. He comes from South India so does not know the language of this area. Our program will have to be in English for his benefit. There has been much talk of doing away with the use of the English language. I believe that is impossible because it is more widely used than any other language. All the educated people know how to speak English.

In the middle of September we held special services for the children. We had a children's evangelist who was with us about ten days.

I am more convinced than ever that the people of Calcutta want peace and they are doing their best to maintain it. The problem is a huge one and few people can realize all the complications. As far as the mass of Muslims and Hindus and their leaders are concerned they want peace. The battle now seems to be against what we would call crime and gangsters. Here they call it goondas. These goondas are out to steal money in any way they can. This last outbreak of violence is now said to be caused by them alone. We are told that 3,000 have been arrested since Sept. 1st. That should make a difference in conditions in this city. We still read of armed gangs robbing people in broad daylight. Aside from the goondas we have large groups of refugees coming in from northern India where most of the trouble has taken place. It is hard for them to forget what the Muslims did to them and they are somewhat antagonistic towards the ones here.

As I write this I can look out on a beautiful sunset. The sky varies from a bright melon to a light pink. In the foreground the tall palm trees stretching up from their bright green base add to the beauty. Sprawling under these trees are the men in their white dhotis, the long cloth the men wrap around their waist that forms a divided covering for each leg. In the dusk we cannot see all the unpleasantness that lurks near by. This is the land of extremes. In no other country can you find the beauty that compares with India's beautiful spots. Often we sit and watch the sunset in silence. After seeing so much that is unlovely it refreshes us to see the beauty of God. And then we think of how God wants to make every human being an example of His handiwork. We can call to mind a few people who display His beauty just as much as these beautiful sunsets.

The monsoons are now drawing to a close but before they let up they brought much water to this part of India and in some places floods have resulted. Not only have the floods bought present distress but they have destroyed much of the rice crops that people were depending upon to bring relief to the already existing shortage of food. In the villages where we have Christian workers the price of rice has already soared to a very high price and is practically impossible to obtain. Some have begged us to take their children and thus save them. We are trying but we seem to be able to do so little.

October 2nd was Gandhi's birthday and a holiday. We celebrated mine and his together. All the teachers and I went down to the docks and took a ferry down to the botanical gardens. We had a lovely boat ride down the Hooghly River and I enjoyed it very much. I think there is nothing like sailing on water. We had our picnic lunch under the shade of some lovely trees and by a pond with water lilies in it. It was nice and quiet even though there were many other people there. We continue to speak of Calcutta as being quiet but "quiet Calcutta" is very noisy 24 hours a day. When it is not 'quiet' we have curfews and there is a deathly silence that is frightening. Calcutta continues to be free from the riots. One of my friends wanted to know if we were going to have to go home because of the trouble. Here we are feeling so good because of the peace we have for the first time since I have been here. We are now hearing about the happenings in other parts of India but for some time we did not hear very much. The situation in other areas seems to be improving. Recent rains and riots have interfered with communication. We have people with us at the present in distress because they cannot get word from loved ones in North India, particularly from the school for missionary children. Some people were supposed to arrive here from that school a week ago and they have not come, and there is no word from them. The rains washed out some of the railway lines but we thought that by this time some alternative arrangement could be made.

The other day I had a very happy surprise. I found some lovely voile. It was very beautiful and of course I could not resist buying some. It is just a little bit over a dollar a yard. I found stamped on the cloth "seconds from U. S. A. "I could not find anything wrong with it. I will give it away as Christmas presents to the teachers to make blouses for their saries. There may be a decrease in products from the U. S. A. I suppose there will always be smugglers. Laws do not seem to mean much to them. I do not understand the thinking of American business men or the public. At a time when we hear nothing but the talk of curtailing all American products the prices rise higher in America. I guess I do not understand economics. The news we get here about the USA comes through a different dye. There have been some good articles defending USA recently. Many think India is pro-Russia but I think the leaders are trying to be good neutralists. I'm sure they will have a hard time maintaining their position. Indians want to be good friends with both the USA and Russia.

Mr. Archibald was injured on Sept. 1 by a group of rioters while taking some of the workers home. It was immediately after the new outbreak and he was rushing them home before it got too bad he thought. Instead he got in the thick of it. He received several cuts on the face and a very bad bruise on the arm. He stayed in bed one day and then was up going as usual. Many hearing the news have tried to enlarge it. The rioters had nothing against him personally or anyone of his color. They were just an angry group and he got in their way.

Just one year ago today I set sail for India. What a glorious year it has been. As I look back over it my heart is made to rejoice again. I say with the Psalmist in Psalm 40 "Many, O Lord my God are thy wonderful works which thou hast done, and thy thoughts which are to us word: they cannot be reckoned up in order unto thee:

if I would declare and speak of them, they are more than can be numbered." I wish to praise Him again for the way He has led me into the place of His calling.

There are many things to praise God for. I will list a few:
- for protection during the disturbed days
- for supplying our physical needs — food, money.
- for giving me good health during my first year.
- for taking the Griffiths home safely
- for giving the Griffiths help in obtaining permit to return
- for sparing Mrs. Ada Lee from another serious illness
- For the countless ways he has used our teachers and workers.

Here are some of our needs.
- for continued help in obtaining food and supplies for all.
- for the closing of school in December and the new school year beginning in January.
- for safe and speedy return of the Griffiths.
- for three more missionaries.
- for money for expansion as well as to meet our daily needs.
- for Divine guidance for planning in the new India among new opportunities.
- for prayer our workers.

\-   for the Church in the new independent India and that the
gospel may continue to go forth unhindered.

\-   for me as I continue to study and also as I begin to take on
new responsibilities.

God has been very near. He has fulfilled His promises to me
and has given me many new ones to stand on. I am claiming Isaiah.
58: 10-12 for this Mission.

"And if thou draw out thy soul to the hungry, and satisfy the
afflicted soul; then shall thy light rise in obscurity, and thy darkness
be as the noon day. And the LORD shall guide thee continually, and
satisfy thy soul in drought, and make fat thy bones: and thou shalt be
like a watered garden, and like a spring of water, whose waters fail
not. And they that shall be of thee shall build the old waste places:
thou shalt raise up the foundations of many generations; and thou
shalt be called, The repairer of the breach, The restorer of paths to
dwell in."

I came to Kaurapukur on October 11 to spend two or three
days. It is the nearest thing to a vacation I have ever had. About ten
days ago I got a letter from one of the girls I met in language school
saying that her coworkers were going away and she would be alone
for two weeks. She gave me a cordial invitation to visit her and break
her monotony. When the Archibalds heard about it they said, "Why
yes, go and stay as long as you like." They seem to think I needed a

vacation so I got ready and came out. This is a regular village and very typical of thousands of such villages in India; yet it is very near Calcutta. To get here I took one of the trams to the end of the line and then I got a rickshaw pulled by a bicycle. That was something new to me. When we came to a large canal I had to get out. We crossed the canal on a "ferry," flat poles tied together. Then we walked the rest of the way. Sometimes they travel the rest of the way in a "shalti" or dug out canoe. This mission is owned by the London Missionary Society. They have a boys' school, a girls' school and village churches. They also do some medical work with a dispensary. The compound is lovely and quite different than our quarters in crowded Calcutta. It really is wonderful to be out here where we hear frogs, crickets, roosters crowing and birds singing instead of all the hubble bubble of Calcutta. It seems to me that Calcutta gets worse. I'm sure it does! Since the people are free to move about they are doing plenty of it. For instance the communist held a rally on Wellington square almost every day last week.

A village in India is different to anything we have in America. The people live in their houses close together while their rice fields surround the cluster of houses. The farmers go out from their house to their little plot of land to cultivate it. Their whole farming system is different and since I have not had first hand contact I will not write much about it. To me it all seems worse than the feudal system of the middle ages. I'm sure the condition of the farm laborers is as bad as the peasants of those days.

Each little village has a bazaar section with the necessary food and supply shops. Most villages have a market day once or twice a week. This is the important time for getting food supplies. The building I am staying in is a paka one. Many buildings around us are of mud walls and grass roofs. Mango, banana and coconut trees surround the buildings. Out beyond our compound are the rice fields. These fields are a lovely site. The rice is tall and green and looks like it will soon be ready to head. The rice stalks stand in water. I have been promised a ride down the canal in a canoe between the rice fields.

Another important feature of this compound is what is called "tank". They are large holes filled with water. They are similar to our ponds but have no streams running into them. This compound has three: one for men to bathe and wash their clothes, one for the washing of dishes and one for the girls' bathing. They are a nice size and of course look grand for swimming but I don't dare risk it because of water borne diseases. Who would have ever dreamed that this American country girl would become a city girl visiting the country?

I came back to Calcutta after a week out in the village. It has been noisier than ever with the biggest puja festival of the year going on. Every day last week I took a group of girls out to enjoy the sights. Durga Puja is known as the Bengal National Puja Festival. Durga was one of their most famous gods. She was supposed to be a combination of three gods combined to kill a very evil god. She has ten hands. All during the week life size images were placed in many places for the public to worship or view. Some of these are works of art. Other than the image there are some sacred scenes like we try to reproduce the manger scene at Christmas time. The whole week was given to festivity. On Friday they went in huge processions taking their images down to the river and immersing them there. This ceremony is a very famous one. I saw all or at least as much as I could. I had been wondering where the beautiful colors that I had heard so much about were. The people here wear white so much, but during this season the women came out in their brilliant colored saries and small children were also dressed in their bright colors. The men put on colored loose pajamas. All of this added to the beauty of the ceremonies.

The Hindus finished this particular puja on Friday and the Muslims began theirs that day. All day Saturday they were very prominent. Their most spectacular scene is their prayer meetings when they gather together in huge numbers and do all movements together. Their festival has ended. The middle of next week the

Hindus have another one. The Hindus all over India do not observe the same festivals.

This afternoon a Bengali Christian Conference will begin. It will last several days. Next week, Nov 3 to 9, we Methodists have our annual conference. It will be held in Pakaur which is 170 miles from Calcutta

Everyone is very proud of the fact that Calcutta is still peaceful. During all this festivity people expected trouble again but instead the Hindus and Muslims tried to show how much they loved each other. For example the Hindus would stop their noisy musical instruments when passing the Muslim mosque when the prayers were in progress. Such cooperation had been very rare. The people of Calcutta are justly proud of their shining example to the rest of India. It looks like war among some groups in other parts of India. Our state government has done some more things of which we are proud. They put down a recent strike that could have been very serious. The way they handled it should be an example to any nation. If the strike had been successful it would have meant that our girls would have had to go without rice and that really would have been disastrous. As long as the government does as well as they are doing we have nothing to worry about. What worries us is the kind of thing I am listening to and that we hear almost daily - a communist rally in the park in front of our building. I bought a book violently against America just to see what it said. I'm thankful many Indians are too sensible to swallow everything they are being told.

The cool season has already begun and it has made a difference in the way I feel. I actually have energy enough so that the work and study are enjoyable instead of a drag. I did not realize the climate was the blame but every body says it does the same to them. It does not seem unpleasant but makes one feel tired.

On Nov 10th we came back from Annual Conference. We were in Pakaur a week and enjoyed it. The railway station is spelled Pakur and the post office spells it Pakaur. Both are written the same in the Bengali language so both are pronounced the same. Conference was a new experience for me. It is not a large conference. There are 23 Indian preachers in addition to the missionaries. There were some principals of schools who always attend the conference as they are appointed to the schools by the Bishop. This year there were seven missionaries and the missionary Bishop. Three of us were new so it only left four of the older ones. In this the Bengal Conference we have work among four language groups: English, Bengali, Hindi and Santali. At the opening session the entire time was taken up debating what language we should use. Since India has gained Independence there is much talk of using Indian languages instead of English. Since English is the only language that is generally understood throughout India it will be a very difficult process. In time we think that Hindi will replace it and many moves are already being made to do this. In many provinces government records are being made in other languages and not in English.

A few people thought we should not use English in the conference so there was a hot debate. It was finally decided that a person could speak in any language he wanted to. People did just that. Aside from Santali, most people could follow what was done in any language so it was not as difficult as it might sound. Since our newest missionaries are Swedish we had the fifth language added. On the last day we had a very good prayer meeting with each one praying in their native tongue. It was an impressive service and the difference in language did not make any difference in the spirit of the service. It now seems certain that I will have to be acquainted with two languages instead of one. I will have to keep my ears open and naturally pick up Hindi. It is similar to Bengali and many of the words are identical so it should not be too difficult to grasp two languages within ten years.

I traveled to Pakaur with our Bengali ladies in women's inter class. Along the way an old woman got into the train with us who had never seen a white woman. It was very amusing to me but she was frightened. I had a kerchief on my head so that made me look strange to her. She spoke Bengali so when she began to ask people questions about me I could understand what she was saying. The first thing she asked, pointing at me, was: "What is that?" They had a hard time convincing her that I was a woman. She thought I was a small boy. Finally I took off my kerchief and showed her that my hair was long. She was almost convinced then but said: "If she is a woman she ought to wear a sari." She continued to be afraid of me until I began to speak to her in Bengali. She finally got over her fear and sat down and relaxed.

Another lady got in the train who was Muslim. She was wearing her black garment that covered every inch of her. To see me she peered through a hole covered with black net. She, too, was frightened and not because of me but because she was afraid she might be surrounded by Hindus. We assured her we were Christians so she felt more at ease. After the train began to move and she was convinced no men were around she began to pull the black purdah aside and to peep out. It gave me a funny feeling to be stared at from behind her black curtain. All I could see was her one big eye. Gradually, she began to pull off the whole thing and we discovered that she was a very nice looking woman and not very old. We also spied the little baby that had been under the robe. It had never made a sound and did not while they were with us as it probably was doped with opium.

I am back in Calcutta amidst all the noises. The drums are beating in the street below. I do not know what it means but it seems to be a sports' gathering. Calcutta is still peaceful and we are more and more confident that it will remain this way in spite of what is going on in other places. We have not kept up with the North India situation during the last week but are conscious that there has been fighting on a big scale.

I certainly am fortunate when it comes to mail. Right here in this same province it takes more than two weeks to get a letter through. In many places there is trouble with the mail. Many letters from the U S are coming in five days especially the ones that are mailed on Thursday. The plane leaves New York on Saturday and gets here on Monday and I get the letters on Tuesday, sometimes before breakfast.

The smoke (pollution) is hanging over us just like a big thick fog. We stay black all the time. The days are very pleasant. Calcutta is still peaceful but a noisy place. We are thankful that there is still communal harmony. We heard a rumor of something that happened in North India. If it is true we are worried. If only I had a radio that could pick up NBC New York we could find out if it is true. We have been hearing quite a bit of news of North India recently. If possible they keep serious news out of this part of India.

Everyone here is busy getting ready for the closing of school. One group of examinations begins on Monday and there will be tests from now until Dec. 20. Two other schools will come here since we are the center for their examinations. There is always so much to these examinations.

It is time for Muhoruum (Muslim festival) again. They do not follow the same calendar that we do so dates vary. Tomorrow night and Sunday night will be the big nights and perhaps we will not get much sleep. There seems to have been something for the people to parade and beat their drums about for the past two months.

The food situation here is much better. New crops are beginning to be harvested and that brings relief. It is orange season again. Soon the tomatoes will be getting ripe and we will like that. We received an invitation to join the other Americans in a big Thanksgiving dinner with turkey and all the trimmings. All Americans in the city will be there probably except the poor missionaries. It really is beyond our pocket books. I really would like to go to see who is here. We have heard that the city is filled with Americans since the English have gone. We meet very few Americans. In times long ago the Consulate has entertained Americans on Thanksgiving but I suppose now the group is too large and things are too expensive to do so. It used to be that they could live much cheaper than they can now. Now everything is so much more expensive. When the army surpluses run out it will be even more difficult. Now there are few imports from America. They say practically none but we can not believe that. They must have the dollar currency to buy wheat.

Mrs. Lee had been much better. She was almost her old self again but about two weeks ago she had another attack that set her back again. She amuses her self. She has a large magnifying glass that she uses to read. She is not able to be on her feet but pushes around some in a chair. She has never been one to give up. I'm sure that it is her will power that keeps her alive.

For the last few weeks I have thought of nothing except our language examination and was busy studying for that. I was examined for three days this week. I finished yesterday so once again I am relaxing and beginning to think of some other duties. I praise the Lord for the help He gave me. Throughout the examination I was conscious that people were praying and I knew God was helping me to think clearly as I answered the questions. I will not know the results of the written part until later but they told me that I passed the oral part. I am thankful for that. Now I can begin to look for real service for the Lord. There will be plenty of studying to do but after the first year we are supposed to be able to do half time work.

During December the temperature goes below 60. A strong breeze is blowing and we are uncomfortable if we do not wear a light sweater or jacket. On the outside the sun is very pleasant. The cool weather is very refreshing to all of us. But those who do not have extra clothes suffer from the cold. This morning I watched the girls come to school and I noticed that many of the small girls were wearing two dresses instead of one. This is examination time for them. The school year is closing. Next week we have a Christmas program and the closing exercises of the school. All the girls who have parents or relatives who will accept them will go away for these holidays. However there will be a group who will stay with us. During their holiday we plan to have holiday with them and will spend much of our time taking them out or playing games with them here. A new school year will begin about the middle of January.

We had a very nice Christmas. Practically every day since my examination has been filled with something special. On Dec. 15 Nehru visited Calcutta for the first time since Independence. We thought it would be interesting to see Nehru, hear him speak and to see the crowds of people so we went to the maidan, the big field where he was to speak. There have always been streams of people on the streets but that day there were oceans of them. We pushed through the crowd got into the ladies lane and to a section near the speaker's platform. All around us as far as we could see there were people. We didn't like the tone of voices and as the time drew near for the hero to come it got worse so we left. Later we learned that all the commotion was because the loud-speaking system had broken down. Many people were hurt in the mad scramble to get near the platform. Nehru came but could not speak because of the confusion. He finally left and gave a radio address. The newspaper said it was the largest gathering in Calcutta's history. I believe it.

On December 19 our school closed. Both here and Elliott Road had Christmas plays for the closing exercises. The children were very cute as they did the nativity play. The girls here at the Square gave a play that had been translated from English. It was very similar to ones we had given with the story given by reading the scripture passages and lots of singing. They did it extremely well because they know how to make it look like a real Biblical scene. It was very beautiful. Even the girls who represented angels looked much as you would expect angels to look.

This year we gave the children their gifts on Christmas Eve. They enjoyed them and had a grand time playing with them afterwards. It was a joy for me to see our own children again all together. The boys are here from the Baptist Boys' School. They certainly have grown during the year. They did very well in their studies. The high school girls are here from United Missionary High School. They have done extremely well and leading their classes. It makes us feel good to have our girls among the upper three of the respective classes.

We have four orphan girls in high school and others who are daughters of the workers. We had a very successful year. The teachers have worked hard. They have greatly missed the Griffiths. In addition to the closing activities of school with examinations and getting ready for Christmas, they have knitted about 25 pounds of wool for relief.

On Christmas day we went to Church at 8:30. The Church was packed with people. Many Christians only go to church on Easter and Christmas. Yesterday the Church could not hold them all. After Church we came back and at 12:30 we ate Christmas dinner. For the first time in many years there were no guests. The Archibalds, Miss Welles, Mrs. Lee and I had dinner together. A few days before Christmas Mrs. Lee got up and walked. She is just as amazing now in her old age as she has ever been. We were afraid that she overdid but it doesn't seem to have bothered her. After we ate she gave the children fruit as it is her custom. Then we entertained the children. Mrs. Archibald took the older ones for a walk down by the river.

I took all the small ones to the 'Square' (park in front of our building) and they had a grand time sliding down the "shooty shoot." They drew lots of attention and especially since there was a memesahib (white woman) looking after them. I heard lots of the onlookers asking the children about me and I could also hear and

111

understand the children's answers. They told them that they were orphans and that we were very good to them and gave them all their clothes and food. Then they told them how good we had been to them at Christmas time. After we brought the children back in the older ones had not returned so we had a three man orchestra brought in to play music for the children. At holiday time such people roam the streets looking for a place to play their instruments and earn a little money. One had a bag pipe, one a drum and the other something that looked like a bugle. They played some good Indian music.

At six we ate rice with good chicken curry and finished the day. All during this Christmas there has been much of the air of Christmas. Last year there was trouble and Christmas was not very different from any other day. Here on Christmas even the crowds in the bazaars would probably exceed the crowds in any city at home. I went to buy a few things and found that I had made a great mistake because the price of everything was higher. However, I was glad that I had seen the bazaar on the day before Christmas. The most interesting was the great quantity of things the Chinese had made for decorations. All kinds of interesting things made from paper. People are saying they will do away with Christmas holidays. I do not believe it after seeing the way everyone seemed to enjoy this Christmas. Then, too, I'm sure it means much for many of the pocket books.

Today in a village many miles from here the Methodists had a get together with eating and sports. Many families from Calcutta went. I went along and we all had a grand time together.

Until a few days before Christmas we had rain. For about a week it was rainy, damp, dark and cold. For Christmas it cleared off and is extremely nice. The rain was miserable but helped clear up the smoke and dirt. Tonight is as beautiful a night as one would ever see anyplace.

I received a Christmas package from U. S. on Dec. 31. The duty on it amounted to about $4. All the dresses are very useful and I'm sure it is worth more than three times the duty. The surprising thing to me is that the dresses fit the children without having to do much alteration.

The communists and some other unions called a general strike for the city. It was a complete failure. It really made us feel good. Many attempts were made to create trouble but those attempts also failed. We were a little frightened and thought something might happen but things went off peacefully and smoothly. Again we say "Hurrah" for the government and people. You never hear much about our Governor in West Bengal but even Gandhi and Nehru will admit he is the brains of the political developments.

Chapter 5

INDIA MOURNS

Today January 31, 1948 all India is mourning. The great leader and father of the nation has fallen. His tragic death is being compared with the crucifixion of our Savior. Gandhi has been shot by one of his own. The longer I have been in India the more I realize what this one man has meant to the people. The masses have looked upon him as their savior. Now he is no more. All about us all mankind and even nature is wearing a mournful look. We are stunned. What will it mean? I believe there are other great men who will carry on. Somehow in spite of all the difficulties, I believe that India will stand and rise up as a great nation. May this tragedy be a source of inspiration instead of discouragement!

Men, women and children are silently gathering on the Square in front of us. How often I have seen them gather there by the thousands and for all purposes but today it is a very different scene. Other times they have come shouting slogans but today the people are streaming in from all directions with bowed heads. From here they will begin this procession of mourning. Five months ago he fasted and put his life in danger that these same people might live in peace. Since that time there has been peace here. Just a few days ago he fasted in another part of India for the same purpose and a change in

115

the attitude of people was brought about. He was a great man with a great soul and truly lived for others.

Everything in this city is completely closed. All offices and means of transportation! Never before have we seen things so completely closed up. I will spend a quite day reading and writing letters.

Our new school year began early in January. Every class is full. Some have as many as 50 and still we had to turn girls away. All the schools in the city are the same. There are not enough schools to take care of the children who want to go to school. The people of independent India are very eager to have their children educated. This places upon us new responsibilities and new opportunities. I pray that we might adequately meet the challenges and be faithful in fulfilling His will for us.

The teachers are so overloaded that they are hoping I will soon take over the teaching of English. It will mean a complete change of schedule and nobody wants to do that until the Griffiths return. By the time they get here it will be time for language school so I don't know what will happen.

Refugees are still coming in and living all over the place. Smallpox is raging and cholera is on the increase. I had another smallpox vaccination last week and it took. I'm very happy it did. Of course I have been droopy because of my vaccination but otherwise I am feeling fine and my energy is constantly increasing. I'm still mending and sewing, mostly at night.

We hear that postal service and travel in Pakistan is in a terrible state. I'm afraid I do not have much sympathy for Pakistan's case in the UN. I do not know the true facts and there are probably very few people who do but when Nehru said he wouldn't accept Pakistan if they tried to give it to him, I believe he meant it. He says he doesn't want the responsibility of it. He's got too much sense and enough to handle without asking for more. I'm sure that by now the Muslims are fed up with the fulfillment of their long fight for Pakistan.

Sometimes mail from Pakistan reaches us within a month and sometimes never. Packages sent from Calcutta, if they ever reach their destinations, have quite different things in them. Someone opens them up, takes out what they want and puts something else in to make the weight. Trains going into Pakistan from India change crews at the boundary line. Trains in Pakistan have lost all sense of schedule. All trains are filled. Many travel without tickets. Light fixtures have been stolen from the trains. Leather coverings off the springs have disappeared. There isn't as much chaos in India but I guess in places it is bad enough. This week rationing was taken off cloth and then suddenly put back on again. The officials are having difficulty in keeping ration shops supplied with rice even though it is the harvesting season.

The cabinet of Bengal had a complete change and now our neighbor, Dr. B. C. Roy, is head of the cabinet. He is just back from the USA. He is a world-recognized physician but we'll have to wait and see what kind of a politician he is. Don't think that things are worse because I have written like this. They're just the same and there are many reasons to be hopeful. There are many dishonest wicked men to cause corruption but as long as top leaders are as capable as the ones we have there is room for hope.

One of the strangest processions I have ever seen has just passed, and it turned out to be only an advertisement of a movie. In front were men carrying many colored paper decorations. Behind people carried a man and a woman in what we call a palki (a decorated seat carried on the shoulders of four men). The walking signboards brought up the rear.

The tragedy of Gandhi's assassination has also revealed in a much clearer light a group of people who are evidently trying to destroy the present government and the modern trends in India. The organization to which the assassin belonged has been declared unconstitutional and many leaders of it have been arrested. The majority oppose them When the majority oppose them can a minority of people overthrow a government and bring about chaos and war? Gandhi is the one binding link in India. If they forget him then there is every reason to believe there will be unheard of chaos with fighting, followed by famine, poverty, disease and all that goes with it. The indications are that they are not going to forget him in such a short time.

Even though it is hard for us to exalt Gandhi to a position almost equal with Christ and sometimes above we see in this the tie that will hold India together. One now can hardly say that India has never heard the name of Jesus. Over and over again during the last week Gandhi has been compared with Jesus. One of the workers tells of a conversation yesterday that she had with groups of people while she stood in line at the post office. She was telling them that Gandhi was only a man and she asked them who Gandhi tried to live like. They immediately answered, "Jesus." One of Gandhi's great aims was to bring all religions together. The newspapers took portions from the Gita (Hindu) Koran (Muslim) and the Bible. That philosophy in itself is one that is a hindrance to Christianity. People accept the ideas of Christianity and at the same time hold on to all that is Hindu.

After school started in January I did nothing but stay in and study. February has started off with a bang. On Tuesday night I went to a musical concert put on by missionaries. Afterwards we had our dinner in a restaurant. Tonight I am going to Salvation Headquarter for a birthday dinner for their only American member here in Calcutta. Tomorrow I will be gone all day. We are attending the closing exercises of Serampore Theological Seminary. William Carey founded the college. Mission Historians name William Carey as the first Protestant missionary. Serampore is not very far from Calcutta but I have not been there. I will see things of historical interest in the museum, and I will see some of the outstanding Christian leaders in this area as well as some distinguished guests.

I received the Bengali language examination results. I am fifth among 18 and passed in the second division with 72% - 645 points out of 900.

By the end of February the cool season left this part of the world. It took every ounce of my energy along with it. It really is not so very hot but it seems to me that the heat is the worst I have experienced. We had been marveling at the cool weather but did not realize it would leave so suddenly. Everyone around here is very droopy. I guess it is spring fever. I have opened all doors, pushed back all curtains, pulled my bed out into the middle of the room and propped myself up under a ceiling fan.

Last Monday was a holiday and we went out for a birthday treat for one of the teachers. We went to the airport which is 12 miles away. We thought we would see the Pan American or TWA flights but they were late and we couldn't wait. We saw an Indian plane land and Bishop Pickett and his wife got off. They left the next day for San Francisco. Bishops and delegates are flying to USA for the Methodist Church General Conference.

The final ceremonies for Gandhi were held last week and the period of mourning ended. Calcutta has really come to life again. In the square in front of us an international youth conference is in session. It is a big thing with delegates from most oriental countries and some from Europe. I'm not sure it is completely communistic but it is very red. In another part of the city a large exhibition is in progress. I will be going to it. There was an exciting hold up in the city today near the American Express. Some of the people staying here were there and saw most of it. It was an armed gang. The government has been trying their best to catch them but it is very difficult. I'm glad I'm a poor missionary and maybe it is a good thing that my dresses are faded. Crime is terrible in many cities.

The stock markets in New York have affected things here. Before I heard about the New York event I went through the Bazaar and cloth was cheaper. I bought a lovely piece of print for Rs2.7 a yard (about 80 cents) They say it will become cheaper, and there will be no shortage. All travelers have been amazed at Calcutta stores. More things are available here than any other place in India and perhaps any place but America. Army surplus peanut butter and jams are cheaper than the American public can buy them. They told us a long time ago the end of these supplies was coming but they still exist in great abundance. If prices continue to go down we will be alright. Recently the price of soap and other toilet articles for our girls has been extremely high, but we are hoping they will come down, too

The Griffiths arrived today. They were delayed a few days because of longer stops in Singapore and other islands. They say it is the best trip they have ever had. All look extremely well. We are glad to see them. Miss Welles left last Saturday. Now the Archibalds will be getting ready to leave.

Chapter 6

CONTINUING THE JATRA

Every Saturday night Youth for Christ meets in the Thoburn Church. I can attend now that they are so near. I am planning to go tonight. I like them very much especially the singing. Nearly all the singing out here is what American youth call slow and draggy. I like both kinds but I find lively American choruses very refreshing.

It is spring now. The old leaves are falling off and new young tender leaves are coming on the trees. In a few more weeks the beautiful flowering trees will be blooming. The gardens around the government buildings are a mass of color.

The Griffiths are busy taking over the work and learning all about the changes that have taken place since they went away. In these days of many uncertainties we feel better with the responsibility resting upon their experienced shoulders. The Archiblads did a wonderful a job in their absence. Now they are getting ready to return and take up their work in the Southern California Methodist Conference.

We need God's guidance for the future. There are many things that we would like to do but it seems that we are bound by many hindrances. We are now discussing what I will be doing after I finish my second year language course. The plan is that I will take the management of Elliott Road. That is where we have our small children. Even though I will not take the second examination until December I will probably assume responsibility of Elliott Road in July. The ten-year lease expires this year. We do not know what the government will do about it. We are in a land that has a new government. They are now forming their policies. It is impossible to predict what they will do. There are many other problems facing us. We are in God's hands and our confidence is in Him.

Our hearts go out more and more to those all around us who are in need. Daily we see the sick, the blind, the cripple and the hungry. We cannot get away from these things. Even if I left India now I am sure these scenes would haunt me the rest of my life. What can I do to help them? We want to continue to give homes to those who do not have homes. We want to bring up young men and women who will make a real contribution to Christianity and to society. We realize more than ever before that it takes more than money. It also takes much prayer and patience.

In the middle of March we had an awful storm here. It rained, hailed and the wind blew. It rained two and one half inches in 45 minutes. I have never seen anything like it before. It really cooled things off. Three days before it had been 100 degrees. The storm brought the temperature down to the seventies and we had to pull out sweaters and blankets. Now the cool spell is over and it is hot again but not nearly as bad.

We have had a very good Easter season. As I was in language school last year at Easter time this was my first Easter with our Christian people. It seems to me that Easter has a much deeper meaning to them than Christmas. On Good Friday we had a service that began at 12:30 and lasted until 3:30. The church was full of people and all remained very quiet and reverent throughout the whole service. The preachers in charge discussed the different phases of the crucifixion. All during the service we prayed that all those present would realize afresh what Christ had suffered for them. As we watched their faces we knew that many of them were thinking seriously. Again on Easter morning we had a long service but a much more joyful one, ending by all taking communion. During the course of the service several babies were baptized. In Hindu society when a person is baptized he loses all caste relationship and as for as his Hindu friends are concerned he is a social outcaste. Thank God many of these hindrances are breaking down. Some Hindus treat their Christian brothers and sisters as one of the family. However we still find many cases where this is not true.

Mrs. Lee celebrated her 92nd birthday on March 23rd. A few days before she was very weak and we wondered if she would remain with us. She told us that she was coming over here to eat with us the day before. We did not see how it would be possible but, she had the will power and she did it with no bad effects. Her prayer was a blessing to all that heard. Now day after day she lies on her bed in a helpless condition. She finds much comfort in the sustaining grace of God. She has always been a strong woman of faith and that faith is still very bright.

In the city all about us there are still numerous problems. Can any city have as many problems as this one? There have been some events to disquiet us but again the government has proven efficient. The most sensational news is that the communists of this province were declared unlawful and a ban placed on them. All their main leaders have been arrested. The government took this strong step after several incidents that indicated the destructive policy of the party. Living here on Wellington Square, which is one of the main centers for their meetings, we have observed their actions closely. We must admit it worried us to see them so active. Then, too, with all the recent developments in world affairs we wondered just what might happen here. For a long time we wondered what the attitude toward the communist party was. Often it seemed to be favorable. So we welcome these strong steps taken by the government. Public meetings have been banned so we are having some wonderful relief from the terrible blare of public address systems. The loud speakers are an awful nuisance when misused or when you have to listen to them day after day and often throughout the night.

Mr. Archibald has been very sick with a very bad infection in his nose. The infection has now been stopped and he is out of danger. In a few days they are sailing for Boston. They certainly have had eighteen months of hard work mixed with many worries. Both have lost in health and are very much in need of rest. His injury during the riots last September has had an effect upon both of them.

One of my jobs is examining the girls' heads to see that none of them went to class with any signs of "livestock." I have done a lot of looking at heads lately so they think I really am becoming an experienced missionary because I can recognize the creatures.

My errands took me to Sealdah station to make train reservations for some friends who are going to Darjeeling next week. Talk about the air being thick with humanity or people swarming around, as buzzards over a dead cow, does not do justice to the scene at the station. Somehow it affected me more than usual. Perhaps it was because I could hardly buy the tickets because all around the ticket windows refugee women were lying around like pigs in their wallow. They were not only lying on the floor but all their left over scraps of food, orange peelings and spilled water was all about them. It was difficult for me to buy the tickets without stepping on them.

127

Oh! What a city! Also, I have seen more leprosy recently and other terribly diseased people.

There are about 60 cases of the plague in the city. Everyone here except me had plague shots a couple of days ago. I am the most healthy person around. Since I am going to Darjeeling I won't need the shots. They are really something to endure. It is hoped that the plague epidemic will not get bad but with such conditions as exist in the city. I do not have much hopes of their stopping it. Cholera and smallpox have been raging a long time.

Mrs. Lee is strong in body but almost completely gone in mind. She isn't any trouble now but has very crazy ideas. Everything that she had wanted most during the latter part of her life has come true as far as she is concerned. So she is happy in her delusions. She tells me about how she has handed out money and food to the needy, the cows that now supply milk to the children and that her son is on his way to India. She has wanted them so badly that she thinks they have come true. Other than that her mind is often very good.

I arrived in Darjeeling May first. I had a very nice trip up. I did not know just what to expect because we had to go through East Pakistan. Before we got on the train in Calcutta we went though customs. The method was identical with what I went through when we got off the ship in Bombay. At the last station before we entered

Pakistan officials came on the train and again looked over our baggage. They didn't open it but only looked at it. We stayed at that station for more than two hours while crews changed. It was night and I was very sleepy so I went to sleep as soon as my inspection was over. This year I came the 40 miles up the mountain by taxi instead of the toy train that I took on my first trip.

The school had been in session more than a month and they were ready for the first examination. After two or three days of study I took the examination along with the others. Most of the others have gone off on long hikes of five and six days. They have gone to all kinds of lovely places. I am not studying but having lots of fun during these days when the others are away. We had planned a morning of tennis but it has been too wet. It is now showing signs of clearing up so we can play this afternoon. On Monday we hope to go horse back riding.

On clear mornings by propping up on my pillows I can see out across valleys and ranges of mountains to the snow capped peaks of the Kanchenjunga range rising more than 28,000 feet. This morning the scene was unusual. It is never the same. The valley below was filled with clouds and looked like the ocean or a bottomless pit. Above our heads dark clouds hung low but on the horizon the uppermost snow peaks were sparkling with the sunrays and a small patch of blue behind them. Around us was a dreary dimness but we

129

could see the sunshine on the snow peaks. As I prayed and had morning devotions I kept glancing at that marvelous scene. It is so refreshing to see some of God's beauty after seeing so much ugliness.

Many people who are working in East Pakistan are in Language School with us. Many tales of woe could be written about much that goes on. To us, the onlookers, it all seems to be so foolish and unnecessary. We do not see how the new country can survive but they have their own land and are determined to keep it going. Mail seems to be one of the worst hit. Sometimes it takes a letter a month to go from India to Pakistan, and some never reach. I know in some cases it has taken two months.

I preached my first sermon in Bengali yesterday. We will have to be giving many of these in class as well as writing essays, compositions and translating from famous Bengali literature.

We are having lots and lots of rain and I don't enjoy it very much. When it does clear up the scenery is so marvelous that it makes up for all the dreary hours of fog and rain. At the moment the sun is almost shining and in a few minutes I am going to a restaurant in Darjeeling to buy some ham and ice cream. I haven't had a piece of ham since being in India. Everybody has been raving about this ham so I hope to get some this afternoon. I also want some mangoes and pineapples. They are in season now.

Since being here I have been studying some and sleeping but it isn't all dull. Last night we had a small party - six of us - four girls and two boys. Four out of the six are Australian. The party was in honor of Harold Neufeld who is a Methodist worker in the Inter-Mission Business office at Bombay. He has been spending his vacation in Darjeeling and is leaving. We had a grand time and it was a lot like my college days.

Tomorrow the Mt. Hermon School is having what we call "sale day." The Governor of Bengal, future Governor General of India, will be there. He is also vacationing in Darjeeling. This year along with our language study we are having a short course in Islamics. We are studying the life of Muhammed and things about the Qur'an as well as present day sects of Muslims. Our lecturer for this is a professor in the Henry Martyn School of Islamics Studies which was located in North India but now in West Pakistan.

Letters from Calcutta tell us that they are blest with cool weather this May. They also mentioned that the "Youth for Christ" are having some trouble. They have been having very successful meetings and many Hindus have been converted. When people start changing their religion then other people get stirred up.

Last night I received a telegram from Calcutta saying that Mrs. Lee passed away on Friday night, June 11. Later I will receive by letter the details of her death and funeral.

I have been feeling extremely good and getting lots of work and study done. It is so good to feel ambitious again. I've caught something that doesn't make me sick but is uncomfortable at times. It is called dhobi's itch. Dhobi means laundryman. It is only in the awkward place that I use to sit on. That makes it inconvenient since I have to sit so much. To treat it I'm painted with gentian violet so that makes me a bright purple in places.

One of the Indian pastors died of cholera in Calcutta. It was a great shock to all of us. He was rather young and one of the most promising pastors. (His daughter, Beulah, married Bill Jones and served with her husband as a missionary for many years. They have now retired and live near Raleigh, N. C.).

Since being up here I have been able to understand Bengali sermons without any effort so I can enjoy them. Usually on Sunday we go into town or down to Mt. Hermon for Sunday morning service. This morning it was so rainy and because I got a typhoid shot last night, I decided to stay here. I read the biography of Sadhu Sundar Singh a famous Indian Christian.

Although it is stormy today last week was an exceptional one as far as the scenery was concerned. In the day time it rained and stormed, but at sunset the snows came from behind the clouds. At night the full moon shone upon them and in the mornings about five the sun rays upon the high snow peaks provided a glorious view. One morning we got up very early and went to Tiger Hill. There we got a brief glimpse of the rising sun shining on Mt. Everest. The scene of the clouds and the rising sun was a rare sight. I felt that it was just another step into heaven.

I came from Darjeeling at the end of June. Two days before leaving I fell down the steps and sprang my ankle but most of the pain was gone before the journey. Now I have very little pain but lots of swelling so I have it bound as tightly as possible and propped up in the air.

Dr. Griffiths met me so I arrived at the Square before breakfast. After the breakfast the Griffiths and I had a little conference and it was decided that I would move over to Elliott Road. Since I had most of my things already packed I decided to move right away so moved on July second. They had already done a lot of changing around and cleaning so everything was ready for me. It is worth at least Rs 500 ($160) a month in rent if not more.

On one side of the second floor there are two sections. The other section will be infirmary for the children. As I come up the steps I enter a big living room. It has a nice living room set in it and will be very lovely with only a little repair. There is also a piano that will not make a sound until it is repaired. The living room opens on to a big spacious verandah where I expect to study and sleep at least 10 months out of the year. From the verandah I look down upon our garden and on to the Elliott Road. From one side of the verandah I enter a large room. It is well furnished with a large desk, a typewriter desk, a dresser, a fireplace with a mantle, two almirahs (closets) to hang clothes in, a book case, a radio stand, two small tables, a bed, four straight chairs and one easy chair. Adjoining it and also at the head of the stairs is another room that I will use as a combination of kitchen and dining room. It has some dining room furniture. In the kitchen I have a table, an electric hot plate and a food cabinet. Mrs. Griffiths has loaned me some of her lovely dishes, so if nothing else I have a lovely set of dishes. Next to the dining room is the bath room. It doesn't have a bath tub or shower but has everything else that is necessary such as the commode and the bucket and mug for the 'pour' bath.

From the living room and from the stairway doors lead to the teachers' room and the children's room. I'm not going all out for housekeeping yet. It is too expensive for one person. Part of my food will be sent over and I will do a little here. Then in the evening I will go over to the Square for dinner. One of the most enjoyable things about the place is the flowers and trees. We have a large compound with lots of fruit trees as well as flowering trees and shrubs. There is a nice space for the children to play. We also have some Indian vegetables planted and hope to get enough for the children to have one or two meals. We think we could even have a cow. That is a dream of mine. The only snag about the place is that it belongs to a trust or something and our lease runs out the first of 1949. We have applied for a new lease and are very hopeful that we will be allowed to stay here. It is in need of much repair but we will not do big repairs until we know we will have a new lease and are certain that we will be here several years.

All day yesterday I was unpacking, but even in the midst of that, I had to stop to comfort a child who had been badly stung by a bee and to take in a new little boy of four and try to keep him from crying as his folk went away. While I was away attending a Youth for Christ meeting and eating dinner, a girl developed an awful stomachache. They called me. I rushed home after dinner but she was asleep and this morning she is fine.

I thought living here would be quieter but it is still in Calcutta and I don't think I ever heard a nosier night than last night. Sleep was impossible because of heat and noise. Coming out of Darjeeling into this makes it worse for me. Then, too, I think I had learned to sleep to the tune of Indian music but last night we had American jazz fresh from America in a dance hall next door. It was mixed with sounds coming from several other houses and the mixtures did not blend. This is a Muslim and Anglo-Indian section.

The Baptist Mission headquarters (English) is a few doors from here. They are the oldest mission, dating from William Carey, and have a very nice establishment near here. I hope to get better acquainted with some of them.

Elliott Road is about one and a half miles from Wellington Square. It is still in the heart of Calcutta. Trams and buses run about every two minutes taking me to the Square or on to the business center. On my mother's birthday we took in a 11 day old baby, Ada Adhicary. We gave her my mother's name as her middle name. So she is Ada Etta. A few days later another baby two and a half months came. She does not have a proper name yet. Little Ada's father died six months ago and her mother died when she was born. A neighbor brought her to us and she was so doped that it was many hours before she showed any signs of life. She was the tiniest little thing I have ever seen. Now she looks much better and weighs four pounds. Neither of the babies are here with me. They are both at the Square. I have enough to begin with - without two tiny babies.

We've taken another child or two here. A few days ago a widow came from the village where we have work to help in the kitchen at the Square. They brought her small girl of about five or six. You should have seen her. She fought like a wildcat when her mother tried to leave her. She kicked, fought and screamed for all she was worth for a long time. Then she decided to give up and is quite happy now. She enjoys playing with the other children.

We have 73 children now. Twenty-five are entirely dependent upon us. Eight pay full fees and all the rest pay from one to eight rupees a month. Many of them only have one parent living. Some are from very poor homes. There are five Hindus and one Muslim. All the others are from Christian homes. Twenty five are from Methodist families and the 25 dependent upon us make 50 Methodists.

Our older orphans are over at the Square or away in school someplace. Last Monday two of our girls went away to Isabella Thoburn College in Lucknow. In this land, as in England, everything depends upon passing the examinations. In order to get a high school diploma the student must pass the final or matriculation examination. This year four of our girls took that examination. All passed and two passed in the first division. To be in the first division is a real honor. One girl got distinction in two subjects. She was a temple baby. (She was born in a Hindu temple in Puri where her mother served the priest)

We've come to the time of the year when things are scarce again and the price of everything is high. The mission is in the need of more money so we can pay our workers more. Some are having a struggle to make both ends meet. Bread is scarce and very high and the same for potatoes. Chickens are a dream now as they are so expensive. Beef is plentiful and cheap but I'm tired of it. Most Indians will not eat beef. Even goat meat is higher than beef. Okra, eggplant and fruits are plentiful but expensive. Cucumbers and a few other Indian vegetables are plentiful but this is the time when the staple crop, rice, is scarce. The Mission has seen real famine so they know how to survive.

We raised the worker's salaries (by faith) and they are all happy. We hope the extra money comes in. They have needed a raise for a long, long time but we didn't see how we could manage. Now we understood they couldn't go on any longer with the small amount they were receiving. God provides. The monthly check from my home church Shiloh was more than the previous ones.

We've got some new buses in Calcutta. They certainly look grand but the old rattle traps are still on the streets. The population here does not decrease. I went to the business section today. I was amazed at the crowds of people. Saw lots of Americans. The new styles are beginning to reach Calcutta.

My work here is supervision of everything that goes on from all the gardening, cleaning up and teaching. We have sufficient staff but there are always little odd jobs to be done and then, too, some one has to make all the decisions. The discipline of the children is a very important job and it seemed that when I first came I did not do any thing but spank children. Now several days have passed and I haven't had to spank anyone. The children are really very good and get along remarkably well together. Now they are looking forward to celebrating the first anniversary of Independence Day, and the big treat they expect to receive. The anticipation of this treat helps them to be good.

We are still facing the problem of what will happen here at the end of the year when the property lease expires. Recently the officials have stated that they would like for us to continue but under the present circumstances we are finding it difficult to finance all the work. This place needs repair very badly and it would run into thousands of dollars. The government cannot afford it and neither can we. There are so many places where we could put large sums of money to very great advantage. So we are thinking perhaps it will be best to discontinue this unit of work. We can take some children over to the Square but not all. It means that other arrangements will have to be made for many of them. It also means cutting down on our work instead of increasing as we would like to do. There are always many requests to take more children. It will be very hard to turn away some we already have.

There have been many flu cases at the Square but the children at Elliott Road have been unusually well. We hope it continues. We had a couple of skin cases for some time. The children are doing fine in every way. It has been very encouraging to watch some of them improve and a little spanking has made a great difference with some; with others, it has been an extra kind word.

I suppose the other world events over shadow news from India. Things here continue to keep people nervous and excited. Missionaries and others must be having a tough time in Hyderabad. Burma is closing her door to all missionaries and fighting continues there. Calcutta continues to be the same unsettled place. Last week a man refused to pay his tram fare as thousands do each day. The tram conductor tried to insist but the man continued to refuse and finally slapped the conductor in the face. For that they took him to the tram depot. A mob quickly gathered, threw hand grenades and bombs at tram officials and rescued the man who refused to pay his tram fare of one anna or two cents. They acted as though the conductor had committed a great crime. Luckily there are millions who believe in paying their fare, and only thousands who refuse to pay their tram fare and other similar things that cause trouble.

During the last week in August I was sick with flu. It left me rather weak but I have fully recovered now and feel better than I have in many months. The weather is still hot but the nights are cooler and that helps a lot. Here in Calcutta we have had the normal amount of rain for the monsoon season but in many places there are serious floods. Thousands of villages have been flooded and many people are homeless. Because of floods and war food has been scarcer here and our ration of rice was cut down so low that it was beyond reason. Dr. Griffiths made several trips to the ration shop and got it increased but it is 25% less than what is necessary. It means we must try to find other things for our children to eat and it is not so easy. There seems to be no end to these high prices and it becomes more difficult for us.

We had several cases of skin diseases and now we are having sore eyes. The sore eyes have worried us because next week the children are taking terminal examinations and I'm afraid several will not be able to do so. During the month we have also had two cases of malaria. We have wonderful medicines that cures it and a medicine to keep it from recurring. It seems to be very successful. Nevertheless, when a child's temperature shoots up to 105 degrees in three hours it makes me very nervous. We have to take one girl away because of a discipline problem. She came to us from the streets where she had been begging. She is much older than the girls of her class and is not learning very fast so we think it best to put her in a school where they teach more hand work. Our two babies are fine. Little Ada has gotten fat and is a beautiful baby. She did look pitiful when we got her.

These days much is happening in India; floods in many parts. The Ganges River is the highest it has ever known to be. That means thousands lose their lives and thousands more are made homeless. In the future it means less food. Already they have cut our rice ration at Elliott Road until it will be impossible for us to make out. Dr. Griffiths is trying to fight it out with the ration officials. Everything with food had been O. K. until now. India is fighting a real war now with Hyderabad, not riots or goondism but troops with weapons. Hyderabad is one of the many princely states of India. When the English left many of these states either joined the Indian Union or Pakistan. Hyderabad said "we'll join neither - we'll remain independent." They were very pro-Pakistan. I don't know about all the developments after independence but the Indian government claims conditions became very bad, and they are going to restore peace. Hyderabad is a large and rich state.

We knew this 'war' was coming and feared what it might mean fighting between Muslims and Hindus in this fair city. The

Muslims have pledged their fullest support to India and everything is fine thus far.

Mrs. Griffiths had a birthday recently. My children gave a program for her and it went over so big that we decided they must give it to all the big folks at the Square. They did so today. They really were wonderful as they gave a short play, sang songs and did other things. For Mrs. Griffiths birthday dinner we had ham and chicken. The ham was a gift from a ship's officer. That is the second time I have had it since I have been here. We had chicken several times lately. We have homemade ice cream every night and it is good!

I felt splendid for two or three weeks but during the last eight days my temperature rises above normal every day and went up to 99.2. So I made an appointment with the doctor and haven't had fever since. However, I will go for a check up tomorrow. I have kept going all the time and done more work than usual but not nearly as much study. Trying to get ready to pass the Bengali examination in December is harder than anything else I have to do. I think when I get that out of the way I will be all right.

We get only a Bengali paper here and I try to get the news from it. I hear English news broadcasts and sometimes get one from New York, but I get as tired of hearing them talk about the Berlin situation as I do hearing the Indians talking about Hyderabad. The best news broadcast is the one from London for the English forces in the Orient. The world is really in a mess. Since the Hyderabad situation Indian newspapers refer to the Security Council as the Insecurity Council. They were really mad at the whole world for the attitude they took in regard to the conquest of Hyderabad. Some editorials were very entertaining. Jinnah, the Pakistan leader, has passed away. Pakistan seems to be getting along just as well without him.

Bishop and Mrs. Rockey were with us for about ten days. He wants us to stay on at Elliott Road and he and the other bishops are the ones who make any official decision. They make no definite offer of funds from the Methodist Board. Sometimes it is rather difficult to understand the attitude of the Board of Missions toward us. It seems that they thought our policy would be changed after Mrs. Lee's death but we had no idea of changing anything. We ask what they mean by some of their statements but they do not clear up the mystery. We hope to remain the same faith mission and linked to the Methodist Church in India.

For my birthday I received two nice apples, the first ones since being in India. We have lots of fruit here but apples are not among them. A man who had just gotten a big shipment of print chicken feed sacks gave me five sacks.

Chapter 7

ENVELOPED IN FOG

In early October when I went to the doctor she explained and said that there was definitely something wrong but she had no idea what and furthermore she could do nothing to find out about it, and that the only thing to do was to go to a hospital for lots of tests. She rather frightened me. I came home and the Griffiths immediately decided that I should go to Bareilly in North India to one of the best Methodist Mission Hospitals. It would also give me a very definite change in climate which would be good. We wrote a letter to the doctor in charge asking him to reply by telegram if it was convenient for me to come.

On the night before the telegram came I got a very severe pain in my lower left side. The pain subsided and soreness settled around my ankle and my fever went up to 103 degrees. This started while I was eating dinner at the Square so of course I didn't go back to Elliott Road. I carried on so in my sleep that I kept both of the Griffiths awake all night. I think they were really worried about me. As soon as daybreak came Dr. Griffiths went to the Presidency General Hospital, Calcutta to see about getting me admitted. By that time my foot was very painful and swollen and red. It looked like I was in for blood-poisoning. I did have a touch of athlete's foot. He made all the

145

arrangements and took me to the hospital shortly after nine. I was taken straight to my bed.

They started to work on me right away. They took blood for test before I got undressed. Shortly the doctor of the hospital came in to see me. His first impression at sight was that I had filaria. That was not at all comforting. In fact, I'd just as soon be told that I had leprosy. At least there is a cure for leprosy but as yet they have found no cure for filaria. The only difference between diseases is leprosy is contagious and filaria is carried by mosquitoes. They have found no trace of it in my blood. They are still testing but I feel quite assured that everything will work out O. K. With this disease they say that I could live and work in the north of the United States but not the year round in South Carolina.

The thoughts of what could happen in the future was a terrible shock to me. It was so much so that I couldn't cry. I was more numbed than anything else. I was told that Dr. Griffiths walked around as though he was in a daze. My fever didn't last so long, just a little over 24 hours but the foot is just the same. Some of my organs refused to function properly but now they are getting better. They still are not sure what it is and they still may find the germ. They say they are planning to take my blood three more nights at midnight to see if the filaria germ is hidden away.

146

I think I am in the best place in the world for tests like these. They have the knowledge and experience of these diseases. They have been very good to me. I am in a lovely clean room for two patients. I have my own private Ayah (maid) who has to be here to give me all my meals, and she does all the other waiting on me like giving me water, combing my hair. The nurses bathe me twice a day and that's something I didn't get when I had appendicitis surgery in USA. This hospital used to be only for Europeans. But it isn't now. The only fly in the soup is the price. I will just have to hope and pray that it will not run up too high. I am near enough broke already. It is quiet here, too, except for the groans of patients.

I've had no more fever and the redness and soreness from my foot is gone. There is still some swelling. All filaria reports were negative and the x-rays showed that both my feet are all right. The doctors are still puzzled about my sudden rise in temperature and my red swollen foot. It has gotten better and they have not done a thing in the way of treating me. They have been trying to find out what there is to cure. They were ready to give me some injections for my foot but they got switched off onto my stomach. So I'm no longer a foot or fever case but a stomach case. As part of this routine they tested my stool. Seeing the results, they decided to make a fractional test. After that the doctor came and wanted to know if he was to go on testing. I said; "Of course, if you think it is necessary." He said:

"I do but it is going to cost you money and I thought perhaps you might still want to go on to your mission hospital in Bareilly."

Since I'm here and they've started it would be foolish to go some place else. This is as good as any place in the world. It is just the question of money. So tomorrow I go on a special diet. I'm not sure what the diet will be. Then on Tuesday they are x-raying my stomach. I presume they are looking for ulcers. They didn't find them when I was in another hospital and I haven't had as much trouble recently as I did then. I thought perhaps since 96% of the people in India have amoebic dysentery that I had that. Evidently they think I have a little more than that.

They still intend to give me the injections as a kind of experiment to see if they can get rid of the swelling. That will last two weeks and I have no idea when they will start them. The doctor is very good. I have confidence in him and am sure he knows what he is doing.

They x-rayed my stomach nine times in all of that area. After finishing the Barium series of five X rays they found that my stomach and bowels were in good condition and no evidence of ulcers. Still the facts of the fractional test could not be denied so they took another series of the gall bladder, four X-rays and they find that my gall bladder is not functioning properly and that it is the root of all my stomach trouble.

I have had four injections for filaria and my latest swellings are on the decrease. This is something new for treatment of filaria (at least in Calcutta) so maybe it will work wonders. They have never proven that I have filaria but there seems to be little doubt in the doctor's mind. They see so much of it here. The doctor has worked hard trying to find out what ails me. We think he has. At least he has found the reason for the stomach trouble and I am terribly afraid he is right about filaria. He hasn't fully made up his mind about how many injections to give me but at the present rate it will take almost a month to finish them. Except for the first few days I have felt pretty good and have found various ways to entertain myself. I have read a lot. One of the Griffiths, along with some teachers or girls, have come every day so that has broken the monotony.

School reopened this week after three weeks of holidays. Our conference meets next week. It is finally settled that I shall become a member of the Woman's Conference but it is necessary to move my local church membership here. In some ways I am almost afraid to become a member of the Woman's Conference. It gives them more of a chance to move me around as they like. They have already mentioned sending me someplace else. I definitely do not want to go. Some times it seems the Methodist Church views the Lee Memorial as a naughty step child. They don't always claim us but, yet would like to order us around as they wish.

I used a blanket last night, the first time in Calcutta since the heat of February. They have already moved all my things back to my old room at Wellington Square. The plan is for me to do odd jobs for the rest of this year. There will be plenty with exams and the closing of school.

We are in full swing of a new school year of 1949. We have every class full and have had to make a double section of one class. I think we must have turned away more girls than we took in. In every other school it is the same way. Everybody wants to go to school and there just are not enough schools. I have two full days of teaching each week and one day of office work. On the other days I am supposed to study, go to the villages and do other odd jobs.

I have been feeling extremely good and have gained four pounds since Christmas. My lowest weight was 113 but now I am 117 again and maybe more. It is good to be feeling so well. For two days now Mrs. Griffiths has been in bed. She has a terrible cold. The pastor of Thoburn Church is leaving this week. Until some other arrangement is made, Dr. Griffiths will act as pastor. He is taking on what should be another full time job.

We have no guests in the house at present and that ought to be news after the coming and going of so many people. It is only a lull before the storm because we expect a boat with several people. Another group is having a conference so that will fill us up again. We have a telephone again. The other night we did not have any electricity. During the day there had been processions and demonstrations and everyone thought something terrible had happened but we soon learned that a cable had broken and it was fixed in about an hour.

Yesterday and the day before I taught all day and had stacks and stacks of papers to correct. Today I will be in the office all day while Dr. Griffiths teaches science. I'm here now waiting for him to come and tell me what to do. Last week I did accounts for him. People have just about stopped coming to get their children admitted into the school. It seemed there was an endless stream of them. I'm sure we turned away more than we took in. Each person thought we should make an exception for his child. All this is a real sign that things are really changing in this land. For so long it was thought improper for girls to get an education and now they are clamoring to attend. Some schools are running two shifts but we felt we could not do that.

At the beginning of the year we closed our section at Elliott Road. We brought about 45 of the children to Wellington Square.

The others went home and some are coming as day scholars. It is very difficult for some but they are managing. Whenever anyone drops out of the boarding section, we take one of those children that was at Elliott Road. The 45 we brought here are the ones who absolutely had no other place to go. Last year we had a little over a hundred here, now we have 150.

I believe that God will heal me and that I can continue my work in India. But the Griffiths actions indicate that they do not have the same faith. That is a disappointment to me.

One of the girls fell from a second story window. She had a bad fall but now is perfectly all right. We wonder how she escaped death. The babies are fine. One of them is in the real cute stage. She doesn't walk alone yet but when we hold her up she really dances a jig. She enjoys hearing everyone laugh at her.

Our smallest baby, Ada Etta, has measles and we are worried about her as she is rather frail. The other baby started walking only three days ago. I taught her to take her first steps and since then she has been keeping it up. For weeks she had been walking around holding on to everything but would not turn loose so I played a trick on her. I made her think I was holding her when I wasn't. When she found she was walking alone she laughed, and clapped her hands. She was more tickled than all her spectators.

We still have chicken pox cases. We had a dozen and today we got another case. It is all over Calcutta and people tell of riding on the streetcars by people who are broken out with chicken pox. They say 57% of the people have it. The cases in the school have varied from very light cases to the more serious types. Some have had very high fever and suffered a great deal. We think there are two kinds. At least one girl seems to have had both kinds. She had a light case and a few days after she started back to school she came down again and was very sick. Many people who have had it before are having it again.

Next week the TB Association and Government are going to vaccinate our children for TB This is new in India and more or less an experiment. The Government has hired a famous doctor from Denmark to do this work and he is going to do our children. Many people in Calcutta now realize the value of inoculations but still there are many people who will have nothing to do with them. They would rather die with the disease. We sent out letters to the parents of the day scholars asking them if they wish to have their children vaccinated against TB and many have answered in the negative. Regardless of all the other terrible diseases in India, T B still takes more lives than any other in Calcutta and to me it is the worst one of all. Last week I spent several hours in the T B clinic and watched the doctor read X-rays and do screening work. Most of the cases had active T B I had my chest screened for a check up and they said it is perfect.

I helped Mrs. Griffiths buy 100 saries. It takes a lot of money just to clothe our children. Mrs. Griffiths will do that while the rest of us are away on our holiday but she already has most of the things collected. Dr. Griffiths will be away at the same time I will but for not as long.

While Mrs. Griffiths is away, Kumudini will come down stairs and room with me. It will be very nice to have a roommate for a change. She is an extremely nice girl. All who know her agree that she is unusual. We are very proud that she is a product of this institution and believe she will do wonders here in India for her own people.

As a result of some discussions and the last meeting of the Lee Memorial trustees in January, I think the relationship of Lee Memorial to the Methodist Church and to the Board is more clearly defined. Many thought that when Mrs. Lee died Dr. Griffiths would ask for the Board to take over the Lee Memorial and they wanted to do so, but when they got an idea of the financial responsibility involved, they were only too happy to let us continue as we are. The Griffiths are under Board appointment and support. Since I am a single lady I can not belong to Board of Foreign Missions. I would have to be under the Women's Division of Christian Service. They were asked to support me before I came. They replied saying they'd wait to see what I was like.

After three weeks of bounding health and strength I am again laid flat, the flattest I have been since last October. Periodically I have had low fever and a terrible achy body. Blood pressure remains low and I stay anemic in spite of tonics and vitamins. With this attack the doctor has a new idea and has started on a different line of treatment. He has not called it any name but he thinks I have an infection of some kind and is giving treatment along that line.

I often wonder what my life is accomplishing. It seems that out here I am not able to do anything much. If there is anything that makes me feel like giving up it is the feeling of uselessness that I get often. I do not mind facing the hard things if I feel like I am accomplishing something worthwhile but when I go on so long and nothing seems to be accomplished it is discouraging. Yes, I need to learn to leave the results with God.

There is unrest in the city again. Bombs, shooting and some people are killed but things are normal in spite of it. When I first came people would close up everything and go in hiding at the least little incident. Now they go on about their business hoping it won't come to closing.

One of our workers came down with cholera in our compound last week. He had a close call but is pulling through. A day scholar died with it last week. All our boarders are well. Two college girls came home from Isabella Thoburn College for summer vacation.

I started for Darjeeling on the 11th and arrived here on the 12th. The trip up the mountain was a pleasant one. Many people are traveling this way and it is difficult to find transportation for all. I came the last 50 miles in an old bus. The driver was very careless and as I was sitting on the outer edge I could see how near he came to the edge of the road. Once he ran into a stone wall and tore the fender off the bus. He drove on a short way until he was able to get another bus.

I am staying in Mt. Hermon School. Mr. and Mrs. Forsgren are in charge of the school. I am staying in one of the teacher's quarters and eating in the dining room with all the teachers and students. All the instruction is in English and they follow the British system of education. They have many races and languages here. There are many missionary children from England, Australia, New Zealand, America and other countries. This year they are teaching American history and other American courses and have more Americans than usual. The American type school is so far away from us in this area that many are thankful that they can send their children here. Other than the missionary children there are the various Indian races. Among them are the Nepali and Tibetan who are very interesting. They are way back in the Himalaya mountains. Some of the children have long trips by foot in order to get here. These two countries have never allowed missionaries to come into their area but yet they send their children out to a mission school. The children and grandchildren of the leading officials of both these countries are in this school.

The school is on a large estate owned by the Methodist Church in India The estate covers quite a large area of this mountainside and scattered around over the hillside at various levels are many cottages. At present all of these cottages are filled with missionary families who have fled from the heat to this wonderful resort. Many more families have begged to come but there are not enough cottages to go around. Missionaries with children in school have first preference, and then after them the young couples who want to study Bengali in the Language School have been accommodated. In some cases individuals have bought their own cottages. The early missionaries had a wonderful eye for business when they planned the mission work and bought the property here and throughout India. They had wonderful foresight and planning and as a result today we can be very proud of all of our institutions.

It is early morning. All the mountains about us are covered in mist and fog. The king of mountains has not shown his face yet. We are eagerly waiting the moment when the clouds roll back and the great ranges and deep valleys shine in all their glory. It is a scene worth traveling around the world to see. To us who have labored in the city teeming with humanity, we think it is a little taste of heaven. Ah, yes! Some day the clouds will be rolled away and we shall see our Redeemer face to face. What a glorious day that will be, and it is worth a life time of toil and struggle in this sin-stricken world.

A Baptist missionary from Assam was ordered to leave India by the government. He is in Calcutta waiting for a boat now. He has a very limited time to get out of the country. He is charged with non-loyal activities. I don't understand everything, but he works among remote hill tribes that are rebelling against the new government of India. Perhaps they think he had something to do with inciting them but I'm sure he would not deliberately do that.

There is lots of opposition to the ruling party in India and especially in Calcutta. Other political groups are trying to get power and we often wonder what the results will be. Recently in a by-election in Calcutta the ruling party was badly defeated. In some of the campaigning there was some violence, but the election went off peacefully. Calcutta remains a "hot spot" in one way or another. I do not like some of the revolutionary ideas of the group that won the election. Perhaps it will bring about a reform in the other group, and there is plenty of room for that.

A week ago yesterday I returned to Calcutta on July 1, 1949. The trip down the mountain was different. There were landslides that had blocked the roads so it caused me quite a bit of trouble. When I finally reached Calcutta I was worn to a frazzle. The heat did not make me feel any better and for the first two days I was dizzy and could hardly do anything. I did manage to do a little unpacking in order to be able to live through the week of examinations. Yesterday morning I finished my Bengali language examinations. It will be several weeks before I know the total result, but I already know the oral results. There were two parts: conversation, reading, and the delivering of a sermon. In the conversation part out of a possible 250 points I received 223 making 89.2%. In this part I was first missing distinction by a point but in the sermon I did not do so well, only getting 116 out of 150. My total percent for the oral is 84 and I ranked second. In comparison with the marks obtained by students in the last few years this is high. I am proud of it. I hope I did as well in the written part but I am afraid I did not. It is a great relief to have it over. I will be considered a full fledged missionary and take more responsibility. Mrs. Griffiths has hinted that she has several things in mind but we have not had a chance to discuss them. I hope I can take some of the load from her shoulders as she has so much to do.

There is a tram strike in the city. Nehru will be visiting Calcutta next week. Preparations for his visit are under way on a large scale. We hope the unruly elements will not cause trouble by their demonstrations against the present government. Calcutta seems to be the key city in this political unrest as she was during the communal unrest. We are close to China and Burma.

We have read about the terrible plane crash near Bombay that killed 35 people including 13 American journalists. Nehru is in Calcutta and in many circles he is not welcomed. More than 500,000 people gathered in one public meeting to hear him. Attempts were made to disturb the meetings but they failed. Calcutta is again the key city of unrest. This time it is all political unrest. Everyone blames the communists but there is a new group who call themselves Socialist Republican. It is they who won in the recent by-election. The man who won was formerly a strong congressman but broke away because of disagreements with the leaders. His brother is the famous hero of India who had a mysterious disappearance during World War II. He fought with the Japanese forces in that war. Among the students he is more revered than Gandhi. This new party will have strength. All of this keeps us in the same old mood of wondering just what will happen. We know by now that anything good or bad can come from it.

A committee is meeting and they are supposed to decide whether I am capable of being Editor of a Bengali Magazine. I have been assistant editor for some time. The editor is going to America on a crusade scholarship. There does not seem to be anyone else to do the job. My Bengali is not good enough for that, yet I may have to do it anyway. The lady, who is going to Garrett, is one of our faithful teachers and my Bengali teacher.

The Board seems to have finally taken full notice of our cry for more missionaries. We will be swamped if present plans are carried out. The Board plans to send single young people for a three year term. They are sending five such people to this conference. Four of the five will be in Calcutta. Two single ladies and two single men. The third single man goes to Mt. Hermon in Darjeeling. Other than this, the Board is sending three couples to this conference Two are regular and will be in rural work. The third one is assigned to the Lee Memorial to await entry into Burma. In all of this we are not getting anyone who we are sure will study the language and make this their life work. These other people will be able to do many things for us especially in the English work. We do have a good deal of that but we also need people for the vernacular work. The couple for Burma seems to be the nearest to getting here as the application for their visa has already passed through our office.

I am teaching or supervising English all day. When they inspected our school they said our English was very weak so we are trying to pull that up first. I have regular classes and give extra help to needy students. In addition I am taking over the publishing of a monthly Bengali paper. It is a big job for me as I'm slow at translating articles and proof reading.

The roof above the girls' hostel is being repaired. Other repairs are necessary. Thieves visited us two nights in succession but were unsuccessful both times. The first night one could not get over the fence and was busy trying to take off the hub caps from the car when some one heard him. He fled and got on the outside. We have tried to take extra precautions so a thief does not have an easy time getting into our place.

The rest of my results of my language examination have come out. I passed the examination in the first division - stood 2nd - another girl beating me by a few points.

We are having trouble with thieves. It looks as though they are determined to pester us. Last night one came up on the third floor into one of our guest rooms a few doors from mine and opened up some suitcases. He made too much noise so fled when a lady screamed. We all got up and searched for him. We think we know how he made his entrance and get-a-way. We are not the only ones pestered. Several times I have been awakened by people yelling "Chor, chor" (thief, thief) and then listen to the chase. We always try to catch them. Recently one of our newspapers reported that there are about 20,000 known criminals including all kinds of robbers in

Calcutta. It might be a nice city if they were all taken away. What worries me is that one of our own workers might be the culprit.

On September 16, 1949 I flew to Gauhati Assam. It was nice to see Bengal and East Pakistan from the air. It is amazing scene especially at this time of the year. The clouds obstructed our view at times but at other times we could see through or between the clouds. What we saw below looked like one vast flooded land. At this time of the year, East Bengal is just that, and that is what it is expected to be. Houses are built on high foundations and in dry season one wonders why they are so funny. During the rainy season they are surrounded by water and people go around in boats or on bamboo footbridges. The rice grows up through the water sometimes seven and eight feet deep. From the air we could see the huts all surrounded by water and then the green fields because the rice plants come up above the water. Sometimes they harvest the rice in boats. Another interesting thing is the way they have gardens. They cut the straw in the dry season and with bamboo and straw make a long float. When it rains and water rises, the floats stay on top of the water. They tie them to a post and plant vegetables on top. Then there are other things that grow in water that they eat. A missionary friend lives under such conditions.

Assam is a very fascinating province in India with more distinct races than any other area in the world. The Baptist (Northern Convention) have developed a great work here. I've come to one of their hospitals for a vacation. Tomorrow the doctor, a girl about my own age, starts examining me. She is going to trace several clues. I have no idea how long I will be here. The three things they are looking for are amoebic dysentery, filaria and gynecological diseases. The doctor here seems to think that my main difficulty is failing to build up after my sickness last fall and getting adjusted to the country. She has filled me with tonics and injections so I ought to be all right.

On October 1 I boarded the plane for the return trip to Calcutta. The mud shot up as our plane sped along the runway. It is a jungle airstrip. We are coming over white clouds and I see blacker ones in the distance. While in Gauhati I went to Shillong which is another hill station like Darjeeling but not as high. It was cool there and they say it is not as rainy as Darjeeling. The only thing I dread about this trip is the landing. As we lose altitude I get a headache. It will be worse this time as I have a terrible head cold. We are not flying very high. There are white clouds above and below us.

The rupee has been devalued. This has caused lots of excitement. We are waiting to see how it is going to affect us. Our dollars are worth much more but we'll have to wait and see if prices go up so high that we do not gain anything. Our new exchange rate is worth about 35% more than the last one. Prices of some things have gone up. Many American products have disappeared or gone underground as the result of the devaluation of the sterling. It is still vacation time from school but we seem to have more work than at any other time. Our boys were with us, 13 of them, along with the girls from high school and Teacher's Training College.

Four new missionaries have arrived to be with the Methodist work here in Calcutta. I am very glad to see them and have spent much time meeting them and introducing them to the ways of the country. One couple will go on to Burma as soon as the arrangements can be made. We have had District Conference, Women's Society of Christian Service Convention and Annual Conference during October. It has taken considerable time since we are the entertaining group for these. All the Conferences were good and worthwhile.

Aside from all the above activities the city has been filled with excitement. There are processions every day; throwing hand bombs, and the retaliation of the police by firing. A tear gas bomb fell in our church gate during one of our conference sessions. The wind was in our favor so only a few of us were affected.

Sugar completely disappeared from the market very suddenly. We are allowed two teaspoons per day. I use more than that in my tea when I can get it. After the disappearance of sugar some people spread a rumor that salt stocks were about exhausted. As the rumor spread people frantically rushed to stores to buy salt at any price.

165

Storekeepers sold it at huge profits. Two days later we learned that salt is plentiful.

There is a strike of street cleaners. In some places garbage, ashes, and other refuse is piled high and the stench is terrific. The public latrines are being abandoned and more people than ever are using the streets. The one trash can in front of our building was filled long ago. A couple of days after the strike began some one put two dead calves in it. Can you imagine what it must be like? The problem was how to get them away and where to throw them. We covered them with lime and bleaching powder. On Monday our Girl Guides went out to clean the street. We attracted a great deal of attention. Literally thousands of people watched us, and among them were, newspaper men, chief executive officers of the city, and probably the Chief Minister of the State as we cleaned the street in front of his residence. Some people objected and heckled us. They said we were breaking the strike and yesterday in the striker's meeting in the square in front of us they condemned our action. We finally found some one willing to remove the dead animals. They came to get them in a truck under police protection. We heard that they had to throw them out not far from here because of the protest of the strikers. Many volunteers are trying to do something about the unbearable situation but the stench and the filth increases.

Would that this were all of our troubles but alas! The things that have worried us the most are still unreported. A small group of people tried to take the Bengali Boys' School away from the Methodist Church and almost did. It has been a long hard struggle, but so far the Government has condemned the action of the group and upheld the church. The group's attempts to gain the property and the school have brought slander against all the church workers including us at the Lee Memorial. The Bishop and Dr. Griffiths have had the greater share of the slander. The group made charges and sent them to the highest officials of the country. Some government agencies investigated and are continuing to investigate. It certainly is an unpleasant way to gain publicity. This has been a great concern to us. It is difficult to know what the attitude of the officials will be in a land that recently got rid of the rule of the white man and that has ordered some missionaries to leave the country and refused to let others enter. We rejoice that so far most things have been in our favor. We may still have a long way to go before church authorities are actually in control of the school again.

Recently the newspaper announced that Indian made cloth would be more plentiful and cheaper. Since devaluation most American products have become scarce. I bought a bottle of what I thought was parker ink — the bottle was the same but the ink is terrible. Somebody has substituted. English and Australian goods are coming in. They are as good and are cheaper. The most serious loss is in the field of medicine. The new medicine for typhoid, which is wonderful, is almost impossible to get. People pay as much as Rs 225 -more than $50 for one dose. Other medicines are scarce. We hope that soon they will be available in India.

The Joneses had just gotten nicely settled when they got word they could go to Burma. They are the first new Methodist missionaries to Burma in 12 years. We surely hate to see them go from here as we like them so much, especially the two children.

America has given Nehru a big reception. He is no doubt a great statesman. We wish that there were about a hundred more like him but unfortunately his kind are very rare here as well as in the world. I saw him before India was free and he was still a common man. Since independence his receptions have been so big here in Calcutta that I haven't dared get mixed up with the crowds. The last time he was here they tried to take his life. In spite of the few enemies, hundred of thousands of people were not afraid to gather and listen to him.

Miss Welles arrives on Saturday, November 19th and Reverend Morgan, the new pastor for Thoburn Church, arrives a few days later. We are planning a big American Thanksgiving dinner. Now we will be eight Methodist missionaries in Calcutta

There were five riots last week but only one so far this week. Only one of them was at our door. It has become a regular sport. A group of 500 or more people met and then marched along shouting. Policemen tag along with them just to see that they behave. Somewhere along the way the crowd throws a homemade bomb at the policemen, a tram or a bus. Then there follows a brief scuffle between the policemen and the mob. Sometimes the policemen use tear gas and then the crowd scatters. Last week all around our building they shot something that looked like big rockets. They were very effective in dispersing the crowd. The crowds throw their bombs. Some were very harmful and a few were incendiary. I always marvel at the way everyone seems to stay alive amid so much fire works.

Yesterday there was a collision of two airplanes flying over the city and they crashed into a hospital and a school. If it had been two seconds earlier it might have been us. Many people saw the crash. I was in the examination hall. It caused lots of excitement here.

The school is in the midst of government examinations that always come at the end of the school term. The children are well now, but we had several cases of flu when the weather first became cooler. About two weeks ago one of our workers died. He was our general repairman and looked after the general upkeep of the buildings as well as many other things. We certainly do miss him as already in the short time since his death a great variety of jobs are waiting for some one to do. He came here during the famine of 1899 as a young boy and had been here all of his life.

Pandit Nehru is back in India and he seems to have had a thrilling trip. His trip has been the main news here for weeks. There have been many more little riots. On Saturday December 12th Wellington Square was the battleground. Since then there has not been another except some fist fights in the university during the teachers' strikes.

The other day in the midst of my Saturday washing and ironing I stepped down stairs for a minute. I noticed a stranger, American looking, sitting on an old bench in the hallway so I decided I'd better see what she wanted. She said if I would give her a bed to rest for about an hour she would be happy. She was looking for some one but hadn't been able to find her. I did so and visited with her a little while, then left her alone. I never asked her name and she didn't bother to tell me. Later I learned that she was the first American Congress woman.

Chapter 8

ON THE TRAIL AGAIN

After Christmas with the festivities, weddings and celebrations, we began the new year with a new school year. Among other duties I took two of our girls to another mission station where they will teach. At the same time I visited the largest leper asylum in India. There I met again some friends and graduates of Marion College

The Communists are on the rampage again. They threw bombs at the police every day last week. Pakistan and India are engaged in an economic war especially on this side in the east of India. As a result vegetables, eggs and other products from East Pakistan are very expensive and some very scarce. It costs more to live since we are having to pay more for food. We are now in the process of trying to decide how to raise my salary. I think it will be the same amount in dollars ($50 per month) but it will be more in rupees. Since devaluation I have had to borrow before the end of the month.

On January 26, 1950 the new constitution of India went into effect. This was the first "Republic Day." India now has her own government. They borrowed from the American constitution and also took from other countries so they have a mixture. Everything will go well if it is administered properly. Two very fine men are at the head. Nehru is the Prime Minister and Prasad is the first President. On Republic Day we went out and mixed with the people. I tried to see parades, but really only saw millions of people. In the evening everything was brilliantly lighted with floodlights.

Reverend James Mathews, who is Board Secretary for India, will visit us this week. Later Miss Colony, the Secretary for India of the Woman's Division of Christian Service, and Bishop Martin will come. Bishop Rockey is with us now but since last July he has been with us so much that this is practically home to him.

About ten days ago my watch disappeared from a table in my room in the middle of the day. We are not sure how it walked out. It would not run on my arm but ran when on the table so I left it there. I had intended to have it fixed but was afraid of what it might cost. I had a little money I got for Christmas and I borrowed a little more so I bought a new watch. It keeps good time so I am pleased with it. I could not get along without one in the classroom. I had to buy a new fountain pen because my lifetime Schaeffer just would not write. I spent money trying to get it fixed. I think it is the imitation ink we get.

Everyone is upset. Hindus are flocking in from East Pakistan and Muslims are on the move in Calcutta. We have not seen anything except these refugees but there are plenty of rumors. Life on the streets about us is much quieter than usual but that is because people are being on the safe side and staying at home. Everybody remains jittery here in Calcutta. They have more real reason for fear than people in America who are so excited about the H-bomb. There still remains hatred and occasional fighting between Muslims and Hindus of the two Bengals- West Bengal (India) East Bengal (Pakistan). No one seems to know the truth and rumors on both sides are terrible. Nehru is coming to Calcutta this week to see what he can do.

Last night just as we were about to go to church a hand-made bomb was thrown at a horse-gari (buggy). The driver, a Muslim, was seriously wounded. He was one we knew, and we are afraid he is dead. This was the second attack on him in front of our building. The other time they missed him and pieces from that bomb fell in two of our classrooms. This time the trouble has not upset our regular activities. Most of the children have attended school regularly

A week ago we took about 200 of the children to the Governor's mansion. A few of the small girls did a folk dance for the Governor. Many people took movies of it and their song was recorded and broadcast on the radio. It was a big day for them.

Max Banker and his wife are here. I knew them at Marion. Max was here during the war. He wrote me about the Lee Memorial before I came out. They are working with the Quakers and are here on business. We certainly are glad to have them and it is so good to see someone I knew at home.

I have had a long day, but an interesting one because I met many new and interesting people. This morning at 7:30 we started out on a picnic with ten of our girls. The girls were all dressed in blue dresses, white shoes and socks and red ribbons. They looked very nice. We got into a truck with a group of Anglo-Indians from a Church of England School and then drove on to a Catholic school where about ten more got in. Then we drove on to the place where we boarded a steamer and went down the river to a lovely garden. The Rotary club gave a picnic to about 375 children from about 20 orphanages in Calcutta.

These rich businessmen along with their wives had a grand time. The children were from all religious groups — Catholic, Protestants, Hindu, Muslim and Ramakrishna. We played games, had races, and ate lots of good things and received nice gifts. The Governor also came by to see them. I enjoyed meeting the teachers and workers from all the institutions. Had a long talk and became well acquainted with the Superintendent of Calcutta Muslim Girls'

Orphanage. They have 230 girls. These are very difficult days for them.

Conditions in Calcutta and Bengal are very uncertain. Many people are begging Nehru to go to war with Pakistan but, whether there is war or not there is rioting and thousands of people are homeless.

Yesterday (March 18, 1950) was Saturday and the first Saturday in months that I haven't had something special on. So I washed and washed clothes, and then did a lot of sewing, mending and then ironed. I worked from six to six on clothes. While sewing I saw a very strange thing on our roof. A monkey stole a kitten and played with it as though it were its own baby. The kitten didn't object and both were happy. They finally moved on to another place.

Conditions as far as actual riots are concerned have greatly improved. I haven't heard a bomb go off in several days. But the refugee problem is terrific. Three or four thousand come into Bengal every day. In the last two months more than a 100,000 have come and the city was already dangerously overcrowded. I can't understand how people go on living. I don't wonder about the strife and unrest when I see their living conditions. It is a miracle that there isn't more violence.

Last week was filled with meetings because Miss Colony was here. Other people came here for the occasion. We discussed all our activities and problems, but there were also some social times. One night we young folk — seven of us- had a party. We had a grand time, so much so that we didn't hear the shooting or the explosions that were going on not so far away from us. During these days the truth is remarkably concealed and rumors fly around all the time. They are ten times worse than the truth.

Last night about three am I was suddenly awakened by blood curdling screams right in front of our house. I jumped up and went to look over the railing without taking time for shoes or anything else. When I got out there, I saw that everyone else had done the same. The screams didn't stop right away and a policeman came. He woke the poor man out of his nightmare. The story this morning is that he dreamed the goddess Kali was after him. Yes, the man was sleeping on the sidewalk.

It took me sometime to get to sleep after that. I heard all the other unearthly noises of the night: A crazy woman and her screams, a crazy man calling his wife, heavy steps of a policeman walking down the middle of the street, jeeps with soldiers driving by and the creaks and groans of ox carts loaded with vegetables going to the market. At last I dozed off for a few minutes only to be awakened again at five by the first signs of day and the terrible but usual cawing of the crows.

This is the first day of the Bengali New Year, April 14, 1950. With Easter and New Year so close we have had a long holiday — at least from class work. I went out to tea today at a Hindu home. I enjoyed it very much.

Nehru and the Prime Minister of Pakistan have displayed a wonderful piece of statesmanship. We can only hope that their people will be convinced of the fact. Two Bengali Ministers of Nehru's cabinet have resigned. They want war; so do a lot of other people and they are not afraid to say so. They are not realistic and don't begin to realize what it would mean. So Nehru does not have an easy job. He deserves lots of credit for the measure of success he is having. Bengal has a history somewhat similar to that of South Carolina. It's people are just as stubborn and rebellious as any South Carolinian. Meanwhile there seems to be a great improvement in the situation here as far as actual rioting is concerned. Maybe they'll at least rest awhile. A series of serious train wrecks are the chief topic of conversation now. They were definite cases of sabotage.

Most Bengalis have reluctantly accepted Nehru's and Khan's agreement and they do not easily forget things, so one wonders what will eventually happen. I see no hope for peace in India for many years to come. When the Hindus and Muslims get through fighting the Hindus will fight each other — liberal or modern Hindus against

177

orthodox Hindus. We are very much afraid of this latter group. Their rule over us would be about as bad as Communist rule.

On May 11th I started my 1950 summer vacation. I am staying in the Selborne Missionary Home in Otacamund, South India. At present there are 72 missionaries here. I only knew one couple and the three I came with. This is a different world.

I have never been more determined to "stick it out" and put in years of service in India. But many times it looks as though I'm going to be forced to give it up. Furlough time will be a very decisive time. I'm already worrying about it.

I am sitting in the sunshine near some big cedar trees in the loveliest place I can find. Birds are singing all around me. It is such a contrast to Calcutta and most refreshing to me. I'm having the time of my life. I spend my mornings reading books- religious, educational and light fiction. I also study and read more Bengali and spend some time writing letters. In the afternoons we usually go out for a couple of hours. Yesterday we went boating on the lake here. It is too cold for swimming. There are also various conferences, conventions, discussions and meetings that I attend so this is like a refresher course for me.

The Government Botanical Gardens are especially nice. They say the loveliest in India. They had a flower show on Saturday. I saw all kinds of beautiful flowers. They also displayed vegetables and other products and even some cows that looked like real cows. The best I have ever seen out here. Saturday was a big day in this small city. Aside from the flower show and all the fuss that went with it the Catholics had a big festival. The famed image called "The Lady of Fatima" was brought into the city and carried through the streets. Crowds of people flocked around to see. I took it all in.

Saturday was also the birthday of a missionary visitor. In his honor an older man took us out to a big Indian restaurant and we ate South Indian food. The old man is trying to make a match but the fellow is definitely not the type I want. I will continue to be an old maid or unclaimed blessing.

When I arrived back in Calcutta after a few days delay I found school going and life going on as usual. I have been busy trying to catch up. Among our orphan children I found three new faces: a little brother and sister came to us after their mother died with TB and another older girl who has been married but her husband deserted her. She looks to be very young.

There was a terrible landslide in Darjeeling. Many say it is much worse than the one in 1899 when the Lee children were killed.

Some of the property at the Methodist School has been damaged and the danger is not over as they are still having torrential rain. Many believe there was an earthquake along with the storm that caused the mountains to literally cave in. Here in Calcutta and on the plains we are having heavy rain until we ourselves feel soaked and everything about us is "moldy." In some districts there are bad floods.

Yesterday we had a worker's retreat for all our workers in Calcutta District. It was held about ten miles outside Calcutta. To get there we had to go by train. The railway stations are still filled with refugees. They are living in the stations. We stepped over them to purchase a ticket. The waiting rooms and platforms are filled. We had barely room enough to walk to the train and then we stepped over the people. They have room to lie down and that's about all and there they eat, sleep and take care of all bodily functions. It is really impossible for me to exaggerate the misery and everything connected with it. It does something to me. I can hardly bear to think of it.

The Christians of Calcutta have united and are trying to take care of the needs of two camps. The conditions of those two camps are even worse than those at the railway stations. Small babies and children die for lack of milk and people are dying of dysentery because they can not get the necessary sulfa medicine. Church World Service is supposed to send milk but it has not come through. Black marketers have taken advantage of the situation and are making lots of money by selling medicines and milk at very high prices. The world is so corrupt!

The school work is going well. There have been no interruptions for some time and that is unusual in unsettled Calcutta. The two babies grow cuter every day. The older one, Anju, who is almost two and a half years is already full of questions and constantly amazes us with her questions. The children have all been well. The weather has been unusually cool for this time of the year.

One of the things that has taken much of my time recently is helping in organizing a Methodist Youth Fellowship in our churches. The young people are responding. We are greatly encouraged as we work with these enthusiastic young people.

Along with all my other duties I have spent time with some of our distinguished visitors. One man has made about 2000 feet of sound movies of our children. Yesterday three women who have been teaching with the occupational forces in Japan visited us. One of them is a member of a church that supports the Griffiths. We have been watching the Korean situation very carefully. We certainly hope that things take a turn for the better.

There was a terrible earthquake in Assam. The center was in inaccessible parts of Tibet. We are anxiously waiting for news from many of the Baptist missionaries we know. I imagine lots of property has been destroyed but we cannot get definite details. One river is drying up and another one is flooding with black water. In one place the road sank 30 feet. We felt the earthquake here and got everyone out of the building. We had a dizzy feeling when the earth rocked like a boat. Some said they felt symptoms of seasickness.

This year we are having peach ice cream often. The peaches are flown in from Kashmir and the price is still low enough for us to buy.

Our newspaper last week was filled with all kinds of disquieting news — earthquakes, floods, drought, train wrecks (sabotage), food shortage and discontent of refugees It is a miracle that India gets along as well as she does. We received a large shipment of multipurpose food and rice from the USA. The shipment will aid relief work.

Last Sunday was youth Sunday in our churches. In our Bengali Church our newly organized MYF had charge of the service. We were greatly encouraged and inspired as we watched them conduct the service and saw the church packed with people- many of them young. I believe God has great things for the church here. We are now planning a big rally to be held in October during our Annual Conference.

Yesterday afternoon after school I went to see one of our girls who has been very ill. The hospital has not yet diagnosed her illness. While there we had a downpour. It rained cats and dogs! When visiting hours were over it was still raining. I waited for it to cease and then started out. I tried to get a taxi but all were in use. Streetcars could not run because of water on the streets. I started walking. Soon I was wading in water almost to my knees. I was able to get on a bus after wading for several blocks. The bus was so crowded that I had a hard time getting out of it when it reached our place. I finally squeezed my way out the door and stepped down into knee deep water and found the downpour had set in again. I was soaked and exhausted when I arrived home. The water ran off the streets as fast as the drains would carry it

God has blessed us by making possible necessary repairs on our buildings and supplying the food we need. Through Church World Service we received barrels of powdered milk for our children. In addition we received other things to distribute to refugees. A couple of weeks ago I visited the refugee camp where some of our Christians have been working. I was surprised to see the happy faces of the children and women. This camp was as crowded as the railway station I described earlier. Here some Christian teachers are holding classes for the children and teaching the women to sew. Rice and milk from America is distributed to them. This work is only among a thousand but there are many more thousands who do not have this care.

Our Annual Conference has just closed. I was received into the Women's Conference as a full member. There were many knotty problems but throughout the discussions there was a very good spirit. There were several good reports of work that had been done during the year. We certainly rejoice in the way God has answered prayer. The members are united and do all they can to build up the church. Just before the conference we had a Woman's Society of Christian Service convention. Delegates came from all our churches. They were a very inspiring group. During the conference we had a large youth rally. During this next year we believe God for even greater things. Another point for rejoicing was the fact that six young men are taking the Conference course of study for ordination.

In late October Miss Welles moved into a house provided by the conference. I am going to move into the room that she vacated. It has new paint and new furnishings. The Griffiths and I are the only missionaries that live at Lee Memorial. Homer Morgan, pastor of Thoburn Church, takes all his meals with us. We are afraid the navy department may call him back into the navy. He was a chaplain for a short time at the close of the World War II.

We received 25 print dresses for the children from Shiloh Methodist Church in Piedmont. We were thrilled when we opened up the package and felt that Santa Claus had come. We are making big plans for Christmas. This year we will have and extra special treat. The American Club composed of consular staff and American businessmen are giving our children a Christmas party. This is something new. It is the first time they have entertained our children. We have received help from the American Information Service this year. They frequently come and show educational films to our school children. These are on the American way of life and include health and hygiene films. They do all of this free of charge. They have mobile units equipped for this work.

School has closed for the Christmas vacation. We hear the joyful chatter of the girls as they get ready to go home. It is not only Christmas vacation but also the close of the school year so the girls are happy over their report cards and news of promotion. We are glad to close another successful year. There has been very little to interrupt the regular routine. While war clouds and riots have been very close they have not disturbed our regular routine of work. Perhaps it is because people have learned to adjust and carry on in spite of disturbed conditions. There is a greater demand than ever for education for girls. We have finished the enrolment for 1951. Now comes the trying time of saying, "No, there is no room for your child".

One of the highlights of our closing exercise was a farewell for Charu Mashi. Mashi is an affectionate term for an elderly woman. Charu Mashi has been with the Lee Memorial since its beginning in 1894. She will go to her home in the village where she will not have to be so active. She has been a mother to hundreds of children who had no other mother. Every one dearly loves her. Often when I went to her room I found her kneeling by her bed with the Bible before her as she prayed. Heaven only knows what her prayers have accomplished. We certainly hate to lose her but we know that her prayers will still remain with us.

Christmas 1950 is over. During this time my father is ill. I long to see him. I cried it out and then went on about our Christmas activities. Our schedule was more than full with many special programs and functions of all types. I felt the people had caught more of the true spirit of Christmas. It was so satisfactory to see so many of the things we had prayed for being accomplished. I am beginning to feel that I am having a part in the work and adjusted to the climate and people. I am looking forward to this coming year of 1951.

On December 28th I left with 15 girls from our school for the youth institute at Pakaur. Before we reached Pakaur our party had increased to more than 50. Everyone seems to be enjoying themselves. I am certainly happy to be out of smoke and noise of the city. I feel so relaxed that I can hardly get any work done.

I spoke at the evening service one night. I spoke in Bengali and it was translated into Santali. It was the first time I had spoken in a regular Bengali service. The service was in a simple chapel. Everyone sat on the floor, and we sat on the floor on the stage behind a special thing that looked like a pulpit with the legs cut off.

This year we have about 35 new boarders. More than half of them are new orphans and the others are needy children. We have one family of five. The father died with typhoid two years ago. Now the mother is in a very critical condition with T. B and we have taken the children. Dr. Griffiths arranged for the mother to go to a sanatorium. A few days after we took them a letter came from America saying they would support five children! God speedily answered our prayers. We have another family of four. The youngest in that family is a little bit older than Ada and Anju. They've worn rags so long that they are excited with their new clothes.

We've been entertaining celebrities again this week. Dr. Fry, of the World Council of Churches, was here on Sunday with a group. They made movies and collected material for broadcast in order to raise money for relief. From Tuesday until this morning, Dr. John Bennett, author and professor at Union Theological Seminary, was here.

The food situation in India is difficult. We keep reading that the U. S. is considering giving two million tons of wheat to India but they never seem to decide. I read in today's newspaper that one senator said Nehru had spoiled the chances of getting the wheat because of his attitude on China. That makes Indians angry. The U.S. is using a supposedly humanitarian gift as a political weapon

I went to a dentist last week and had a tooth filled. Some how or another he must have injured my gum because I got an infection that has been annoying. I have a bad cold again. The weather is still pleasantly cool. Last week we received a CARE package with 120 yards of beautiful white cloth. The person in U. S. paid $17 for it. To buy it here it would have cost $60 and since it came through CARE it is duty free. It'll make wonderful petticoats and blouses for the girls. Price of cloth has gone up a lot. This afternoon Mrs. Griffiths is buying cloth for the children's dresses. Many new dresses have to be made.

When we read the "Times" we get the jitters. The world situation is bad. Recently, we have become more disturbed about the state of affairs in India. The party in power wants to postpone elections. Food situation is bad. There has been a lot of Anti-American feeling lately. The Indians don't appreciate the remarks the American press makes about Nehru.

Strange things happen. In addition to food shortage, there are other shortages. Last week I needed newsprint paper to print our Bengali Magazine. So I sent for some but soon learned that there was none available. With great difficulty I succeeded in getting newsprint paper but at a much higher price than before.

Yesterday at about 5 a m I woke up and remembered it was my day to be on "duty." After some procrastination I crawled out of bed and took a cold shower. By the time that was finished the bearer had brought my two cups of hot tea with some bread and butter. I hastily drank the tea and then went to see how the children were getting along. I found them up, wide awake and busily looking at each other's heads. They were looking for those tiny pests that are so plentiful out here. I asked them to stop long enough to have morning prayers. One of the older girls took charge of the short prayer service. Before we finished Mrs. Griffiths had come and was waiting to inspect their heads. She inspected them one by one and most of them were lice free. When she had almost finished we discovered that two girls were missing. We began to search for them. The children searched the whole building but could not find them. Finally we went into our auditorium and found them behind the curtains of the stage, pretending to be asleep. By this time everyone was excited. I shook one girl but she did not move. I was frightened and began to wonder if she had smothered to death. After a few more shakes she rose up as one from a stupor. She was an excellent actor. One glance at their heads explained everything. They spent the rest of the day trying to get their heads clean.

On May 8th school closed for the summer holidays. That night two of my friends and I took the train and started for the Himalayas. Our first stop was at Benaras, the holy city of India. We spent two days visiting Hindu temples. We took a small boat and went on the sacred Ganges in the early morning while the people were bathing and performing all the rituals connected with their worship. Many Hindus believe that going to Benaras, bathing in the Ganges and worshipping the idols will save them from rebirth — being born into this world in some other form after death. The morning we were there the river bank was crowded with people who had come from all parts of India. We took a short journey beyond Benaras and visited some places connected with Buddha and the founding of the religion known as Buddhism.

From Benaras we went to Agra. We stayed at one of our Methodist Schools known as Holman Institute. The main attraction there is the Taj Mahal, one of the most beautiful building in the world. It was built in the days when the Muslims ruled this part of India. The famous Emperor, Shahjahan, built it as a memorial or tomb to his wife. In Agra we visited other places of historical interest such as the large fort. From Agra we went to Delhi. Again we stayed with Methodist missionaries and saw some more of the work of our

Church. We had a short visit with Bishop Pickett. We visited New Delhi and saw the beautiful new capital buildings. From Delhi we got on the train again. This time the train was very crowded as we traveled by 'Inter' class. We went a cheaper class to be able to make our money stretch out to do many things we wanted to do.

One week after we left Calcutta we arrived in Landour; Mussoorie, U. P., a beautiful mountain spot. The last four miles we came in a 'dandy' a big chair carried on four men's shoulders. We walk and climb everywhere but we were advised to be careful until we get adjusted to the high altitude. The common type of transport for new arrivals is the 'dandy'! Even though we are at an altitude of 7000 feet we find it is warm here. The temperature is in the 80's, but it is a lot better than 110. The nights are cooler. We are reading, writing, studying, hiking and attending conferences and institutes. There is a large school for American children here. Many parents come during the hot weather on the plains to be with their children who are in school. There is also a hospital to take care of the medical needs of the missionaries and others. There are probably a 1000 missionaries taking refuge from the heat.

I have been doing a good bit of cooking and have enjoyed it. I've been able to get things to have very good meals. It has been fun to try to cook again. We have also had opportunity to do a lot of walking. I finished my course of medicine for amoebae. They made some more tests but did not find it again so I hope it has cleared up. Even when it has rained I have not had the achy bones and muscles that I had before.

Today we went for a picnic and a long walk. We walked about seven miles. The scenery was lovely. We must have climbed up near 8,000 feet. All along the way we could look down and out across the plains below. The number of streams and rivers that we see is the most interesting feature. One or two amusing incidents happened. All along the way many pahari (mountaineers) passed us or met us. They are always friendlier than city people, and they nearly always greet us and often try to talk to us. We don't know much of their language but do know a tiny bit of Hindi and so sometimes can communicate with them. One place they asked us where we were going and if we were going to return today. They made good suggestions as to where good picnic spots were. At least 90 per cent of the people we saw asked us what time it was. We never could figure out if they really wanted to know or whether they just wanted to talk to us and hear our broken Hindi.

One place we met a whole herd of cows. We were remarking about the expressions on their faces when one young heifer charged toward us but turned and went by. I started on when I heard a loud scream and turned to see one of the girls just behind me beat the same heifer away from me with her walking stick. It was a close shave for me. I had on a red dress with flowers, and I had lengthened it by putting two strips of red cloth on the bottom of the skirt. I guess the heifer didn't like the red. One man stopped and asked us the time and after he had our answer he pointed to my red strips around my skirt and chattered away as if he was well pleased. When we listened carefully and asked a few simple questions, we finally understood him. We learned that he was saying that his wife wears something just like that. These hill women do not wear saries but bright colored full skirts.

On June 18, 1951 we left Landour. We came straight through and had a long, hot, dirty trip. The hot wind began blowing in our faces before we were down the mountain and never have I felt so hot before. I felt as though the heat would suffocate me and two or three times I was wet with sweat. It rains but it doesn't seem to cool things off so we just steam worse than ever before. Dr. Griffiths is having a series of boils.

We hardly know what to think about conditions in this city. I try to keep from thinking about them. Conditions do not get better. After weeks of getting ration cards, permits and going to and fro to the store Mrs. Griffiths finally came home with Rs 1,100 ($366) worth of cloth and saries. She was able to buy one sari and four yards of cloth for each girl and teacher. They usually get six saries each summer that last them during the year. There are plenty of high priced saries available. Rice ration is very low now. People get enough for three days in a week. By adding other things they have to make it stretch. The people here do not like wheat food like the people of North India but they are glad to have it rather than nothing. Cloth to make dresses for the small girls is very expensive. It might as well not be available. What is available is not practical for children's clothes. All the Indian mills seem to be turning out rayon these days.

On the Fourth of July the American Consul entertained all Americans. They say there are 250 Americans in the city. I think they were nearly all there. It is the first time in years that the missionaries have joined with others in such a function. I don't know who had to make the biggest compromise- they by condescending to be friendly, or we by ignoring their cocktails. It was my first cocktail party. Many of the Americans now are very friendly toward the missionaries. The Consul-General comes to Thoburn Church occasionally.

One of the missionaries, and my best friend, has typhoid in Pakaur. Fortunately they have some of the new drugs for typhoid on hand so she started taking that right away. The last we heard she was much better with no fever. The medications for all the diseases are wonderful. We are fortunate to be able to get them.

There is lots of talk here that is not consoling and many people are very pessimistic about the outlook for the very near future. I do not see how an upheaval of one kind or another can be avoided. There are already some strikes and talk of other major strikes that would paralyze the country. The trouble between the Muslims and Hindus is on the increase again. Elections are being held and many more will be held. These are not peaceful and the Congress Party is losing out. Some say that things are rapidly developing in favor of the Communists. We know they thrive on unrest and dissatisfaction in any country. There is dissatisfaction here and the communists are evident. Almost every day we see a procession carrying the communist flag.

Things are moving very rapidly for me. Already I am thrilled when I think that in a few months I will be in the U. S. A. Reservations have been made and the date of arrival in New York is about December 15. Developments around us are most disturbing from time to time. I am so glad I am in God's Hands. He knows all about me.

We are encouraged by the work of the Church even though other things may look dark Spiritually, the people are advancing and I believe that people are learning some valuable lessons in overcoming difficulties. Often it is difficult to imagine the innumerable hardships that these people constantly face. I have often heard it stated in the

195

pulpit that discouragement is one of the greatest weapons of the devil. I'm sure it is true. An Indian Christian has so much to be discouraged about, and yet is going on in spite of it. The other day I met a casual acquaintance on the street. In order to be friendly and make conversation, I asked him how he and his family were getting along. His answer floored me. He said: "We have cholera in the family. One child died and another is very serious but the others are recovering very nicely." The next day in talking to another friend I learned that two of his children are ill with typhoid. Neither of these men would have told me if I had not inquired about their family and both were going ahead and doing their work as usual. The longer I stay here the more I realize what Christianity has done for America. We know that many have neglected their religion or have none, but still the Christian principles abound every place. I hope we shall never lose sight of them and their value.

This being the last Saturday of the month is the day for a district meeting. All the district pastors and workers have come into Calcutta for the day. The teachers of the schools have gone to special lectures arranged by the Teacher's League. This afternoon and tonight there is W. S. C. S. meeting and Quarterly Conference. In addition to this I have to meet with a small committee from various missions to discuss production of literature for our Christian homes. We have a wonderful movement called "Christian Home Movement" which works in educating mothers and others in how to bring up the family. This is a very needy area. Recent figures showed that 23% of all babies born the first six months of this year died.

The Calcutta area has had lots of rain but in many other areas they are having dry weather. The rice cannot be planted in the dry areas, and that means the probability of another year with a crop failure. One wonders how a country like this can keep on going without rice. Our children are eating bread made of wheat. We get a kind of whole wheat flour that they use to make chapatties, a kind of unleavened bread. Then they eat it with a vegetable curry. Two weeks ago we got the ration as usual but evidently the flour has been adulterated with some stones. All the teachers and children got sick. You can imagine what a job it is to keep them satisfied. Our teachers and children have been very good and do not complain very much. But often we hear people say we are going to die if we don't get rice.

We have three days of holiday this week because of Independence Day. I don't like school holidays because I am usually busier than at other times. This one is no exception. Practically all the Methodist Missionaries of the Conference are here. Bishop Rockey arrives today. It is his first visit with us since last conference and since his return from America. He'll be a very busy man.

Smriti Das has returned. The Bishop has appointed her principal so she will take that off Mrs. Griffiths' shoulders. But there are still the thousands of odd jobs in the hostel and with the children that can require a lot of time. One of the girls tried to commit suicide. She took something that was very harmless but caused a stir among the girls. Other girls have been sick and have required attention. One case is still bed ridden and we do not know just what is wrong.

We had a storm last week. I have never been in any thing like it. The sky seemed ablaze with continuous streaks of lightning. The thunder was deafening. We were in class but it was impossible to hear each other so we just sat and watched the storm. After about an hour of which half an hour was really terrific, there was a flash of lightning that caused fire to go in every direction from all the iron and electric bulbs in the building. We were left stunned - more from fright than anything else. It was fully ten minutes before I knew that the building had been struck by lightning. It is a miracle that no one was hurt. Only one teacher claimed that she felt some electrical shock. In one classroom some children got some scratches as the falling electric light bulbs fell on them. People from outside who saw the lightning hit our building said it was really a sight. Many of them rushed to us. One doctor came. They expected to find children injured or killed. The actual damage was minor. The wiring had to be checked. Fuses and bulbs were burnt out and things like that. The lightning hit on the roof and bored a neat little hole through to the third floor; going through brick cement and an iron beam. It was a neater job than any person could have done. The children were very calm during the storm and seemed to accept it as just another adventure. After the storm was over all the students marched up to the roof to see what the lightning did. They had a very good object lesson in science and a great example of the way God takes care of us. Hindus joined the Christians in giving thanks for God's protecting care over us.

We have been having a revival in the school. A children's evangelist led the services. He has preached once every day and twice on some days. He has given them very good sound gospel messages. The children have been very responsive. We are praying that their experiences will last. The services have been well attended by the Hindu students. It was optional for them. Many of them even came back for some of our evening meetings.

On September sixth a thief succeeded in overcoming all barriers and entered our building. He came to my room, unlocked the place where my money is kept and got away with all my money and my fountain pen. The total amount of money comes to about $100. I had just received my monthly salary. I also had some mission money. The place from which he took the money is only about six feet from my bed. Robberies are very common and almost everyone becomes a victim. Our place is barricaded like a fort and still they get in. This is my first real loss.

I am preparing lessons to teach at the Youth Institute next week. As these have to be done in Bengali, it will take me about three days to get them all worked out. There will be a special Literature Conference and a Fair of Bengali Christian Literature. I am also expected to take part in that. Then in the middle of the week we go to Asansol for the Youth Institute. Immediately after that we have a W. S C. S. convention here in Calcutta and as soon as that is over we have Annual Conference.

On my birthday every one must have been awfully sorry for me because my money was stolen so they gave me many nice gifts. They are things that I can always keep to remember India by.

Everyone thinks it is practically settled that I shall not be coming back. Two weeks ago, after my flu, I went to the doctors again. Now they say that I definitely have filaria and should not return to India. I'm waiting to see what New York will say. If the medical office in New York comes to the same conclusion then I guess I will give up all hopes of returning. Thus far it has been impossible for me to lose hope. God has done many wonderful things. I believe He can do something about this, too.

I have made my bookings as follows. I sail from Bombay on November 15 on the S. S. Strathmore. It stops at Port Said and Marseilles, France before going on to England. I plan to get off in

France and visit the sister of my language teacher who works in Paris with UNESCO. Then I will go on to London and visit the family of my roommate in language school. I sail from Southampton on the SS Liberte with expected arrival in New York on December 14.

At our Youth Institute many of the young people consecrated themselves for Christian work on the last evening. I think it was the best service I have attended since being in India. Right after that I came back to Calcutta and just got back in time for the W. S. C. S. Convention. We are just beginning the Annual Conference. We are watching the Egyptian situation very closely. If things are too unsettled the boats will probably be redirected around Africa.

Chapter 9
CHANGE OF DIRECTION

I left Calcutta on the November 8, 1951 for furlough. I visited the Wesleyan work just north of Bombay and had a lovely visit with the folk there. When I returned to Bombay I found that we have to report for customs inspection immediately. Then, too, we learned that some friends of ours were arriving in Bombay today on another boat so went to the docks to meet them. We had dinner on their boat tonight. We sailed the next morning at 10 a.m.

We arrived in Marseilles on schedule and I went from there to Geneva. While in Geneva we went up into the Alps and also to Berne. We had a good visit in Paris. Tourist agencies have all kinds of conducted tours. I saw many interesting places. Europe seems so small compared to India or U. S. A. I came from Paris to London on Tuesday (4th). It took about eight hours. The English Channel was very rough. I was only on the boat for an hour and a half. It was equipped with these new things that keep boats from rolling. In spite of that I had my first experience of being seasick.

I am enjoying my visit in London. I am also taking the conducted tours here. I am staying in the home of the girl that I roomed with my first year in Language school. She has not come home yet. Her parents are treating me just as they would treat her. Tomorrow I am going to the home of another friend from India The next day we sail from Southampton That is about two hours from London by train. I am getting excited about getting home. I have already had many emotional reactions. I did not know that I missed some things as much as I have. The preparation and decorations for Christmas in each place has been most thrilling. Staying over in New York an extra day to see all the stores ready for Christmas will be well worth it. The places we visited have not been as cold as I expected. I was in some snow while in Switzerland. My old clothes are doing a good job of keeping me warm.

I arrived in New York on schedule. Faye Wood and her two children met me. Faye is originally from Piedmont and her brothers and sisters attend Shiloh. The Medical Office tested me thoroughly and reported that they saw no reason why I should not return to India. Hallelujah! They did not find filaria and reported that even if I had filaria they were sure that modern treatment could control it. (On another furlough they did find the filaria parasite).

Later a missionary personnel committee interviewed me at Duke University. They reported that I was acceptable. I was commissioned as a missionary in early 1953 at Buck Hills Fall. The Woman's Division gave me a scholarship so I could attend Emory University and obtain an M. Ed in Elementary Education. Each quarter I was able to take at least one subject in Candler School of Theology. I enjoyed Emory. My roommate became a life long friend. A group in the School of Theology were preparing for missionary service, and I joined a mission fellowship group. At least three others of the group became missionaries under the Methodist Board of Missions.

I was able to go to Piedmont often and frequently I obtained a ride with a theology student. I did lots of speaking in South Carolina. I completed my degree and started my journey back to India on August 16,1953.

I arrived here on September 15th exactly one month after I left home. Three days in New York and five days on the S. S. Queen Elizabeth passed very rapidly and soon I found myself among the crowds of tourists in London. There I saw the fading splendor of the historic coronation of Queen Elizabeth.

I looked forward to getting on the S. S. "Stratheden" and the longer time for relaxation. I was not the least bit disappointed. The voyage from London to Bombay was everything a tired, returning after furlough, missionary could have asked. The sea was calm, the breezes cool, the food excellent, and the people friendly. There was time for sleeping, reading, playing or talking with interesting personalities. Miss Colony, our secretary to India, was my cabin mate. It was a privilege to come to know her better as a person rather than a name signed to a letter. Among the passengers were the American Ambassador to Ceylon, the Indian Ambassador to Egypt, the speaker of the Indian Parliament, the Registrar of Bombay University, professors and Australian business men and others.

There were interesting things to see along the way, like the coastline of Spain, the Rock of Gibraltar, the African Coast, a stop at Port Said, followed by the journey through the Suez Canal and the Red Sea where we could dimly see the outline of some of the mountain ranges mentioned in the Old Testament. In the Red Sea the heat was the worst I have ever experienced — much worse than Emory in the summer of 1952. We stopped at Aden, a small British Colony on the tip of Saudi Arabia. From there we came into the Arabian sea and felt the cool monsoon breezes.

We arrived in Bombay on Saturday, September 12th. It was impossible to get everything finished before the offices closed at noon so I stayed in Bombay until Monday evening. I caught the train for Pakaur. As I traveled across India my heart was filled with joy and peace. I look forward to the next few years with keen anticipation. These days are such important ones for India. Everywhere we see signs of India's growth. On the other hand, we find many who are pessimistic.

I came back to India at the close of the monsoon season. It has been a good season and a bumper rice crop is expected. From the train we saw the beautiful green fields. I have never seen India so green before and so beautiful. Here in this section we have had too much rain and some crops have been destroyed.

The Bishop and his cabinet appointed me as Headmistress of the Bengali Day School in Pakaur. Pakaur is located in eastern Bihar (pronounced Bee-Har and Pa-koor). Though small, its population is made up of several races and religions. The majority of the people in this state of Bihar are Hindi-speaking. Along the border of Bihar and West Bengal are large numbers of Bengali- speaking people. Another group, in this section, are the Santals. They are aboriginals.

On Christmas Eve the MYF had a carol singing party. I attended that. On Christmas day we had a service at eight o'clock in the morning. Everyone came to this service in their new clothes. In the afternoon the MYF took their drums and went through the streets singing the Christmas songs. Today they went out into the surrounding villages. Last evening I had my Christmas dinner with the pastor and his family. Today I have had a fairly quiet day and am having a chance to answer some of the letters that I have neglected for such a long time. I am now sitting in front of my fireplace. It is night and a little cool. A fire is not absolutely necessary but feels good and looks wonderful

We have another week's vacation in our school. I am busy getting people to work on repairing the school building. It will be wonderful to have a roof that does not leak when it rains, and we will be able to keep things from decaying and the insects from eating things up.

In addition to the school work I am Conference President of the WSCS. This week we had a District rally. About 100 women came to the rally. They walked long distances. Even though they do not have very much they are learning the joy of giving. The WSCS groups in all of India have united in several projects. They are beginning a new project to help support a nurse in the new mission work in Nepal.

It is now April. I am sitting inside my room with the doors closed. Outside the wind is whistling through the mango trees. Were it not for the fact that I am dripping with perspiration, I could imagine that it is a cold winter wind. It is mid-April here in Eastern India. This year the dry season is drier than usual. The temperature is the highest it has been in 30 years. That whistling wind is filled with dust and we have to find refuge from it during the noon hours behind our closed doors. During April and May our school hours are from 6 a.m. to 11 a. m. School has closed for today and except for the noise of the wind, it is quiet outside. Even the crows have stopped their cawing!

With this season come diseases and fires. This year there are many fires. The wind catches a spark from an open fire for cooking and sets a grass roof on fire. In the matter of seconds the whole village is aflame. Three days ago 103 homes burned in a village about three miles from here. I went out to see the scene. It was tragic but the way the people were already at work cleaning away the smoldering ashes and gathering thatch to rebuild their homes surprised me. Perhaps I had expected them to be wringing their hands in despair. Today I received a letter from the father of one of the students who lost his home in this fire. He wrote to say that he would not be able to pay the school fees for May until June, and asked me to kindly excuse the delay. I admire that man for his self-respect.

My work in the school has included many things. Supervising and planning the repair of the building has taken most of my time. In spite of the office work and the building repairs there have been opportunities for contacts with students and teachers. These I enjoy more than anything else. In one of our staff meetings the teachers insisted that I must do something about the irregular attendance of the students. So I began to study the problem and to deal with truants. I have learned many things about the students through dealing with this problem The problem is a complex one. Unfortunately the festival occasions of the three religious groups do not coincide. It is impossible for us to give school holidays for every festival. So frequently students are excused for their festival. Each Friday the Muslim students are excused for two hours so they may attend their prayers. We have just been having the auspicious time for Hindu weddings. Many students were excused for wedding festivities which is a two or three day affair. One or two of the students themselves were married.

All the students who were absent did not have legitimate reasons, however. I had to punish a truant or two and educate a few others on the importance of regular attendance at school. One day the teacher of Class I brought me a rather large boy for a first grader. She complained that he never returned to school after the lunch recess. This was his first year in the school. When he came to the office he was afraid of the strange looking foreign principal. I dismissed the teacher and began to get acquainted with the boy. He was wearing worn clothes; yet, they showed care as they were clean and mended. He began to tell me about his home. He and his mother live alone. They have a little mud house and a tiny plot of land and a goat or two. His mother is uneducated. When I finally came back to the problem of his missing school, he began to cry. He explained that his mother did not know that he was supposed to come back to school and she sent him to look for the goats. Now he has educated his mother. She is anxious for him to have an education so he comes back to school after lunch.

We have another boy who will not stay away from school. One day I took a boy from class V to the Mission dispensary because he had a sore on his foot that would not heal. The sore was the clue that led to the finding of leprosy. We explained this to the boy. The doctor arranged to give him the treatment that is very successful in curing the disease. Then we sent the boy home. In a few days he was back in school wearing shoes that covered the sore. I sent him home again. Soon he was back in class. Each time I sent him away he was very despondent because his education was going to be interrupted. Some members of his family came to plead that he be allowed to remain in school. Finally we reached a compromise. The boy is studying at home. We will make arrangements for him to be examined and promoted.

Outside of school hours my activities reach out into the community and church. We have had a very good Easter. Last night, Monday after Easter, the young adults gave a splendid drama. It was based on the persecution of the early Christians. As the young people played the part of those who refused to denounce their faith one felt that they were not acting in a drama but speaking from their hearts. I find these young people keenly aware of the uncertainties of these times. I pray that their experience of full salvation will be so real and deep that it will give them the strength and the faith of those early Christians. Signs of growth and progress in India are numerous. The local Grow-More-Food officer sends a man to spray our fruit trees and often comes himself to help with our gardening problems. The Anti-Malaria team sprays our compound periodically. There are large projects like the Damodar Valley Project similar to our TVA, and then there are numerous tiny projects that do not get any publicity. A few days ago I saw the farmers digging what we call a 'tank' which is a pond-like reservoir. During the rains it will fill up with water. Then the farmers will be able to irrigate their crops and have fish, too. This one was a community project aided by government funds.

The masses of people are friendly. In the late afternoon, just before dusk, a ride on my bicycle through the rice fields along a narrow path is a pleasant experience. There are many people out at that time. They are always friendly and stop to ask where I am going and why. Yesterday a woman stopped to tell me she had been taking

212

her daughter to the Mission dispensary and that she was getting well. Her expression as well as her words conveyed her gratitude. Others stop to tell me that they are the father of such and such child in my school or that they attended the school themselves. Others stop to stare at the curious stranger and to listen to her try to speak their mother tongue. They do not see me as an American but as a person from the Mission that has been ministering to their needs for nearly a hundred years.

In October the rainy season gave way to cooler breezes and drier, cooler days. The rainy season is the time for rice planting. The fields about us are beautiful again this year. To the north of us there has been excessive rain with floods. To the south there is drought and poor crops. Here in this limited area the crops are good. Prices are a little lower. Eggs are twenty cents a dozen, goat meat, twenty five cents a pound. We cannot get any other kind of meat. For vegetables we have okra, cucumbers, eggplants and an assortment of Indian greens and squash. Now I am getting the garden ready for the cool season when we have tomatoes, carrots, peas, cabbage and other vegetables.

Let me explain the meaning of the words and initials in my address. Bihar is the name of the state. Santal Parganas (S. P.) is the name of the district or county. It means the place of the Santals, a tribal people. The place of the Santals is inhabited by other groups such as the Bengalies. The district is divided into three sub-districts. Pakaur is the name of one of the sub-districts as well as the name of our post office. The Pakaur sub-district is almost as large as my home county and in some respects the Pakaur sub-district is much like some of our small county seats. There is a court and many of the departments of government have a branch office here. There is one man who is the head of the sub-district called the sub-divisional officer. Our work brings us into contact with these officials, particularly the educational officer. They are friendly and helpful.

Our new school year began the first of July. We have 215 students on our roll. During the rainy season some of our students have to swim part of their way to school. Some come part way by boat. They come from villages as far as four miles away.

In class four there is a girl named Taherooni. She is about twelve years old. She comes to school every day with an older brother from a village about two miles away. She is very ordinary looking and one would not choose her as an outstanding student. The unusual thing about her is that she is the only Muslim girl from her village who is trying to get an education. One day her father came to me and showed me a letter he had received threatening to do harm to the girl if she remained in school.

In India, as well as other parts of the world, some women are still kept in purdah (behind the veil). Taharooni has reached the age for purdah, but she and her father are determined that she shall have an education. In spite of letters and criticism she still comes to school.

I have been to Calcutta quite frequently. Mrs. Griffiths and some of the others from there were here last week for the WSCS convention. The WSCS groups in India are certainly progressing. I am thinking of one particular group of about 20 members. The highest paid one among them earns about 200 rupees per month. That is about 65 dollars. To buy an ordinary cotton sari costs 12 or 15 rupees and a nice one costs about Rs 30. Most of the group earn fifty or sixty rupees a month. Yet they gave more than 600 rupees to missions this year. They earned much of it by working and selling things they made. I do not know a more active group or a group that works as hard as they do. The money they give goes to an orphanage, the Bible Society, for T B and leper patients as well as a project in Nepal. We will be very happy when all the groups learn to give like this.

Here in the quietness and beauty of our mission compound, in the absence of elaborate decorations, Christmas has a new meaning for me. Now it is easier for me to have a mental picture of the Bethlehem scene. As I see more of the people that Christ came to save my prayer is: "O Savior, help me to know how to get the Christmas message to them. Answer those agonizing longings of our hearts which never find words."

During Christmas we worship Christ. Christ died for us, Christ rose for us, Christ reigns in power for us, Christ prays for us! Can anything separate us from the love of Christ? "For I am persuaded that neither death, nor life, nor angels, nor principalities, nor powers, nor things present, nor things to come, nor height, nor depths, nor any other creature, shall be able to separate us from the love of God, which is Christ Jesus our Lord."

Even though the Christians are only a small minority in this area, everyone knew about Christmas. For several days before people in shops and offices wished me a happy Christmas. Our celebration consisted of school programs, church services and special dinners. On New Year's Day, 1954 we had a fellowship dinner. All the Christians of the local church were present. The young people went about singing Christmas songs and other songs giving the story of salvation. Between Christmas and New Years they went from village to village singing their "kirtens' (a type of Indian songs). The Conference MYF held its annual institute with us in Pakaur during the Christmas holidays. Fifty young people met for four days of study, prayer, and fellowship. I was reminded of the first institute that I helped to organize four years ago. This year I had little to do with organization as those who were delegates then have grown and are now the leaders. They take all the responsibility for their activities. It is a joy to sit back and watch them.

At the meeting of the Annual Conference the cabinet decided to transfer me back to Calcutta. Moving time gives me a chance to look back upon my work and evaluate it. The year in Pakaur has been taken up with repairing a very old building. Contractors for such jobs have not been satisfactory so I had to do planning, buying and supervising of the workmen. It has been a real education for me as I have learned so much about buildings that I never knew before. Along with putting on a new roof, putting in new floors and door frames, we have carried on our school program without interruption. We have 215 students in grammar school. Now that we have a nice building it would have been nice to stay on and develop a better school program but the Bishop and his cabinet thought my services were needed elsewhere. This week an Indian woman who is well trained and experienced took charge of the school.

The job or the name of the appointment that I happened to be asked to fill is not the important thing. There are always people to serve. God has sent me to serve those who need Him and His love. During my first term I had the privilege of serving the orphan children at Lee Memorial and earned the privilege of being an "auntie." Here, in addition to the children in the school, I have had the unique privilege of getting to know what we call the coolies. As a newcomer several years ago, the plight of the coolies was a shock to me as it is to most travelers in the Orient. It seemed to me that they were treated worse than animals. This year as I have had numbers of coolies working for me, I had to learn how to treat them as they should be treated. Numerous barriers filled me with frustrations. Last week I felt rewarded for my efforts when an old Muslim coolie brought me a dozen eggs as a gift. The price of the eggs was a day's wage, and for a feeble old man with fatherless grandchildren it was an expensive gift. Another day I was very happy when one of the Muslim masons referred to the school as "Our School." Since then he has asked to place his two small grandchildren in our boarding.

I see numerous opportunities ahead. My appointment reads: Women's Work, Calcutta Bengali District. I will live at 130 Dharamtala Street, Calcutta 13 — about two blocks from my first home in India, Lee Memorial. In one village the committees have decided to develop what we call a village center. The idea is to concentrate in one village with an intensive program of social and spiritual uplift. I have not yet visited the village that has been selected in this district. It was selected several years ago and a building built and some work is in progress. I hope to do much more. The need for leadership in Christian education programs, particularly church schools, is very great. In a city like Calcutta there are endless opportunities for work. My field is very large. I pray that God will help me concentrate my efforts in the right direction. I hope in some way to make our churches more vital and spiritual.

Before settling down in my new appointment I have an opportunity to go and observe work that is being done in other parts of India. I have been chosen to represent our conference on the Board of Governors of Isabella Thoburn College. After attending the annual meeting next week I intend to visit some of our other Methodist stations- particularly village work. In this way I hope to get help in developing our work in villages near Calcutta.

My father passed away in February 1955. Again I felt the love and support of many of my supporters. In addition to attending the Board of Governors meeting at Isabella Thoburn College, I was chosen to accompany Mrs. Frank Brooks, President of the Woman's Society of Christian Service in the U S A, on her tour of India. We visited all the conferences.

As I have taken up duties in this Calcutta Bengali district I am keeping the needs in the various areas before me. At present I feel as though I have not even made a beginning. When I took over, the district had seven churches and two village schools. Six women known as Bible women were of retirement age. I am retiring each of them and taking time out to get each happily settled.

Gradually, I hope to build up a new staff of helpers and a very effective program. Today the schools are closed and summer vacation begins for us. Next week I go to the mountains for a month. This year I am taking 25 teachers from the schools in the conference with me for a short "workshop." It will not be too intensive as the teachers need recreation as well. Miss Smriti Das, a returned Crusade Scholar, will lead discussions in Child study and teaching methods. I am trying to prepare some discussions in religious education. As we will be near the Dr. Stanley Jones Ashram we expect to attend the devotional meetings in the Ashram.

I returned to Calcutta at the end of June and made a fresh start in the district. Yesterday I attended a funeral in pouring rain in one of the villages. On this rainy morning I have been going through old files and again rethinking plans for the whole district. There are many problems and there are many opportunities.

I am very happy to be in this type of work; however, I do miss the organized routine of a large institution. I seem to spend all my time making plans that are never carried out. Nevertheless, gradually I hope to see some things accomplished.

Before the monsoon set in I spent most of my time in Nihata Village Center. I have a room there and enjoy staying in it.

Nihata Village Center and Church

Development in the community is very rapid. A new road has just been completed and it is now possible to drive there all year. Our property is very near the road, but a small strip of land between our property and the road keeps us from having a driveway. We are negotiating for a small plot of land that will give us an opening to the new road. The government has opened a large high school about two miles from the village. Most of our Christian boys attend that high school. The session for girls is held in the early morning from 6 a. m. to 10:30 a.m. A few Christian girls go by train to the early session, but it is too much to ask of them. We still have to depend upon the large boarding schools in Asansol and Calcutta. The pastor and I held supervised study every night for students in the government schools before the final examinations.

For many years we planned to have a dispensary in Nihata. I have tried to find a nurse. As yet my efforts have been unsuccessful. I have interviewed a number of nurses but all have refused to go. I think the main reason has been that they are not assured adequate help from a qualified doctor. That is our main problem. I am not in favor of placing a nurse there unless we can be sure we are going to have a doctor ready to help us. Now instead of trying to find a nurse I am going to try to find a doctor who will visit the village regularly once or twice a week. I must frankly admit I have little hopes of finding such a one. We have a Bible woman there who also does the work of a midwife but she is old and crippled and should retire.

The Nihata area has a number of Christians. A large number of them belong to the S. P. G. Church (Anglican). As I review the last ten years it seems that the church has retreated. In our church we have closed some churches and it seems the other denominations have done the same. Nevertheless there are still people in the villages of that district who are known as Christians but the church has failed to educate the second and third generation Christians. According to statistics, the District (24 Parganas, West Bengal) is one of the most densely populated places in the world. In government schemes the building of roads and putting in electricity is progressing very rapidly. Calcutta itself is growing and greater Calcutta is taking in more and more of these villages.

Another one of our centers is Champahati where we have a school. The school there is very, very run down. I thought it would not be possible to find a building that was more run down than the Pakaur School building but Champahati is worse. In our April meeting it seemed to be the consensus of opinion that we should close the school, or at least turn it over to someone else. The problem at Champahati is very complicated because of an old quarrel that dates back to Bishop Fisher's time and has been renewed from time to time.

The Woman's Division, has kept a school there all these years even though the Christian community broke away from the conference. We kept a school there but put as little money as possible into it, letting it die a slow painful death. My visits there are depressing. I decided I would not remain inactive. I wanted to either make a good primary school or close it. The Finance Committee gave me permission to do what I could. Since our meeting in April the Christian Community has ousted their anti-Methodist leader and reported that they are now willing to cooperate with the Conference and accept the pastor that the Bishop appoints. Now I do not know what to do. There are fourteen Christian families there and there is no girls' school in the immediate vicinity. At present I shall repair as my budget permits. I hate to turn a school building that is so dilapidated over to government or anyone else.

During the rainy season I am concentrating on Calcutta. Even so, I find myself making two or three trips out to the village each week. So often I have felt that it would be impossible to be a village missionary and a city missionary at the same time. First I tried to get acquainted with the villages where we have churches. With good roads as well as frequent bus and train service I can work in both the city and the villages without much trouble.

This week has been the week for the WSCS meetings. I have attended four. This month the women are opening the blessing boxes for Warne Baby Fold. The four meetings provided a great variety. In Nihata the meeting was poorly attended because of heavy rains and an epidemic of typhoid. The women there still need a lot of help. Here in Calcutta at Central Bengali and Thoburn Church I found many women at work. The group at Hatibagan, in Calcutta, is probably our newest society in the Conference. There I found a group of 20 women very eager to learn and to grow.

Irma Felchia, who has just taken her second year Bengali language examination, is helping me in the Hatibagan Sunday School. Another community is at Beliaghata. Already I have plans for opening a primary school there in January in the Lee Memorial property.

Perhaps my most difficult task thus far has been retiring the six Bible women who have already worked long past retirement age. I have had to spend a lot of time counseling each individually. I hope the day will come when retirement will not be such a crisis in the lives of our workers. They will live on their Provident Fund as long as it lasts. Paid to them at the rate of Rs 30/- per month it will last an average of two years. During the 20's and 30's their salary was extremely low. When it was raised the basic salary was not raised but a dearness allowance given. As a result their Provident Fund is very small. I think we need to do something about the Provident Fund of our lower paid workers.

These days we are seeing many developments and improvements in the city and the villages. The outlook of the people is much more optimistic than it was when I was in Calcutta before. I enjoy walking the streets, riding the trains and mixing generally with the people. I guess I really belong here because I like the city of Calcutta — most people hate it! I like my work in the villages as well and I hope I can organize an effective program in both.

Calcutta still has very serious problems, and problems that are almost impossible with which to cope. Refugees are still coming from East Pakistan. This morning's paper reports that more than 4,000 people came from East Pakistan last week. During June more than 11,000 came. There seems to be no reason for this migration. A missionary working there reports that there are many false rumors spread in the villages. The villagers believe they are in danger so get frightened and leave. She further reported that there was a scarcity of food due to floods last year.

I had another acute attack of what is diagnosed as filaria. I was very happy to receive the news that the Woman's Division Committee on Pensions has recommended that I be given credit for the years that I served at the Lee Memorial Mission. They will pay both my share and the share of the Woman's Division for those years.

One of the projects that I support by getting donations of funds and books is this Christian Information Center and Free Reading Room at Thoburn Church. It is managed by Samir Ghosh, a lay member of Thoburn Church and a recent convert from Hinduism. The following is his report.

"Apart from other literary work, the Christian Information Center has taken a major part in His service. The main purpose of this reading room is to establish contacts with non-Christians. The idea of starting a reading room was in the mind of Rev. Homer Morgan, Pastor, Thoburn Methodist Church, Calcutta. When I heard about it, I was very impressed. I am a convert from Hinduism and I always feel the urge to spread His name to other non-Christians so that they may have the same satisfaction, joy and peace as I have received. I know from my personal experience that there are many young men in Calcutta who are interested in Christianity, but they are not finding any suitable place to satisfy their desire. So I volunteered to start the reading room. It was settled that the reading room would be kept open from 5:30 to 7:30 p.m. From the very first day people started coming into the reading room, and still I have so many inquirers that it is often impossible for me to close before 9 p. m. The Reading Room is in the vestibule of the Thoburn Methodist Church which is on one of the principal streets of Calcutta. Its wide open doors invite people inside. They come without any hesitation. Whenever anyone comes inside, he is received cordially and we try to help him get the right kind of reading material he wants. If he wants to know about Christianity we talk with him, read from the Bible and try to extend our faith to him. We tell people our Christian experience and about the love of Christ. When they leave they carry with them a pleasant recollection - something to think about Jesus Christ and a handful of free literature to read at home. We invite all to attend the church services and to take part in the activities of the church. Here we meet people from all classes and standings in society — Hindu, Muslim, Roman Catholics, Brahmin priest from Kali Temple, university students, college professors, rich and poor. Some of them are seriously interested in Christianity, and some are attending the church services. Two of them are so convinced that not only are they attending the church services, but they are taking part in

MYF and other activities. They most probably will embrace Christianity very soon.

We have distributed thousands of free leaflets and gospel portions; sold or distributed a number of Bibles, gospels and other books. Bishop Pickett said that this Reading Room is the only one of its kind in India, and this kind of evangelism is highly praiseworthy. It has been praised by all the bishops of India.

Recently, we started a children's section but with a poor stock of reading materials. We hope to start a youth section very soon. We look forward to raising it to the standard of a first class library for Christian books where Christians from all over the place will come to study and satisfy their doubts."

It is puja time again. The loud speaker is blaring out melancholy songs in the highly decorated pandal of worhip next door. The fair, beautiful image of the mother goddess, Durga, stands in the center of the pandal, and hundreds of men, women and children mill around — occasionally performing rituals — but mostly having a good time. There are hundreds of such pandals over the city and there seems to be a contest to see which one can have the most impressive one. In this we see Hinduism with all of its festivity. The festive spirit is much like what we call the Christmas Spirit. The giving of gifts, buying new clothes, going home, bright lights, music, and feasting are all a part of the celebration. What then is the difference between this festivity and ours? That is the question that we should honestly ask ourselves in order that Christmas may truly be much more than celebration and festivity.

There is something about this large city that grips me. It is noisy, dirty, and very overcrowded. What do I do? I visit and supervise two village schools. I visit in the homes of Christians in the city and in the villages. I take an active part in all the services and functions of three church congregations. For the last three months I have been ill. Not bed-fast, but not able to carry on all my normal activities. This week the doctor has given me permission to take up full-time responsibilities again.

The poor homes of Calcutta are more pathetic than those in the villages. When I go visiting I turn off the wide streets to a narrow one and from the narrow one to a dark passage-way between old houses. Eventually I come to a small dark room that houses a family — sometimes a dozen people. We try to encourage these families in various ways. We have been able to give milk, clothes, and medical aid to many needy ones, but the constant unemployment problem, together with diseases, makes a real solution seem impossible.

The outlook in the villages is more hopeful. There the people through community projects are finding some solutions to their problems, and their lot is improving. Progress is slow but very definite. The farmers are optimistic as they see new roads, irrigation projects and new schools developing about them. This year there have been many floods in various parts of India. The immediate area around Calcutta has not been affected. Heavy rain caused some damage to the rice crop. Still a good harvest is expected. The grain is just beginning to ripen.

This type of new village well is one kind of improvement

Once again God has proven that He is greater than all circumstances. He has been with me in a very special way during trying experiences of the last few months. I have tested His promises and found them true. I have a very deep and real sense of the abiding presence of the Holy Spirit in my heart. I look forward to and pray for a revival here in Calcutta in February as all unite and prepare for the short visit of Billy Graham.

On Sunday morning after service at our English — speaking church I noticed a blond American dressed in Indian clothes lingering near the door. I took the opportunity to welcome him in our midst. I introduced myself as a missionary working in Calcutta and then waited for his introduction of himself. He looked at me, dressed in my American nylon dress (three years old), and replied: "I work in a village where the people are." I was taken aback at his words but he did not give me a chance to express my surprise as he went right on expounding upon the merits of working in the village areas. One would have thought he wanted everyone to forsake the seven million people of this city. What I did not have time to tell that man was that two or three days a week, I pass the street dwellers, climb over the refugees living in the railway station, press my way into a suburban train and travel out beyond the city limits to the beautiful rice fields and village homes nestled together under palm trees. What a difference! It is like two worlds — the city and the village. These days there is tremendous emphasis upon village work and many of my correspondents write: "I do not quite understand what you do." I am giving a brief outline of what I am trying to do.

I work in a district which includes Calcutta and villages outside of Calcutta. We try to look after the "whole person" so our work is with the schools, churches and other institutions.

I. Secular Education

    A.   Supervision of Day Schools

        1. Nihata — A primary school (four classes) with 135 students in a rural area about 20 miles from Calcutta.

        2. Champahati —A primary school with 70 students in a small town about 16 miles from Calcutta,

        3 Hatibagan — A new school just opened in one of our churches located in a very poor section of Calcutta.

        4. Hindi School — This primary school has just been opened in my house. Hindi speaking students are one of the minority groups in Calcutta.

    B. Cooperation with Boarding Schools — Where there are no schools, or when a child has finished the local primary school, I help the parents make arrangements to send the children to a boarding school. This January I helped children get admission into eight different boarding schools — one as far away as Bareilly, U. P. (Northern India).

C.   Chairman of College Scholarship Committee — Our conference has no college so we send students to Lucknow or to a United Christian College here in Calcutta.

II. Religious Education and Literature

A. Church schools

B. WSCS groups

C. MYF groups

D. Audio visual aids — I have a slide and filmstrip library for the use of all the churches and schools in the district.

E. Literature — This includes translation work, printing, and selling. We all realize the importance of Christian literature in the language that the people can understand.

III Medical and Social

This is a big field and is not clearly defined as some other parts of our work. Once a week with the help of the members of the local WSCS, I distribute milk powder, cheese and butter oil to the poor. Recently the relief committee of the Bengal Christian Council made us the sole distributing center for central Calcutta.

Most people come to us seeking help in finding employment. This is a very serious problem in Calcutta and is made worse because of the constant influx of refugees from East Pakistan.

In one village I employ a midwife. I spend a great deal of time helping people contact a doctor or hospital where they can get free medical treatment. We are particularly interested in TB patients and refer them to a Christian Sanatoria in other parts of India. Eight per cent of the people of Calcutta suffer with TB. This is caused by the poor economic conditions. The Christian Council is constantly seeking for ways to improve the economic condition of the people.

One phase of my work cannot be classified under any heading but it consists in serving on inter-church committees. A missionary in Calcutta is always expected to serve on committees of the Christian Council, governing bodies of institutions, the Bible Society and other organizations. This takes up a great deal of time.

At present I employ 23 people to help me carry on the work of the District. They are a very loyal group and sometimes I feel as though I am not doing anything but sitting back and watching them carry on the work. In addition to those on the payroll, there are volunteers who work very faithfully. It is a joy to work with them. For instance, I spent more than three hours today in counseling with workers in the churches who are not on our pay roll.

It is my desire to help, encourage, and inspire village teachers, pastors, Bible women and lay people in their own Christian life and witness. I enjoy visiting in the homes and sharing the joys and sorrows of the people. In the villages it is peaceful and serene and very refreshing to sit in the shade of some tree drinking coconut milk and talking to the people. There I relax as I forget the noise of peddlers, motor horns, streetcars and agitators shouting slogans. When I get back to Calcutta the sight of the multitudes moves me and I find myself praying, "Oh God, help me to make the love of Christ known and felt among these people."

There have been many notable events in Calcutta recently The visit of the Russian leaders and the visit of Billy Graham. What a contrast in the type of visitors. Billy Graham was here only one day and a half. He made a real impact upon the city.

My health has greatly improved. As the intense heat begins there will be fewer trips out into the villages but more concentration on literature work and other things. The nature of our work changes with the seasons. February and March are especially suitable for doing village work.

The sight of a garbage disposal truck gaily decorated with castaway Christmas trees and tinsels awakened me to the fact that the Christmas season is officially over and the new year of 1957 has begun. Trimmings have been packed or discarded and houses no longer have the air of festivity. In some humble places in order to preserve gaiety, the decorations are allowed to remain until they disintegrate and become a part of tropical dust scattered abroad by the hot scorching winds.

There is always sadness about these physical attempts to hold on to the Christmas spirit. My prayer is that we learn to preserve the true Christmas spirit through out the year.

I have had many remembrances from friends at home My friends here in India have also been very kind. It always seems as if I receive so much more than I give. Two gifts stand out, one from a Hindu refugee woman from East Pakistan and another from a Muslim woman. Several months ago the Hindu woman was brought to me by a member of one of our churches. He had taken her from the streets into his home and treated her as a member of his family. Investigations failed to locate any of her relatives and appeals to various organizations to take the destitute woman had been futile. In the meantime our Methodist friend reached retirement age and no longer had any way of earning an income to support his family and those he had befriended. When he appealed to me I felt very helpless as I have no home for destitute women and seemingly no one to help her or the Christian family. But when he with tear filled eyes, said to me: "What am I to do? I cannot turn her out on the streets again." I knew I had to do something. It was a long slow process as all rehabilitation is. The refugee woman succeeded in getting a job early in December. She received her first pay a few days before Christmas.

She brought me about a tenth of it as her Christmas gift and said, "I know you will not use it for yourself but please take it to help someone else in need." Then she stood before my picture of Sallman's Head of Christ enrapted with devotion and adoration. Thus a simple woman - whom I have tried to teach to read - teaches me how to worship. She has asked for baptism but we have asked her to wait until she is absolutely sure she knows what she is doing.

The Muslim woman lives across the street from one of our churches. But living across the street from this church is not like living across the street from St. Pauls or Judson Mill church. Across the street from this church is a bustee. Chicago has slums, Bombay has chawls, Hong Kong has roof dwellers and Calcutta has street dwellers and bustees. A bustee was originally a part of a village. The city has grown up around it and over it. Behind a modern five or six storied building of concrete, steel and bricks that face our streets one will find hovels made of crumbling clay, decayed bamboo, and flattened rusty tins. It is there that the poor live in a community type life — one family each in a small room which opens onto a common courtyard where they share bathroom and kitchen with several other families.

In the church across from one such bustee, hidden by shops, I supervise a day school. Children from the bustee come to the school. They are Christian, Hindu, Buddhist and Muslim. Even though they live so close together there are strict social rules, They have a mixing that at first glance appears unrestricted and unsegregated. Here the segregation is not in where one lives, goes, or sits. It is in what and how one eats and marries.

The Muslim woman in the bustee across from the church has looked upon me as her friend. I have given a place in the school to her two sons. She comes to me with some of the problems in her life and usually demands no more than a sympathetic hearing. On Christmas morning she came to my house with a huge bowl of delicious chicken curry. She said, "I know it is Christmas and I wanted to do something. I got up at four in order to get this ready. All the time I was cooking my neighbors were taunting me and saying, "Why are you cooking on Christmas? Have you, too, become a Christian?" Yes, I am touched. I have a sense of satisfaction because I have been able to help a few.

But alas! I am still disturbed. Experiences as I have described above are like an oasis in the desert. We like to bolster ourselves by dwelling upon them. While we dwell upon them, we close our eyes to the family with the newborn babe who lives on the sidewalk along the wall of the Mission compound that provides a home for about 100 orphan children. We help treat ten TB patients, but for dozens of others we turn our backs. We try to push them out of our minds.

We are doing a wonderful work with the help of church friends. But it is not enough. Huge programs of relief are not the answer. They are necessary but they do not solve the problem. Christian giving is motivated by Christian love for a person in need and not because we want to save him from communism. We must give milk, cheese, employment and other things but all of this giving is in vain unless we give Christ. Christ gives hope, courage and love to endure want and suffering. I fear that my efforts of giving Christ have not been as successful as the giving of relief supplies.

Some of our neighbors live on the sidewalk

Calcutta is a huge metropolis which is often criticized for its deplorable condition. Those who criticize seldom say anything about its problems. The war, the Bengal famine, partition, the continuous influx of refugees and the recurrence of national calamities such as the flood in September and a tornado this spring contribute to the conditions that I see about me.

It is estimated that about 4,000,000 refugees have come from East Pakistan to West Bengal since 1947. During 1956 the average influx was 30,000 every month. The presence of refugees creates many social problems with the greatest being unemployment.

A recent survey made by the Calcutta University has published some shocking statistics. Among the households surveyed, in an area representing one-fourth of Calcutta, they found that 61% of the households with two or more members have no separate kitchens, 50% no bathrooms, 26% no tap water and 6% no latrine. Forty-two percent of the households have a monthly income of Rs 100/- or less. Sixty three percent of the persons in the age group 15 to 24, who are seeking jobs, are unemployed.

Do these statistics mean anything? There are case histories that will illustrate what they mean to me. Mary, a bright young mother, is the product of a Mission school! When I first met her she came seeking employment as her husband had lost his job and could not find another. For several months I have watched this family struggle. The beautiful young woman lost her stately bearing. She has been sick. There is not much resemblance to the Mary of nine months ago. During the past few weeks I have been trying to help her earn money through her sewing. The gleam of hope in her eyes is very encouraging.

Another is John a young man I have known for a long time. He married a girl I knew. They had three children. The problems in his life became too much for him. He had a mental break. Finally, he became so bad that the family could not keep him in their small room with all the children, and they had the police take him and put him in jail. I, along with the family, felt the frustration of trying to get him into an institution where he could get some help. It was impossible. He died in jail. Now the mother must support the children. How can she do it?

There are scores of others in desperate need. As an average employed man, Joe, has a job making a little more than Rs 100/- per month and lives with his family in a room little more than 20 sq. ft. He regularly supports two relatives in addition to his wife and child. He is very active in church. He has a very deep faith and a strong sense of social responsibility. During Christmas he worked very hard and took a leading part in planning all the activities at the Church. The day after Christmas he collapsed. As I visited him I learned the story of his struggles from his neighbors and friends. His brother lost his job several weeks before Christmas. Joe took his brother and his family into his home and shared everything he had with them. Joe's wife was sick and had to have medical attention. The salary that was barely enough could not stretch so far. All tried to live on one scanty meal a day. The rent and other bills were due. Weak from lack of food and exhausted from constant strain, Joe could not take it any longer, so collapsed. He made a speedy recovery. He expressed it thus, "I lost my moral courage." The moral courage of these people is tremendous. There are hundreds of beggars on the streets of Calcutta as any tourist will describe, but there are MILLIONS in need who would not dream of begging.

What can I do? What can the church do? We have Church World Service supplies and we are very happy to distribute them. I give milk regularly to three hundred families. Our churches in Calcutta have their social service committees. They provide pensions to some, scholarships to children, special technical training to young men, and many other things. The need is tremendous and their resources are limited.

Through Church World Service and the National Christian Council a vocational guidance course has been set up in many schools in close cooperation with the government. We have a TB committee that gives medicines and wholesome food to families, where there is TB which is the number one health problem of Calcutta. Under the auspices of the Christian Council an economic life committee is at work. All pastors and Christian workers make it their responsibility to try to obtain employment for the unemployed members. We are constantly trying to devise new ways to help people earn money. One such project is the making of paper bags from old newspapers, magazines, and other waste paper. These paper bags are sold to shopkeepers. Paper that is not fit for bags is sold for pulp. I collect paper from our schools, church members, and friends. With what I get five families are able to supplement their income. Two families depend entirely upon this means for their livelihood. More than 50 other families have requested me to give them paper, but my supply of paper does not go so far.

Other women try to earn through crocheting lace, making jelly and home items. We find that the market is already full of all these products. Competition is very keen. Yet we do make a little profit.

Part of the love offering from the South Carolina Conference has been used as a revolving fund to help in this project. It is wonderful to have this extra money to fall back on whenever we have a loss in some experiment. At this point we need prayers more than anything else. I pray that God will give us wisdom to devise means of rehabilitating the needy ones spiritually, physically and emotionally.

It is now twilight. After several days of very oppressive heat, a cool breeze from the south has begun to blow. A few minutes ago I took a short walk. It seemed that the entire population of the city had left their tiny, dark and sweltering rooms and were out enjoying the breeze. On all sides familiar faces cordially greeted me and I thought I am no longer a stranger in this strange and complex metropolis. These people are my neighbors. Once again the parable of the Good Samaritan disturbed me. I wonder how Christ would have related it if he had been living in Calcutta. Would it have been something like this:

"A certain refugee went from his mother land into a strange country. There he fell into hard circumstances. He was unemployed, underfed and ill. By chance there came a certain Christian worker that way. When he saw him he passed by on the other side saying, "I am busy in my own religious duties. Taking care of these people is the responsibility of the government and the Red Cross.

"And likewise another Christian worker, when he was at the place, came and looked on him. He had pity upon him and wanted to help him but, he, too passed on the other side praying, "Lord, you know, I have my budget. I cannot do any more than I am now doing. Forgive me, Lord.

"But a certain other Christian worker, when he came, went to him. He gave him food and clothing and began to make arrangement for his rehabilitation for he had the loyal support of his church. He knew that church would repay whatever he spent."

This year of 1958, instead of beginning new things, I am trying to strengthen the work already in progress and prepare for furlough. A colleague who is already carrying a heavy load will have the additional responsibility of supervising the work of those employed in the district. This is possible only because the workers themselves are learning to carry responsibility.

Once on a special festival a rickshaw puller brought me a small earthen pot with some paper flowers. He remembered that I had befriended him and showed his appreciation in this way. Today as I walked home from church I passed a street dweller. His earthly possessions, consisting of a small tin trunk covered with an old worn canvas, were beside him. On top of the trunk was one small marigold tastefully arranged and defying all the ugliness about it.

My friends are not only among the poor but among some who have more such as a Rajah who is as much at home with a group of missionaries as he is with the leading citizens of the city at the Governor's mansion. Another friend is a rich Punjabi Sikh who claims to be saving money to start an orphanage. Evidently he takes Lee Memorial as his example. He visits there often. Another friend helps me read some of the classics of Bengali literature and is trying to introduce me to all the numerous varieties of Bengali sweets.

During my years in this huge metropolis, Calcutta is often described with various uncomplimentary titles. I have discovered nobility in the mansions, in the slums and on the sidewalks. I have discovered the noble and artistic Bengalis with their enchanting arts of literature, music and dance.

Can any American understand India? I wonder. A life time is not enough time to learn her languages, her history, sociological and religious developments. Each linguistic group has a culture, art and history of its own. I still have many exciting discoveries ahead of me.

What about the missionary in India? The answer is rather vague. There is no doubt that his past is greatly appreciated and admired. Emulation of the "missionary spirit" is constantly preached. Still the missionary in India today feels as though he is not needed, or not wanted. Great and learned people hold discussions on the place of the missionary in the new India. These discussions often result in wordy descriptions of the type of missionary needed and wanted. These ideas are rather vague to me. So I analyze, meditate and pray.

What is a missionary? From the birth of Christianity a missionary has been one who, forsaking all, has given everything in sacrifice and love. During the last two centuries he has won honorable mention by leaving the physical comforts of his culture and going into remote areas of the world where he patiently endured diseases and discomforts while he steadfastly preached the gospel, fed the hungry, healed the sick, befriended the friendless and taught the seeking.

Today missionary life is easier.   It is not filled with innumerable dangers such as starving or dying from snake bites. Most of the tropical diseases are being conquered. Airmail letters and newspapers keep missionaries in close contact with loved ones and people around the world. World travel is fast, safe and comfortable. In lands where the missionary has gone the church has been established and the local people are carrying on the functions of the church faithfully.   Some even say the missionary is a vanishing species. Have they forgotten the Great Commission? Or, do they think the task has been completed? How will the missionary and the church fulfill this call during the next two centuries? People are still hungry, sick, friendless and seeking. The missionary is not primarily a teacher, a preacher or a doctor. A missionary is one whose sole purpose is to follow Christ and obey His commands and precepts regarding service to others. He trains and adapts his talents according to the challenge confronting him. May the missionary forever be the symbol of the love of God!

With these thoughts that have grown out of my experiences here, I prepare to leave India in May. On the way home I shall observe some work in other fields with the view of better preparing myself for work here. I hope to arrive home in Piedmont sometime the latter part of September. I am looking forward to meeting old and new friends.

About a week before my boat was to sail from Calcutta in May, I canceled the sailing because I could not get the "no objection to return." I had had the wrong information and thought I could get it without staying the full five years since I had stayed one full five year period during my first term. I plan to leave sometime after September 12 and still plan to visit Hong Kong and Japan.

A few days after I canceled my sailing the boat I was booked on was caught smuggling gold. They found gold hidden all over it even in water faucets. That complicated matters and the boat was not allowed to sail on schedule. I still do not know if it has left Calcutta. Everyone decided I should not stay in Calcutta during the heat so on very short notice I came to Shillong, Assam.

Shillong is beautiful and I am crazy about it. I wonder why we haven't come here more often. The altitude is high enough to make it cool yet the hills are rolling and covered with fresh green grass and pine trees. The town has many beautiful gardens and the appearance of being the cleanest place in India. Even though I have heard much about the Assam hill people I was not prepared for the difference. Being in Shillong is like being in a different country. The

Welsh Mission Hospital here is like a dream. I am staying on the hospital compound in an empty bungalow where the missionaries are on furlough. I have my meals with the doctor in charge. He is from Wales. He seems to be a real genius. We have running hot and cold water and so does the hospital. Houses are earthquake proof and are a different style. The bungalows have polished wooden floors. The hospital has polished cement floors with white tiles half way up the walls so it looks very clean.

The church here is large. Last Sunday there were services all day long in the same Prebyterian Church building. Services were in various languages. At 5p.m. there was an English service in one of the churches. The sanctuary was full and 300 or more with only a dozen or so Europeans. Several congregations are enlarging their buildings because they cannot take care of all who attend. The churches contribute to a central fund and maintain about two thirds of all mission work. The grant from Wales is very small. The hospital is entirely self-supporting. They have more Christians in their Assam Mission field than in the "home church."

When I returned from Shillong I helped to initiate a new project among the refugees from East Pakistan in West Bengal, India. During the past two weeks I have spent most of my time visiting the Sodepur Tarapukuria Government Refugee Colony between Calcutta and Barrackpore. It was not until today that I was able to go back to

Halishar near Kanchapara. Things do not move as fast as we would like to see them move, but we trust they are moving. I am finding the work very fascinating. Each day I have interesting experiences and some times the temptation is to spend all my time visiting the refugees in the colony.

The club in Halishar gave me detailed information regarding each family in the colony. I have not had time to visit every family but have visited about half of them. I have found the information given very accurate. There are 160 families. In these 160 families there are 252 men over 18, 219 women over 18 and 380 children making a total of 851. Occupations of the men have been listed as follows: three in tobacco factories, 32 in services (clerks), 15 in business - mostly in the colony itself with tea shops, cloth shops and 66 are on daily wages. The employment of the 66 is very uncertain as it means working as badlies (substitutes) in the factories in the area. Days of work given is most uncertain. The people of the colony are generally from a very good class. Many are educated up to high school and some even more. They had small businesses and their own homes with a little farm land in East Pakistan. It has been a joy to meet this type of refugee. I find evidence in every home that the people are trying to earn money. Several have looms. They claim that they do not earn anything and have given me the reasons why. In one section of the colony several families cooperate in making mud tea cups. They have difficulty in transporting them to the market. I found some widow women making paper bags. They buy the paper. One woman had a young son helping her. Another widow without a son said she could not make a profit because she had to pay a coolie to bring her paper and to deliver her finished bags. There were a few other crafts. One person has asked for a sewing machine. We might be able to solve some of their difficulties. It is a slow tedious process and a matter of helping a few people at a time. I am convinced that it is the solution to the economic problem as a whole. Government has sanctioned two further classes of a weaving center and brush factory for that colony.

The first few visits in the colony have convinced me that we should start medical work immediately. Then, quite by accident, I found that the government health service is already providing medical facilities. Three times a week a registered doctor, compounder and assistant visit the colony. They have a small grant for the medicines and give free medicines as they can. For some reason these medical facilities have not been accepted by the people. As I investigated their complaints, I found that it is probably because the doctor has not been able to cure their chronic complaints of rheumatism and gastric troubles. Neither can we. There are some pathetic cases of undernourishment of children. I would like for us to work with this medical team by supplementing what they are able to give.

Adjoining this colony there are two squatter colonies. They have already approached us for help and I have already started some investigation of their conditions. It seems on the surface much worse than the others. There will be about another 100 families in those two colonies. In both cases the government is in the process of legalizing the matter or acquiring the land for the squatters. The landowners are trying to make a big profit by asking Rs 1000/- for their plots of 21/2 kottahs instead of the government rate of Rs 600/-. In the meantime the squatters live in their bamboo matted huts that are becoming very decayed. In the Sodepur colony itself quite a number of the bonafide residents have rented one room or a portion of their house to someone else. It is estimated that there are at least 50 families renting in this manner. We are constantly asked to provide milk for these families as they are also needy refugees. We have not done so up to now, but I am inclined to include those families with children in the distribution of milk and other food supplies.

I had a very interesting day at the Kalishar Mullick section. The people preparing the information for this place have not quite finished their work. I expect to get it tomorrow. I am told that there are 500 families there. It is a large colony and covers a large area. My first impressions are that it has very good scope for development. There is more space for setting up some kind of work and the need is much greater than in Sodepur. The people themselves have suggested pottery works as a possible industry. I met the man who is congress president of the entire Halishar Mangal. That includes three colonies.

In some cases the refugee stipends are not paid on time and the refugee has to borrow money to pay back when he receives the stipend. If we had careful, conscientious workers we could also help in that problem by making loans that would be collected.

It is very difficult to know how much I can effectively use in the way of the special grants. I know from my experience here in Calcutta with TB patients that the need for medicine is always very apparent. Many medical programs fail because they do not provide medicine. Those who are living on a shoestring cannot afford medicines. Most clinics provide a small basic supply of medicines and prescribe others that must be purchased. In Halishar one of the refugee doctors provides a private practice in the colony. In Sodepur colony there are four cases of diagnosed TB living among the 160 families. Several other cases are in hospitals, and there are other suspected cases. Government gives some help to these cases.

I have written the following fictitious article which I entitled "The Homeless." The characters are composites of some of the homeless I knew.

John spread his bedding roll on the side walk so that a thin ray of light from the hallway of the tenement building fell across his pillow. He carefully folded his only white shirt and placed it under his pillow. From his pocket he pulled out the "Time Magazine" that an American lady had given him. He settled back comfortably and began to read. As he read of far away places - as far away as the moon he was oblivious to the dampness of the pad on the hard concrete and the patter of the monsoon rain. The rattling of the streetcars, the clanging bells of the rickshaws, the roaring engines of buses and the voices of hawkers blended into one joyful song of normality.

"Sahib, Sahib!" Ram excitedly shook his arm, "There is golmal down at Wellington Square."

"Riots? Riots! What's it about this time?" John muttered not taking his eyes from his magazine.

"I don't know, but I think the dock workers are striking for more wages."

"The ungrateful dogs! They have jobs! They get paid, don't they? I think they ought to fire the whole lot and give some of us a chance to work"

"Here comes Samir. Let's ask him what it's about? Samir, did you see the trouble down at the Square? I saw the police knock one man out cold with his club."

"Yeah, a group of dock workers were trying to get in to see the Prime Minister and the police had orders to keep them out," replied Samir.

"Isn't the Prime Minister willing to talk to them?" Ram asked.

"Sure, but not to a big mob at one time," replied Samir. "I hear that they are going to ask for volunteers to work in the docks tomorrow."

John sat up and exclaimed, "Volunteers, volunteers for slaughter by a crazy mob."

"No it seems the union has agreed to let the government unload the perishable food from the ship. Especially all the wheat that has come from America."

"Could I volunteer?" asked Ram

"Sure, I think I'll go and try. Why don't you join us, John? Maybe we can earn a few rupees. Enough to buy some new clothes for the pujas."

"I'll see" muttered John as he settled down to read again.

Ram spread his old tattered piece of canvas beside John while Samir went to the old watering trough to take his daily bath. He was already thinking of the pujas. He must make money for a new sari for Rani and his daughter and some new clothes for his son. The girl would soon be old enough to marry. Without anything he could not go home at puja holiday time. Three months earlier he had spent his meagre saving for his ticket to Calcutta. For three long months he had trudged the streets of Calcutta looking for a job. He was strong. He could do coolie work. But always there were thousands of others like him. Occasionally some kind person let him carry a load. With the pice (pennies) earned in this way he was able to have a meal once

255

a day or four times a week. But Rani and the children expected him to come home with new clothes and money for the marriage feast and a dowry. He slept fitfully as he dreamed of fighting his way through a mob to get into the dock area.

Samir slowly and deliberately poured the water from the watering trough over his body. His mind went back to the days in the village in East Pakistan. Nostalgia overwhelmed him as he thought of the puja festivities. As a child he had often counted the days and the hours until the great day. He had danced excitedly about the courtyard as the women prepared sandesh, jeelabies, kir and scores of other delicious sweetmeats. As he thought of them the emptiness of his stomach felt more like a hard knot drawn too tight. What had happened to bring him to this type of animal existence? After he finished bathing he sank down beside Ram and John and due to exhaustion, went to sleep. As he slept he relived the bitter mob fighting between Hindu and Muslim, the burning villages and the long flight from Mymemsingh, East Pakistan to Calcutta, India - or Hindustan, the refuge for Hindus.

As quietness crept over their refuge under the portico of the tenement building, John put his magazine under his pillow and stared wide-eyed into the rainy night. He was a relic of the British Raj in India. Was there a place for him in this new India? He dreamed of far off places - England, Canada, America and Australia. But who was there to care for him? He was not a refugee that could appeal to the United Nations. He had relatives in England. Did they know of his existence? Among his mother's people here in Calcutta he was an outcast. Friendless, jobless, homeless, hopeless he looked upon the dim outline of the church across the street. He tried to pray. But there were no words to express the great emptiness of his life.

John, the Anglo-Indian; Samir, the refugee from East Pakistan, and Ram, the village peasant, with the aid of police protection, entered the dock area and were given temporary work unloading the ships. John found lodging in a YMCA hostel where once again he slept on a bed with a mattress and springs. He hoped the work would last long enough to permit him to buy a new sheet so he would not have to sleep on the old dingy, threadbare one that he used on his bed of mortar.

Samir and Ram did not move from their refuge. Samir spent his money eating in the restaurants and satisfying his hunger for fish curry, sandesh, and many other varieties of Bengali sweets. Ram ate two cheap meals a day and tied a few more annas in his dhoti each day. How many days would it take him to earn enough to pay back the money he owed the money lender who charged 25 per cent interest? He knew the money lenders. He knew that they were harassing his wife for the interest on his debt. He knew he must save and then get Samir to help him send a money order to his wife.

The job lasted two weeks. As John was about to rejoin his friends on the sidewalk, an Australian tourist staying at the YMCA noticed him and heard his story. He knew his government was granting special visas for the Anglo Indians and helping to rehabilitate them in the outback of Australia. He investigated and was able to help John migrate to Australia where he began a new life. With the aid of friends and hard work he married and lived a normal life.

Ram sent a money order to cover the interest on the debt for four months.

Samir began to explore all the possibilities of work. He finally found a job as a cook in a Christian hostel. The missionary in charge was good to him. He never earned enough to move out and live in his own home. Like most of the other employees, he lived in one small room. Later he married and had three children that were brought up with scholarships from the hostel where he worked.

Ram was illiterate and in debt. He could not find work. When the money lenders began to harass his wife again she decided to leave and brought her two children to Calcutta. As they had no other choice, they lived on the side walk under the portico of the tenement building. According to the last information, they have been living there for thirty years. Ram and his father earn money by pulling rickshaws. The son and daughter, now grown have both married, live with their parents in that same spot. The sidewalk population increases as new children are born in this home. According to the statistics, most of them are like Ram and his family. Village peasants, harassed by landlords and money lenders, flee to the city thinking life will surely be better there. And in some ways it is better. They have food, clothing, work and a place to cook and bathe. If, and when, you visit Calcutta and see the thousands living in the open, remember Ram. While he is a fictional character I saw colonies of sidewalk dwellers who were not fictional characters. I saw their numbers increase. I, personally, used a rickshaww pulled by one who had lived on the sidewalk for more than 30 years. He had grandchildren living with him that we tried to help educate.

When I was planning my furlough I wrote to the New York office and asked if I might visit some other countries instead of spending time in one of our universities studying books. This request was granted so I planned this long trip home in order to see the work of the Methodist Church in some other parts of the world. I have been doing this for six weeks and have found it a very rich experience.

I left Calcutta September 22, 1958 on a slow British India boat that had 30 first class passengers, 80 second class and about 1,000 deck passengers. The first stop was Rangoon, Burma. The day I left Calcutta the newspapers announced that the military had taken over in Burma. We did not know what to expect but as far as we could observe, and what the missionaries told us, it had not yet made much difference in their lives. They were expecting change later. The missionary that I visited was very happy because they had just had word that some property that had been confiscated during World War II would be turned back to them. I was constantly reminded that this small nation has been in constant turmoil since World War II because of the political situation. The church works under difficult circumstances. It was in Rangoon that I got my first glimpse of the strength of the Chinese churches outside of China. The Chinese church in Rangoon was growing rapidly.

After Rangoon we sailed for three more days and then came to Penang, Malaysia, a very beautiful place. I visited three stations in the country. The church seemed to be predominantly Chinese. The population of the country is made up of 40% Malay, 40% Chinese and 20% other. Indians form a very large percentage of the other group and there are several Indian Churches, mostly Tamil which is the predominant language in South India. The church is not allowed to do any evangelistic work among the Malays. That is law. Most of the schools and churches are very large and looked wealthy compared to our Indian churches. Many of the churches use the English language for services, and in them the predominant group is Chinese.

My first glimpse of the Methodist Church was just at the close of the World Communion Service at Wesley Church in Penang. The

Indian doctor who did the medical inspection on our ship was a South Indian Christian with a brother in Calcutta. He was especially kind to me; took me right to the church in his car. As we drove in the church compound there was a sea of cars before us. I found myself wondering just where I was. It seemed that many owned cars and those who did not have cars had motorcycles or bicycles. I found myself constantly amazed at the high standard of living among this group.

I stayed the first night with Miss Clancy and then got a ride to Ipoh with a former English missionary who now works for the Malaya government. I had two nights in Ipoh with Mr. and Mrs. Tom Browne and then caught another ride with one of the WDCS missionaries in Kuala Lumpur.

In the Indian papers I had often read about the insurgents and some had even said that it was not safe to travel because of them. I took two long trips in motor cars. Every mile or two there were police check-points. The police checked to see if anyone was taking supplies to the insurgents. Many have been captured. I went through one area that was supposed to still have some insurgents who have not surrendered. These insurgents do not seem to disturb the life of the country. Some of the missionaries felt that the church was predominantly the upper class Chinese. I felt it a very wonderful thing that we have such a live church among this group of people.

Most of the churches and parsonages are built with funds raised locally. The schools are large, modern and locally supported.

We passed through the rubber plantations. The people of Malaya have tin and were disturbed because Russia is competing with the country by selling it at a much cheaper rate. They fear a depression in the country because of this competition.

From Kuala Lumpur I went to Singapore. It is made up of 90% Chinese. It is not a part of Malaya and will not gain independence from the British until next year. Malaya and Singapore have always cooperated very closely in every respect. There now seem to be signs that this cooperation will decrease instead of increase. Malaya seems to fear the huge Chinese majority in Singapore. It will be interesting to watch political developments in that part of the world.

It was almost a week from Singapore to Hong Kong. I associated with two newly arrived special termers and an older missionary ready for retirement (WDCS) and a Chinese pastor and his family. We had wonderful times sightseeing, eating Chinese food and drinking coffee after church meetings. In spite of the millions of refugees living in shacks, on roof tops, and in 9' x 8' rooms of multistoried apartment houses one had the impression that the people in Hong Kong and Kowloon were among the happiest of the world. It was hard to remember that most of them, including the Chinese pastor's family, had suffered persecution and separation from family. Everyone seemed happy and proud to be in a British Colony. I did not hear any criticism of the foreign ruler. We learned about the horrors of things going on in the People's Republic of China by reading the local papers.

While in Hong Kong I took a short trip to Macau (Portugese Colony) and saw the grave of Robert Morrison, the first protestant missionary to China. I also saw the cross on the ruins of an old church that inspired the author as he wrote "In the Cross of Christ I Glory." As I, too, viewed that cross the spiritual lessons and blessings of the last few months seem to come into focus. Kingdoms may rise and fall, but the Christ of the cross will continue to tower above the wrecks of time. This is being illustrated again today in that very place that is separated from Communist China by only narrow gulf It is also being illustrated in many other places. Having a brief share in holding up the message of the cross gives me supreme happiness.

I worshipped on two Sundays with a different group each time. Both groups were made up almost entirely of people from the Mainland. We Methodists did not have a church in Hong Kong until a few years ago. Now we have two churches with about 200 members each. Each is raising money to build their own sanctuary.

One group now meets in a garage converted into a church and the other rents a YMCA hall.

The concern of the Christian world is evident on every hand in the large Social Service projects of Church World Service, Friends, Lutherans and others. They work separately but cooperate very closely. There is still much left to be done. But coming from Calcutta, it was wonderful to see the church doing enough to make a difference.

Hong Kong is a favorite place for tourists. It was filled with tourists who frantically bought the handicrafts of the refugees. One could not help but feel that this tourist trade was a great factor in helping to keep these millions alive and happy. At the same time, I wonder how the pundits of the world will be able to keep the market from being over saturated.

On October 20th at 10 p.m., with a full moon above and the glittering lights on the island, we pulled out of the harbor. It was a perfect end to a wonderful visit. The next morning we awoke to feel something of the strength of typhoon Lorna and then had three rough days to Kobe, Japan.

Early on the morning of November 2 we began to see the smokestacks of Japan, and realized that Japan is really an industrial center as Kobe and Osaka stretch out along the bay. We were also very soon aware that Japan is a different nation with distinct characteristics. English was not so common but frequently we heard a quiet voice say, "Excuse me, I like to speak English," and took time to converse with a very keen Japanese student.

I visited Hiroshima where the first atom bomb was dropped killing about 250,000 people. I was amazed that the entire city had been rebuilt. One damaged building has been left standing near a memorial and a museum of the atom bomb destruction. I met one of our pastors who had lived through the disaster and had a great part in organizing peace movements that now abound in the city. I met the American doctor who is in charge of the Atom Bomb Casualty Commission and is still doing research on the effects of the bomb on people there. The Woman's Division supports three large projects there a Girls' High School, a Woman's College and a Social Center. All were completely destroyed, but have since been rebuilt and are more than twice as large as they were before.

From Hiroshima up through Kobe and Osaka to Tokyo, I was impressed with what appeared to be a total recovery of the nation from a devastating war. Rarely was the war mentioned. The press sometimes used the phrase "present prosperity". I constantly asked myself, how? How can so many people have this measure of prosperity on such little land and with so few resources? Japanese products are very good. Trains are fast and run strictly on schedule, practically to the minute. The trains were extremely crowded. I was amazed at the quietness, discipline and courtesy of the Japanese. I compared, or contrasted, the Indian, Chinese, and Japanese. Why are they like they are? Would the Indians have been more like the Japanese if they had not been ruled for so long by outsiders? They were ruled first by the Muslims and then the British.

The church in Japan was forced to unite during the war and is still a united body. The church is very well organized and seems to be doing a tremendous lot of work even though the percentage of Christians is less than one percent. I saw projects in Kobe, Osaka, Hiroshima, and Tokyo. My main interest was the Community Center in a poor section of Tokyo among the street cleaners and the rag pickers. Like everything else in Japan it is well organized and efficiently run.

Japan was cold, and some days I was miserably cold as there was no heat in many places. The scenery is different. Even though many of the cities are new, they are not ultramodern like Malaya. Colors are gray, interiors of houses are very simple and beautiful. Flower arrangements were found every place, including the bathrooms on the trains.

After two weeks in Japan I boarded another ship, the President Cleveland, for the west coast of USA. The interesting trend throughout each country has been the tendency to adopt western habits of food, dress, houses, and gadgets. In some countries they seem to be losing their own identity. But Japan has retained much of its ancient culture.

The most wonderful experience has been the fellowship with the Christians. I was moved to tears every time I listened to a group sing familiar tunes with strange words. A song from the heart of a Christian is truly heavenly music. In spite of war, famine, floods, persecutions and sorrows, Christians the world over can raise their hearts in joyful singing. Praise be to God who gives us the victory.

Chapter 10

A CONFUSING CROSSROADS

I reached New York on cloud nine! Miss Colony, who had been so nice to me, destroyed my euphoria with one simple sentence: "As you know our Central Treasurer, Bessie Hollows, is retiring. WE have decided that you are the person to succeed her." It was the greatest shock of my life. What about my dreams? What about the needs of the people in Calcutta? I could not say yes immediately. They sent me on home to think about it. Eventually I said "yes." Why? My mother influenced me more than any other person. Without my telling her anything she sensed that something was wrong. She asked me what was bothering me. I poured the whole thing out to her. She was shocked that I would consider refusing. She expressed her belief that what the authorities of the church asked us to do was God's will for our life.

In August I had three weeks in the Woman's Division Treasuer's office in New York. In blood tests at the AMMO, they found that filaria active in my blood. My work during September and October was most interesting. I worked with our Woman's Division Observer at the United Nations. We planned and carried out seminars for many WSCS groups from various parts of the United States. I helped with about 25 or 30 groups. In addition to the things that most tourists do at the UN, we arranged speakers from some of the foreign delegations, or some of the specialized agencies such as Technical Assistance and UNICEF to explain the work and purpose of their projects.

During the time I was there there were two special seminars. One of them included three days in Washington, DC with speakers from the State Department and the Labor department. I felt it was far more worthwhile than reading books in the dusty stacks of some university library. During the month of October, my name was added to the list of the Speaker's Bureau for the UN. I spoke a few times and was getting invitations to speak on the "World Refugee Year" when my choice to sail for India came.

In mid November I sailed on the S. S. CRISTOFORO COLOMBO enroute to India via Italy. It has been a wonderful furlough filled with travel, speaking, attending conferences, visiting with friends and working in the New York office, Department of Christian Social Relations. I have enjoyed every minute.

According to schedule I arrived in India in the middle of December 1959, spent Christmas in Calcutta and moved to Lucknow to take up my new duties the first of the year.

Lucknow is the capital of the state called Uttar Pradesh. It **is** an old city built first by the Muslim rulers before the British came. The Muslim influence is still evident. The climate is very nice from November to March. In May and June the heat is extreme with dust storms. In July the monsoon gives some relief from the heat and dust. The monsoon usually lasts until the end of September.

This city was one of the early centers of mission work for our church. The Isabella Thoburn College is located here. I live about two miles from it in an apartment near our Publishing House. I am near the Bishop for this area, Bishop Sundaram, and the Commission on Christian Literature and the School of Accounting and Office Management. A few blocks away is Lal Bagh School and Nur Manzel Psychiatric Center. Central Methodist Church serves a large Hindustani Community and Lal Bagh Church serves others through its English services.

Nehru once referred to India as being in the bicycle age. That statement has been frequently quoted. Here in Lucknow we are very much aware of the bicycles. Our lovely broad streets are filled with them. We have the red and green traffic lights but even so we have traffic jams. There are plenty of cars and buses also but the bicycles set the pace.

271

My job as Central Treasurer of India for the Woman's Division of Christian Service, Methodist Church, is an office one. I receive and disburse the money that the Woman's Division sends for more than 200 projects in India and Nepal. This has meant that I have had to adjust to quite a different type of work than what I was doing in Calcutta. In addition to the office work I am invited to "sit" on various committees that discuss problems, plans and policies of the Church and some of our All-India Institutions.

These first five months have been filled with learning. In addition to learning routine, names and addresses, I have learned more about the scope of our work. In the midst of it I still find myself asking if this is God's will for me. This is so different. This is not what I expected when I responded to God's call. I am by nature an adventurer. I like to go to new places and meet new people. There is a romance about the remote places and the pioneer fields. But God has not led me to these. Could it be that the type of pioneer work of which I dreamed has vanished? The stations in India that were remote five years ago are no longer remote because roads have been built and bus services introduced. Schools have cropped up like mushrooms in the jungles and in the mountains as well as in the cities.

In the midst of the figures and the committees, I am acutely aware that the demands of today do not include the privations, the sacrifice of material comforts as it did for our predecessors. But still there is much to explore and discover. There must be a new discovery of people, people as they are and not as we have tried to mold them. The boundaries of the fields to be explored are not clearly demarcated. They are not concrete or physical. The NEED is here. It is spiritual. It is the need to explore anew what God can really do with a spirit-filled life.

So my mission today is to discover in new ways the power of prayer, faith, and a spirit-filled dedicated life. My mission is to discover God anew. My mission is to discover the potentials in people and God working in them. I pray that church people will find their Pentecost so that the church may be as the church on that first Pentecost: bold, confident, united and effective.

During my furlough I saw our Christian women in the U S A at work. I saw them presenting their gifts. The figures in the books before me tell me in a much more impressive way the magnitude of their gifts. But still I ask myself is this all? What are we holding back? Are we betraying Christ with our money? Do we give our pennies and dollars in the collection plate as a wealthy Hindu flings a pice toward the beggar at the temple gate? Or, is our gift like the widow's mite? In a future age will our beautiful churches be as incongruous in their surroundings as the gold-domed temples rising above the poverty of India? It is so easy to let go of a bit of our wealth that we do not need but so difficult to let go of ourselves. The gift of money must be secondary. Christ gave Himself and asks no less than our complete self in return. This includes all we have — our talents, our prejudices, our pet ideas, our intellect, our time and our money. We become His stewards.

I seem to be preaching, I am preaching to myself. I need it. I pray that I may BE what God wants. I realize the "doing" is secondary but my actions do not always bear that out.

Until December, 1960 my office was located in Lucknow. In December I moved to 22 Club Back Road, Bombay 8 where I live and have my office. The main reason is that there is this spacious piece of WDCS property here that needed to be better used. In Lucknow we had a wonderful apartment that could and should be used by some others, and I was renting it. Too, I am happy to be here near the banks and the Inter-Mission Business Office.

I have no intentions of making this a permanent address. We are already making plans for my successor. We hope to find an Indian woman to do this job. There are many who are capable and willing so it is a matter of deciding which one can be released from the important task she is now doing. Within another year we hope that one will be released to take up this work.

I had to change our office help because of the move. During the change I have had to do the work myself. I do not have an accountant or a stenographer but hope to have both in the very near future.

The money which the Woman's Societies in America give to the Woman's Division is divided into many portions. A very large portion comes to India. It comes into a bank account for which I am responsible. I am a link between the donors and the work in India. Occasionally I have the opportunity to visit and see first hand the work to which the money is sent.

One of the recent events of interest was the Central Conference which was held in Hyderabad from December 30 to January 7. Our Central Conference corresponds to the Jurisdictional Conferences in the United States. The eleven conferences in India sent delegates. Formerly Pakistan was a part of the Central Conference, but this year they formed their own provisional Central Conference. Our Conference was presided over by our four Indian bishops. Most of the delegates were Indians with a sprinkling of American missionaries. There was no election for bishops this year. The subject of church union caused the most excitement. There is already a Church of South India. Now there is a scheme for having a United Church of North India. Discussions and negotiations have been going on for many years. The time for decision has arrived. A large group wanted to delay the final decision once again but the majority felt the day of decision had come, and the matter was referred to the Annual Conferences for their vote in 1962.

All of India is looking forward to the visit of Queen Elizabeth. During the last year or so the Indian capital has entertained numerous heads of state, but this time it seems that this visitor is, without a doubt, the most important one yet in the eyes of the Indians. Her welcome will be different. It will also be very special.

One of the latest signs of industrial development is the appearance on the market of an Indian made washing machine. The washing machine with the Indian made refrigerators and sewing machines bring further changes in the homes of middle - class Indians.

I am longing to settle in one place or at least one job. The Board is most anxious to have an Indian because of experiences in Congo and Cuba where the money had to be suddenly turned over to the nationals. Here they want to have some one ready. I had a person who was most acceptable and willing to come this spring. I thought her appointment was going through and then the "powers" that be decided she could not be replaced in her present job. I think they plan to appoint her a year or two from now but one never knows.

India is happy over the Kennedy election. According to the Indian papers, Pakistan is just a little nervous for fear the U. S. policy toward Pakistan will be changed. I missed by a few days being a guest in the same house with Cynthia Bowles last summer while on a visit to Pithoragarh. I mention her because the thing that pleases India and distresses Pakistan is Bowles, former U. S. Ambassador to India has a place in the Administration.

India's third five-year plan has been launched. Campaigns for the elections in February, 1962 have begun. The most destructive monsoon in half a century has just receded, leaving behind it unprecedented floods in numerous places. Emotional integration is a very popular subject for discussion by politicians and the press. Communal riots in some places and the long fast for a Punjabi State illustrates the need for emotional integration. All must think of themselves as Indians and not as Bengali or Punjabi, Hindu or Muslim, high caste or low caste.

The church is greatly affected by the problems of the State. Does the Church control its own course or is it riding the tide of events toward an uncertain goal? What will be the impact of the meeting of the World Council of Churches in New Delhi in November?

The church I attend is one of 21 congregations in this city. The worship service is in English. The English language binds us together. The worshippers come from seventeen different languages backgrounds. During the last ten years the "English Medium Churches" have had a new birth. At the time of independence they were thought to be the dying churches. They have been wonderfully revived. There are other churches using Tamil, Telegu and Marathi languages as they worship. It is estimated that there are about 8,000 Methodists in greater Bombay. They are growing in membership, financial contributions and activities. In one Conference session I heard a district superintendent report many new converts and new members in his district. He gave a report of a detailed survey he had made. The average income per person in that district was said to be Rs. 50 per month (about $10). Yet that district has a very high percentage of giving toward the support of the pastors.

Through participation in some of our committees relating to this office of Treasurer, I have become more aware of the relationship of the Indian church with the American church. There is no doubt but what it is truly an Indian church. The professionals in the study of missions refer to the church today in contrast to missions a few years ago. The missions established a number of years ago have now become independent churches. Young churches have matured and grown up. What is now the relationship between the church in India and the church in America? Is this relationship what it should be?

Our own Board of Missions has been studying these and other questions.

India has the honor of having the first national mission treasurer. He is my colleague. He receives and distributes the funds sent through the Commission on Missions via the Division of World Missions, and I receive and disburse the funds sent by the Woman's Society of Christian Service. We work together very closely and will have a joint office as soon as the necessary space is available. S. B. Tewarson, the new treasurer is a dedicated Christian and one of the humblest-men I have ever met. The Division of World Missions has chosen well in selecting him as Branch Treasurer for India. My role is to channel all gifts in the spirit of love intended by the donor. The church here is learning to receive in a Christian way, and through its own program of stewardship is learning the joy of Christian giving.

Today November 9, 1961 the citizens of Bombay are observing the Diwali festival. It is the festival of lights. Each evening this week the houses have been gaily decorated with lights. In ancient times this was done with tiny earthen lamps called dipas. Today some of the modern people use electric lights while others cling to the "dipa." It is a unique scene to see the houses decorated with the dipas alongside the fancy, modern electrical illuminations. It has also been a time of sending greeting cards and giving gifts and a general spirit of goodwill. I keep wondering who is imitating whom as I see so much that reminds me of Christmas during this particular festival in Bombay. Everything is here except the Christ Child. He is missing.

Bombay experienced the heaviest rains in 44 years. In other places there is a shortage of rain. The people of India have responded generously to the Prime Minister's relief fund, and through that and other funds, much has been done to alleviate the suffering of the flood victims. But the effects of the flood remain for a long time due to the destruction of crops as well as property.

Our newspapers are filled with the news of the Nehru-Kennedy talks. Last night I visited our neighbors who are from Sweden. Over our cups of Swedish coffee we discussed world affairs. My Swedish friends seemed to be better informed and have much stronger opinions on the Kennedy administration than I. When I noted this he said, "You see, he (Kennedy) is not only President of the United States, he is the leader of the Western World and what he does affects us in Sweden just as much as it affects Americans." This made me realize again how closely related the world is.

Bombay's notorious October heat is with us. This is the time of the year we literally earn our bread by the sweat of the brow. The blinding glare of the brassy skies has sent those who can afford it to neighboring hill resorts. One wonders if the weather is to be blamed for frenzied moods. Strikes and strike threats are numerous. The crew of an American tanker left their ship abandoned at the entrance of a city dock bringing shipping to a standstill for 35 hours. One of the leading newspapers of India was not published for two weeks while management haggled with members of the union. City textile workers downed their tools and the streets of Bombay appeared empty as the taxi drivers kept their taxies off the streets one day as a part of their agitation for higher fares. However, the critical situation on the Indo-China border has led to the early settlement of some strikes and postponement of others.

Strikes, oppressive heat and the Indo China conflict have not dampened the fervor of religious and cultural activities that are beginning the post monsoon season. The never ending queues snaked their way past the Mahalaxmi Temple as Hindus celebrated Dussera. An art exhibit of handicapped people was very popular. A novel attraction was the photographic exhibit of ancient and modern hair styles. Raginia and his dance troupe performed in the open air theatre of Rang Bhayan.

For the Methodists it is the time for the annual conferences. Six of the eleven annual conferences have already met, and among other business voted on was whether to join in the scheme for church union in North India. Three conferences voted against and three voted in favor of it.

My appointment has given me many opportunities to see the work of the church in India. There have been many highlights for me. Attending Dharur Jatra (Jungle Camp-Meeting) was one highlight. About 6000 people camped under the trees for a week of special meetings. The Methodists in the South hold this meeting every year.

During August I organized a retreat for our women appointed as District Evangelists. Forty-five workers representing the 11 conferences attended. Miss Joy Jacob led our devotional meditation on "Know God, make Him known." As the women shared their experiences we again felt that the Church is alive! There is health and vitality. There is concern about church buildings. There is also concern for congregations. There is discussion of organization and over organization there is also care for the individual. There is a great deal of human striving; there is also much praying. There is much ignorance; there is also deep faith. There is the burden of gaining daily bread; there is also a hunger for fellowship. There is a lot of cheap, unhealthy literature, but Bibles have never sold so well. There is much sickness; there is also much healing. There are tremendous problems; there is also God. We pledged ourselves to know Him and to make Him known.

Unlike other places, Bombay has no Mission school or hospital as a show place for visitors. During the last ten years hundreds of factories have been built in suburban Bombay.

Thousands or even millions have left their villages and moved into the city. My accountant is the wife of one of the pastors who works among many who have recently moved to Bombay. Her husband has five congregations. Last week I went with them to worship with a congregation in the suburbs. It took us two hours by city bus to go the 15 miles to reach the place of worship. Along the way we saw factories for canning food, making sweets, lanterns, iron grille work, glass, rubber, scooters and more. All are monuments to India's recent developments.

We found the group meeting under a small rented shed. Fifty adults and 30 children packed themselves inside and others looked on from outside. In the previous months services were held in an open area but that plot was taken for another high rise building. These Christians are collecting money to buy land for a church. Plots are expensive. It will take $13,000 to purchase the land. Most of the members of the congregation are unskilled laborers and earn by carrying bricks and mortar on their heads for the new buildings. They are determined that there shall be a new church in this new area of Bombay.

I have accomplished my "Mission" for this term. Miss Chanda Christdas has been appointed as my associate and is in training to take over the entire responsibility about the middle of next year (1963). I shall have a "short furlough" in the U.S. before taking up another appointment. My health is the best it has been in several years. I have thoroughly enjoyed living in Bombay and being the link between the donors and the church here through the distribution of money.

Enroute to the USA I had ten days in Jordan and Israel. The guides of Israel were much more eager to tell about modern history than they were ancient Biblical history.

I arrived in New York on May 28. The doctors at the AMMO in New York recommended some medical treatment. One of the recommendations was further surgery on the deformed fourth and fifth fingers of my hands. I was able to find an excellent orthopedics doctor near my home in Greenville, S. C. He has had lots of experience operating on the fingers of my relatives. The surgeries were performed and I now have beautiful fingers. I had some rest and time with my mother before beginning itineration.

It is wonderful to be with my mother so much of the time. At 73 she is still a remarkable person. She has lost most of her hearing and is gradually losing her sight with a slow developing cataract. Even so she takes care of herself, and also takes care of me. She has a beautiful vegetable and flower garden. With the splints on my fingers I have continued to mow the lawns for both her and my brother. It is good exercise and therapy. My brother is one of the few full time farmers left. He has a dairy. He has more and more paper work so has set up an office. If it keeps up he'll have to hire a secretary. We have had lots of rain and two or three bad storms this summer. My brother has so much feed he does not know what to do with it. The grass and weeds have grown very fast. He has very little hired help.

Various members of my family have been in and out all summer and my baby sister who teaches music in a high school in Kentucky is here now. The biggest news is that the first great grand-child for my mother has arrived.

On August fifth I started speaking. I attended the Conference School of Missions for one week. From this fall the WSCSes will be studying Southern Asia. The school trained those who will teach the course in the local churches. The women worked very hard and I enjoyed the week.

After five months in South Carolina I returned to India at the end of October and moved to my new appointment at "Bethel" Gomoh, Bihar, India. "Bethel" is the name of our house, Gomoh (Go mo) is the name of the post office and Bihar (Bee har) is the name of the state. It is about 100 miles from Calcutta or six to eight hours by train. It is not far from Bokaro which figured in the news last summer in connection with the United States aid to India and the building of a steel mill. Most of our work in that area is new.

285

One of the chief concerns here is the rapid rise in prices of almost every commodity. During the last year since the Chinese attack on India there seems to be a general overall increase of about 25% in prices. In West Bengal, what is known as the "poor man's rice" has doubled in price in some places. All the experts are duly concerned, and we expect that "the poor" will quickly get relief.

Further statistics from the 1961 census were released last week. They show that the proportion of Christians to the total population has slightly increased during the period from 1950 to 1960. They also show that the Buddhists had a very large increase. Another statistic is that among the 3,000,000people who migrated from East Pakistan to Eastern India about 1,000,000 were Muslims.

We had a very good Annual Conference. One of the most impressive things for me was to recognize the spiritual growth and maturity of several who were struggling beginners a few years ago. Often in the midst of our struggles we fail to recognize growth. Coming back after being in other parts of India for several years I was able to recognize growth in several directions. During the year under review one member of the Annual Conference volunteered for Mission Work in the Fiji Islands. He and his family will be going there this month. They are sponsored by the Methodist Church in India. Our Bishop preached a sermon on "Our Mission Today", giving the thought that every Christian is a missionary commissioned by Christ to witness for Him.

Chapter 11

EXPLORING INDUSTRIAL DEVELOPMENTS

On Tuesday November 12, 1963 I moved my things from Calcutta to Gomoh. The first day I spent in Dhanbad which is our business center, about 30 miles away. The second day was spent in helping to entertain a visiting a Bishop and his wife. After that I was able to unpack and settle myself in two rooms. I am living and working with an Indian woman by the name of Miss Singh. She is due to retire in a few months.

Gomoh is a small place and the Mission Compound is a very large portion of the village. The other main thing is the railway station. There seem to be only two automobiles that work and both of them belong to the church. We are in the midst of a building program. During the last five years the church has made this a large center with a school, hostels and church. My work for this first year is mostly with the churches throughout the district.

Yesterday, on my first Sunday here, I took a trip out to the extreme end of the district. Miss Singh and I, with our driver, left here at 7 a.m. We drove through some forests and low hills. As I watched the scenery I soon realized we went on a long route just to get across the river. After about an hour and a half we came to a thickly populated area and looked down from our road into the deep gorge made by open pit mining. Soon we came to the Bokaro thermal power station said to be the largest in Asia built a few years ago with American aid. About a mile from the thermal plant we came to our church. At 9 a. m. we attended the English service in the church. All the members are Indian, but since they come from widely scattered parts of India the only way they can communicate is with the English language. They also use some Hindi which is the national language. After the service a reading room was dedicated and opened. I had the honor of cutting the ribbon. We try to have reading rooms or libraries with most of our churches.

From Bokaro we went to Kathwara where the pastor of the Bokaro circuit held a service in the home of one of the Christians. The majority of the congregation was Tamil from the Madras area of India so the service was in Tamil and Hindi. The pastor preaches only in Hindi and English. After the service we went to another church on the circuit where Miss Singh also supervises a primary school. After a short visit with some of the Christians we returned to Bokaro for our noon meal in the home of one of the laymen.

In the afternoon on our return to Gomoh we visited two other places. All of these places are now cared for by one pastor by using a bicycle. He has at least 15 miles to cover. Our district superintendent is trying to raise money for three motorcycles for the pastors who have such huge circuits in these exploding developments.

In early 1964 Miss Singh and I made a definite division in the District work. I took Jarangdih and Asabani schools and she took the hostel and school in Gomoh and the Goshala primary school. I made several trips to the Jarangdih school with Miss Singh. The first week of January I came by train and spent the day in the school. Each time I returned to Gomoh very much dissatisfied with my visit and understanding of the area. The round trip by car is 80 miles and more than three hours in the car. It seemed to be a terrible waste of time and gasoline. Then I tried the train. Even first class cost only one fourth as much as the trip by car, and the time spent for the trip is about the same. There are only two trains each way every day and it means either getting up at 4 a.m. or taking a noon train and returning at about 10 p. m. At most of the stations there is no transportation, no bus, rickshaw, tonga or taxi. Usually I want to do something besides visit the school so it means walking several miles if I go by train. One solution is a bicycle but the roads are rather up and down. There are no lights at the Jarangddih station. One night I purchased the ticket at the station and crawled under a freight train to get to the opposite side where my train was approaching.

I decided to spend several days in the area. The guest houses attached to the projects are comfortable. They have single rooms with attached bathrooms with hot and cold running water. They charge me the same rate their own staff pays. During this week I have tried to visit all the colonies where Christians are living in these two circuits of Bokaro and Bermo. Even though the pastor and I started out at 8 a. m. each day and returned at 9 p.m., we have not been able to get to all the places. We have ridden by train, public buses, school buses, with Catholic sisters, and in trucks hauling coal to the power plant. We have walked six to eight miles a day.

The Bermo circuit stretches out over a big area with its numerous bazaars. Now much of the town is being shifted to a new location since the National Coal Development Corporation (NCDC) has decided to dig it up to get the coal underneath. We visited one of the newest colonies called Ghandhinagar. We walked two miles along a black dusty road which wound around the mountains of coal. Constantly the trucks hauling coal passed us, raising the black clouds of dust which enveloped us until we could not see to thumb a ride. We stood on a hilltop just outside the home of one of our Christians from Moradabad and had a good view of the new colony as well as several others that have now been completed. Road construction and building are going on. We feel the throbbing of new life. Already members from both Bermo and Jarangdih are living here. The Christians showed me the plot of land, well located, which they are trying to get to build a church building. It is centrally located among several of the new colonies and is also near some old bazaars. Other towns on the Bermo circuit are Kargali and Phusro. A good road has been constructed from Phusro to Chandrapur.

The Bokaro Circuit area consists of a large thermal power station and the colony of about 4,000 people. I cannot get over the fact that a place that looks so nice as this has practically no arrangement for public transportation. We arrived at one home (of Kolar background) to visit at about the same time as the stork and found the father frantically trying to get a jeep to take his wife to the hospital. He finally succeeded. The church here was built by the layman, Mr. Rao, who was in charge of the construction of the project. He is now at Chandrapura, also in this district, and a church there will be dedicated next month.

The members of the Bokaro church live in this colony and in other colonies, five to twelve miles away. There are also two villages with Christians. We visited one of them. Some of the members come from Gomia where there is a huge explosive factory and a colony. Others come from the colony of Kathara where the largest coal washery in India is being built. We want to build a new church there and negotiations are going on for purchase of the land.

As the Christian people from Jarangdih and Bermo scatter to new places because of their transfers in the Damodar Valley Corporation or National Coal Development Corporation, they come and request the pastor to visit them so the two circuits become larger and larger. Already they need to be divided. I can easily visualize this part of the Dhanbad district dividing and becoming the Hazaribagh District in the future.

The Catholics and Protestants cooperate in many ways. The priest in charge of this area called on me and we visited for about two hours. We discussed our mutual problems and ways in which we can cooperate. He made a specific proposal for our Jarangdih schools and asked me to wait until he consulted his bishop before exploring it further. The next day he went to Hazaribagh to see his bishop, but he had an accident on his motorcycle and has not been able to return to Bokaro.

In Bokaro there has been a Bible study group. Until November it was led by an engineer from England who worked on the construction of the explosive factory in Gomia. He has been transferred to Bombay. It was a real inspiration to meet people who were members of this group, or who had been at one time or another. Some have been promoted and transferred and are too far away to attend. The pastor is continuing the studies. The Catholic father regularly attends these studies. They are now studying Acts.

We have yet to see a satisfactory written statement from the National Coal Development Corporation from whom we rent or lease the land. Verbal promises are many. We also realize that their position keeps them from putting things in writing — lest at some future date we bring a complaint against them due to damages caused by mining under our property. I mentioned that many Christians have moved away.

There are seven circuits in the District. Each has its own unique feature. We have four primary schools, which I help to supervise, and one large high school with dormitories for both boys and girls. The high school has been developed during the last ten years, and is still in the developing stages with building construction going on. At present we have about 700 students with 120 of them living in dormitories.

One of the primary schools is in a backward village. It is difficult to reach as it is five miles from our main road. We can go during the dry cool season but in the rainy season it will be impossible to reach it by car.

Gomoh is a small town with a population of 10,000. On one side of the railway track is a large colony for the railway employees and on the other side is a typical Indian bazaar with houses cluttered around it. Everyone tells me how fortunate we are now that we have electricity, a paved road and running water. In the near future we may have a telephone. Here in Gemoh we can get the things that Indians subsist on. For other things, which are luxuries for some but necessities of life for me, we go to Dhanbad 24 miles away. We buy our vegetables from the weekly "hat." The weekly "hat" reminds me of the farmer's market in South Carolina. One of the most difficult adjustments I have had to make from city to village life is learning how to stock my cupboards since I cannot buy things any time I like.

I am enjoying being in a place where we are beginning new projects. It is an inspiration to meet with groups who are busy building the church in new places. The enthusiasm of the driver of a bull-dozer in a new construction project still lingers with me. He took me to the spot he and the building committee had chosen for the church in that place. The church is a very small minority - about two percent of the total population. There may be about 100 witnessing Christians in a new town of 4,000.

Today, March 1,1964 I thought I would have a nice quiet day but one person in trouble, a staff member, came and I listened for about two hours, and that with cleaning my room and a few other jobs took the better part of the day. I am not complaining. I am trying to give you an idea of what life is like. One night, when I got home at 9:30 p.m., my driver reported that we had gone 180 miles. I did business in seven different places. It took me a couple of days to recover after that trip.

This morning, August 13, 1964 I woke up at 4:30 a.m. My mind immediately revolved around the thoughts of the evening before, and I was wide awake. The food situation had reached a crisis. I knew I must do something to alleviate the hardship of my 25 employees. I remembered my gift account and my plans to use it in putting some extra touches on our new buildings. But in the early hours of the morning I decided this free money must go as relief to our workers. Having made this decision I got up fixed my breakfast, and had my devotions. I read from Soul Surgery by H. A. Walter. His thoughts on incisive personal work were a great blessing to me and helped to attune my soul to the Divine Spirit.

After breakfast at 6:30 a.m I wrote a check to the manager of the Boys' Hostel from my gift account and read the newspaper. The newspaper contained good news for us. The Department of Education of the state announced its policies regarding private schools. Most of the rights we had been seeking through our state Christian Council were granted.

At 8:30 a. m., I started out in the car. As the driver and I went through the bazaar a Sikh man stopped us and asked us to tell his brother that his wife had just given birth to a baby boy. We stopped at the post office, collected our mail and went on our way. After four miles we stopped for petrol (gasoline) and to tell the father about his son. The new father keeps a sweet shop on the Grand Trunk Road so he rewarded us by giving us some delicious sweets.

Having completed this errand, we drove along the Grand Trunk Road for about 50 miles. It is an ancient road about 300 years old. It is lined with great trees which at many places form an arch high overhead. It was a clear, bright day after several days of constant rain. The colors about us were brilliant, blue sky with white clouds, light green newly transplanted rice fields edged by the darker green hills. In many places the farmers were still busy with transplanting, and occasionally we saw a woman in her ancient topless dress.

Throughout the drive Parasnath Mountain dominated the scene. Sometimes the 4000 foot peak was clear cut against the blue sky and the white temples stood out. At other times the peak was hidden by clouds. Today the drive took me past the Konar dam and lake which is one of the great artificial lakes built under the American aided Domador Valley scheme patterned after the Tennessee Valley Authority. I stopped by the lake and drank some of the coffee I had brought along in my thermos.

After about two hours we reached the Block Development Office at Gomia. I gave them copies of the deed for the newly purchased land at Kathara and applied for its mutation. This is the final step in a long series of transactions to get a plot of land for a church and school in the great coal mining development. I wish we had kept a record of the number of miles we have traveled and the number of hours spent trying to get this plot of land. It would be an impressive record. Now begins my trek to various offices to get building supply permits.

We left the Block Development office and drove through the colony built around the Indian explosive factory. This is a town of about 4000 with modern township planning features. From there we drove 12 miles to another modern township named Bokaro. Along the way we passed many of the old typical villages with their mud houses. We stopped at the church in Bokaro and found that the pastor had not returned from a stewardship conference in Lucknow. As we were leaving the parsonage I met one of the members of the church. He invited me to his home. I had a nice visit with his family even though I found it difficult to communicate with his wife who speaks only Tamil. The husband is very fluent in English. He told me of how he had just received an answer to prayer. He had been praying to God for clothes for his six children and he had just received a letter from a relative in South India who wrote that he had mailed a package of clothes for the children. The family was so happy that they insisted we share their noon day meal of dal and rice with them. By the time we finished our meal with them the train had come. We returned to the parsonage and found the pastor. With him I arranged to bring a guest speaker for the Sunday services.

Then I called on another family, also South Indian, and all the family members spoke English. The husband attended the stewardship conference in Lucknow with the pastor and gave me a very enthusiastic report of it. The wife served coffee and we had a good period of fellowship.

From Bokaro I went eight miles to Jarangdih. I visited our primary school and gave the four teachers a gift of about $5 each as a special relief during the food crisis. It was a surprise and an answer to prayer for them. In this school we have about 80 children in one room with four teachers. Sometimes during the day one can find a different language in each corner of the room, English, Hindi, Urdu and Tamil. During their recess a group of boys surrounded me and mustered up the courage to ask for a new soccer ball. They showed me the old one which was completely worn out.

After school we started for Gomoh. We returned by another route, which took us through mountains and valleys of black coal. In this area they use the open pit system of mining. We drove along the ridges and looked down into ravines made by removing the coal. After leaving the coal mining region our road wound through forests and in the midst of a lonely forest we passed a car having mechanical difficulty. We stopped and my driver, who is also a good mechanic, tried to help repair the car. After about half an hour he decided he did not have enough tools to fix the car. We gave a ride to two of the men to the nearest garage. As we drove along we conversed in a mixture of Hindi and English. I learned that they were business men dealing in supplying building materials. They in turn learned about the activities of our mission. In the course of the conversation I mentioned the difficulty we were having in getting building supplies. They asked me what I needed and before our journey ended had promised to supply some roofing materials for which I had been searching for six months.

Back in Gomoh at 5:30 p. m., I fixed my supper with a special treat of corn on the cob. This was a gift from a neighbor. After supper I took a brief rest, read some more from the book, "Soul Surgery".

This morning, August 14, 1964 two orphan boys from the school hostel came to remind me that they needed clothes for Independence Day celebrations. At eight, Mr. Baker, an elderly Anglo-Indian who is suffering from cancer, came to see if I had any further work for him. I have been giving him some painting work in order to help him earn some money. He stays here in Gomoh with his daughter who has eleven children. The son-in-law has a very difficult time trying to feed every one in the house.

At 8:30 I left the house to go to complete transactions which I began in the car yesterday for building supplies. I stopped at the office of the Bishop Rockey High School. Hizekiel Pershad, who has recently become manager of the school in place of a missionary, decided to go with me. So on this two hour drive we discussed day to day affairs of the church and school and brought each other up to date on our various activities. We found our business men and gave the order with part payment for the supplies. They promised to deliver after three weeks. Mr. Pershad looked for other building supplies needed in the construction of the new high school building. After this we went to the largest vegetable market this side of Calcutta. I bought some carrots and apples. Both are a special treat for me.

After that we went to the bank. Getting our checks cashed took the usual time of one hour. The driver looked at radios while we were in the bank. For months he had been talking of purchasing one. Today he made up his mind and chose one. According to my agreement with him, I paid for it and he will refund by paying me monthly installments from his salary. The radio cost about $35 and is made in India. It will take him 18 months to pay for it. The driver is a Muslim and has been driving for some one in the Methodist church for about 20 years. Before that he drove for the military and likes to tell about driving the American General Stillwell. He and his wife live next door to me. His wife observes "purdah" so never leaves the four walls of the compound. She will enjoy the radio.

302

After paying for the radio, I bought some cloth for shirt and pants for the two boys who called on me early this morning. Then Hizikiel (Indian for Ezekiel) and I decided to have lunch in an air-conditioned English style restaurant for a change. We usually take an Indian lunch at the railway station. After lunch we returned to Gomoh and reached there at about 4 p.m. The rest of the day was for reading, writing, cooking and visiting with callers.

Today is India's Independence Day. I attended the flag hoisting ceremony in the school at 8 a. m. This was followed by a variety program in the open air. It rained several times during the program, but still most of the program continued. At noon there was a soccer game between Collins Institute, a Methodist school in Calcutta, and Bishop Rockey High School.

But before the game I packed my suitcase and went to Dhanbad to attend an orientation course on Industrial Evangelism. I stayed in the Anglican parsonage. The first meeting was a laymen's rally with laymen coming from all churches including the Catholics. The meeting was well attended. There was a service, followed by discussion groups when the laymen discussed the problems facing them and what they as Christians should do about them. At the last minute they found that they did not have enough leaders for all the groups so I had to try to lead a discussion in a Hindi-speaking group.

There were lively discussions on whether they should make special efforts to spy out food hoarders.

The next day was Sunday. I took one of the members of the Special Industrial Evangelism team to the Bokaro Church. We left Dhanbad at 7 a.m. Our route took us through more coal mines and past the site for the Bokaro steel mill. The aerodrome and offices for this project have already been built.

At 9 a. m. we reached Union Church at Boakro. The guest, Miss Maynard Smith, gave the message. She worked for many years with a church in Sheffield, England. In her sermon she told us how she felt the church had failed among the factory workers of England and urged us to see that it does not fail among the coal miners and factory workers of India.

It poured rain all day so many of the activities planned for the day were canceled. We did some visiting in the homes, and had another service in the evening. The next morning we drove back to Dhanbad. The pastor and two laymen going to the Orientation Course went with us.

For two days pastors and laymen discussed Industrial Evangelism. As we talked together many of our feelings and impressions became strong convictions. We defined Industrial

Evangelism as helping the laymen to live a victorious life, overcoming the evils and temptations they find in their communities and places of work. The front line of the evangelistic movement of the church is led by the Christian laymen. The role of pastors, missionaries, and church workers is to encourage and support laymen through Bible study, prayer and visitation. Many Christians are isolated from other Christians and do not have any opportunity to attend regular worship services or other activities of the church. Each layman represents Christ in his work and life so the task of the paid workers is to minister to him.

The decisions made in these new industrial towns plot the course of India's entire future and affect all of India — even the 80% who still live in the villages. Christians have a special responsibility in this development.

The meetings finished on Tuesday. I returned to Gomoh late that day. Wednesday was spent catching up on my home work which included washing, ironing, writing, reading, and doing accounts. When the people learn that I am at home they drop in. Mr. Baker came again and I gave him some money. He returned a hymn book which he had borrowed from Thoburn Church in Calcutta and asked me to see that it was returned there. He told me that his sufferings would soon be over. I wondered what he meant as he looked strong even though he did have cancer.

In the late afternoon I took the ten minute walk to the school campus. When I arrived there Mr. and Mrs. Pershad suggested that we visit some of the homes in the community. We visited two homes. I returned to my home at about 7 p.m. When I reached home someone was waiting to tell me that Mr. Baker had thrown himself under a running train at 5:30 p.m. being killed instantly. Without entering my home, I went to the home of his family to comfort the wife, daughter and grandchildren. From there we went on to the police to see about getting the body. The police released the body to us when they were convinced that it was a case of suicide.

But there were many problems in arranging the funeral for a suicide case whose relatives were Catholics. Mr. Baker had left the Catholic Church and joined the Methodist Church several years ago. The body remained on a stretcher on the station platform all night. The carpenters who were working on the new school worked throughout the night to make a coffin of wood covered with white cloth using a black lining. We placed the body in the coffin and then started to the cemetery. The cemetery was more than a mile on a lonely hill outside the town. To get to it we had to walk a mile on a hilly footpath. The pallbearers had a difficult time. When we arrived at the cemetery we found that the grave diggers we thought had been at work since dawn had just begun the tedious process of digging a grave in the stony mountain side. After some consultation we decided to go ahead with the funeral service so some who had to go to work could leave. The pastor of our local Methodist church conducted a very comforting service in English.

The pastor and I decided to stay with a few relatives and close friends. We found a shady tree. While the grave diggers worked for three hours we sat and talked. I spent most of the time with three teen-aged grand daughters of the deceased. They were full of questions about my beliefs. We talked about some of the differences in Catholic and Protestant beliefs of life, death and salvation. The girls shared many of their own personal and family problems. Rarely have I been more aware of the presence of the Holy Spirit as we sat together waiting to commit to the earth the final remains of one who made many attempts to live a Christian life. In the end, with a body filled with cancer, he succumbed to the hold of alcohol and then found life too much. The young granddaughters were receptive to Christian teaching as they talked of his life.

I returned home at 1:30 p.m. and found that the mailman had delivered a letter which Mr. Baker had written to me shortly before he ended his life. He was effusive in his praise of me. Why couldn't I have done more?

As I had an appointment in the school office to discuss budgets, I did not have time to linger with my thoughts but hastily had something to eat and then went to the school. The hostels were having a difficult time meeting expenses and feeding the children as prices continued to rise. So again we discussed ways to cut expenses and possible ways of increasing income. This budget session lasted about three hours. Then I came home, read the newspaper and Reader's Digest. I dressed to have my evening meal with the Pershad family.

As I mentioned earlier, the Pershad family have recently replaced a missionary family here in Gomoh. One of the things they expect to do is to entertain American visitors. Occasionally they have an European style meal and invite me to share it with them. At these meals Mrs. Pershad learns to cook new types of food and the three children — two boys and a girl - learn how to use the knife and fork properly. They think it is fun. Mr. Pershad has a Ph. D. in economics and is also an ordained minister. He is the son of a Methodist minister and grew up in the villages of Agra Conference. Mrs. Pershad has an M. A. in sociology. The father and mother of Mr. Pershad live with them. The family is a wholesome one with a real zest for living. This evening I took my projector and slides and showed them pictures of my home and family. I finished my week with a very delightful and refreshing evening.

Wherever I go, whether it is crossing the Atlantic on a jet plane, motoring on India's roads, calling on government officials, or bicycling through the rice fields all quickly come to know that I am a missionary. Immediately the conversation turns to religion. I have a tremendous responsibility. I am happy for those who share it with me through their support materially as well as spiritually.

Bishop G. Sundaram dedicated the new church at Chandrapura on September 13, 1964. Chandrapura is one of the newest townships of this area, built around a new Thermal Power Station under the Damodar Valley Corporation. The new station has six units with a total capacity of 750 mega watts which is the largest power plant in India. The power station has an imposing look with its very tall masonry chimney tower, and a 10,000 foot coal conveyor belt for mechanical feeding of coal from nearby Dughday washery. The entire foreign exchange for the construction has been met from United States aid amounting to 30 million dollars.

The dedication service was well attended by Christians and non-Christians alike. The small simple sanctuary could not seat even half the people. Many laymen participated during the service. Bishop Sundaram in his message described the building of Solomon's Temple but reminded us that in the end Solomon counted wisdom as the greatest gift of all. At the end of the service we went out into the compound for refreshments. A spectacular sunset remained like a halo over the occasion.

Plots of land have been purchased in two other places. I am now busy in one place trying to make arrangements for the construction of a building which will be used for both school and church. The other plot is near the new Bokaro Steel Mill about seven miles from Chandrapur

This week we said goodbye to Dr. and Mrs. Walter Griffiths. They leave India after 44 years of service. The last 24 years were at the Lee Memorial Mission in Calcutta. They brought me to India and have looked after me ever since. Saying goodbye to them brings back many memories.

The year immediately past has been my hardest, fullest and happiest. I have been robbed, ill and persecuted. In the midst of these I have received healing, rich blessings and the joy of victories. As I go into the new housing developments where people are literally beginning a new way of life, I feel that I am doing pioneer work. The people leave the mud villages or the squalid slums of the cities and come away to these lonely places. They construct new towns, thermal power stations and factories of many types. The factories and the housing development around them are special areas. The experiments in town planning and community living are bound to affect all of India, even the 70% who still live in villages.

From my office I can lift my eyes to a mountain rising up to 4,000 feet out of the valley. On the highest point I see a white temple silhouetted against the deep blue sky. Not long ago I climbed to the temple. There in the ornate temple is only a preserved footprint. It is believed that it is the footprint of one of the gods who walked here many thousand years ago. Once a year many pilgrims from all over India come, climb the hill and worship at the place of the footprint.

From the top of the mountain one looks out across the Damodar Valley and the Chotanagpur plateau. The valley and plateau are rich in mineral resources. But the people who live here have been among the poorest in India. The poor farmers have scratched the soil above veins of coal, kyanite, iron ore, copper ore, mica, chromate and have tried to live on their meager harvest of grains. Now technology, industry and modern science are moving in. They hope to transform the whole area. Until now the factories and new townships are like little islands in a sea of jungle and mud villages. Lifted out of their setting they are impressive. But here they are dwarfed by the magnitude of poverty and needs about them. Still, the fact that industry has begun has ignited a fuse of hope that burns and often turns into impatient anger.

Chapter 12

WHO MOVED THE GOAL POST?

Suddenly I was requested to return to work in the Treasurer's office in Bombay. The Woman's Division wanted Miss Christdas to move to New York to be a part of their staff. Accepting the request was a very difficult decision. I struggled with it for several days.

I am one who believes that it is dangerous for one individual alone to decide what God's will is so I asked my Bishop and cabinet to carefully consider my future assignment. I have learned to love the Evangelistic work in the new developing areas I believe that God will give me the strength to do the task He wants me to do.

I moved to Bombay and became Central Treasurer for India December 15, 1965. I returned to Gomoh for Christmas. I took the Christmas service at the new Chandrapura Church. During the last Annual Conference session I was admitted into the Annual Conference on trial and hope to go on to ordination. The day after Christmas I left for Lucknow to attend the Central Conference (of the Methodist Church in India). It is similar to Jurisdictional Conferences in the US. The main item of interest was the election of two bishops as Bishop Subhan and Bishop Mondol retired.

Dr. Harry Denman from the Board of Evangelism stayed throughout the Central Conference and gave many inspiring messages. Mrs. Osgood represented the Committee on Structure of Methodism Overseas (COMOS). Our Executive Secretaries, Henry Lacy and Chanda Christdas, were present. Miss Christdas was a lay delegate from Hyderabad Conference. There were fraternal delegates from Pakistan and Malaysia. The work of Andaman Island was transferred from Malaysia to India.

From June 1, 1965 our church has one treasurer's office for all funds received from the Board of Missions. I am now Assistant Branch Treasurer of the World Division of the Board of Missions. My office is in the Inter-Mission Business Office where about 90 mission organizations cooperate in business matters relating to travel, foreign exchange, banking, insurance and shipping. This office was organized in 1934.

At the time of moving my office I moved my residence also. Instead of living in the guest-house, I now have a separate apartment in our Robinson Memorial Church compound. Robinson Memorial Methodist Church serves the Kanerese and Marathi speaking congregations. It is a large building and centrally located. It has a busy schedule of church activities for ecumenical groups as well as for our Methodists. Back of the church is Wicke Hall named in honor of Bishop Lloyd C. Wicke of the New York area. It is a two-winged, three-storied building in which I live. One main feature is the social hall, a very busy place, especially during the wedding season. There were many wedding receptions during May and June of this year.

I go by taxi two miles to the office each morning. It costs about forty cents. Often I take my lunch. Occasionally I eat in one of the numerous restaurants in the area. Our office is air-conditioned except when there is a power failure. There are frequent power failures during the hottest season of the year just before the monsoons come. This year during June electricity was rationed and no business office was allowed to have air-conditioning. We were literally steamed for about ten days. Now the monsoon is in full swing in Bombay and rains are heavier than usual. Last week we had record-breaking rains. It rained incessantly for several days with about 15 inches in one 24 hour period. I feel that life in Bombay is easier than in many other places. There are rationing and rice less days, but letters from friends in other parts of India remind me that the food shortage is more acute in other places.

We feel closely associated with the total work of our church in India through the office work. We are a staff of eleven in the Methodist department of the Inter-Mission Business Office.

Recently I visited a slum area of Bombay with the wife of one of our pastors. She has ten classes for adults with a total enrollment of 170. She is teaching them reading, writing, family planning, cooking, sewing, hygiene and other subjects. In one of the centers some of the members gave a program using puppets. During the program the jet airplanes from the nearby airport flew overhead. The fast suburban trains buzzed by a short distance away. Yet the scene in this slum area is one that is repeated hundreds of times in villages throughout India. These people live in much the same way as those do in the villages. Since they have come to Bombay they have realized the importance of education and are most anxious to learn. As I sat and watched the program I realized the range of our church in India, and particularly in this city of Bombay. The adults have formed several evangelistic teams that sing the Gospel message with the help of drums. Through the classes, and the evangelistic teams, more than 100 have become Christians.

What can we do to correct some of the false reports that are being scattered abroad? We do not profess to know the full truth. An American told me today that some U. S. newspapers reported that Bombay had been bombed four times. I certainly know that is not true.

We lived in war-time conditions for 23 days in September. Since the cease fire anxiety has receded into the back of our minds. The recent experience of war had a remarkable effect upon India. Politically India is stronger than ever before. Shastri, our Prime

Minister, now draws the crowds and receives the respect formerly given to Nehru and Gandhi. Self-reliance is the new word of the day. The spirit is "We won the war and we did it alone." One man has explained the difference between Self - Reliance and Self - Sufficiency. According to him, the policy of working toward Self - Sufficiency has been wrong because of its narrowness. India needs to negotiate with others from a position of strength rather than weakness. And India has just proven her strength in war with Pakistan. India is a united country and not about to fall apart because of hunger and language differences. The price of meat has come down to the pre-conflict price in Bombay. We have just entered the season when vegetables are always cheaper. There are still long queues at the ration shops for rice, wheat and sugar.

The newspapers and officials are encouraging all to believe India can produce the additional eight percent of food grains needed to feed her people. The new slogan is "Jai Kisan Jai Jawan." "Salute the farmer, salute the soldier." India's new found faith in her own ability marks another step forward in the building up this, the largest democracy in the world.

All of our missionaries remained in their stations during the war. Two of our missionary stations had a very difficult time. They were Fazilka which is two and a half miles from the Indian border with Pakistan, and Jodhpur in Rajastan and Batala had bombs which did not explode.

The major political problem in India today is the conflict with Pakistan. The greatest social problem is the food shortage. The major religious problem concerning the church from outside is synthesis of religions. India in order to promote national integration and unity is trying in every way possible to synthesize cultures and religions. Many Hindus worship Christ along with Krishna and other gods. Many Christians fail to differentiate between true Christianity and the one-religion idea. I feel this is the most dangerous problem as this is often subtle and difficult to recognize. There are scattered cases of persecution of Christians. When persecution takes place, it tends to unite the Christians and make them stronger.

The major problem within the church is rivalry and striving for status and recognition. Elections for office in the local official board and other offices are highly contested. At present, in Bombay, there is a court case about the election at a fourth quarterly conference. Some members of the quarterly conference are trying to prove that the election was illegal according to our church discipline. The church is fighting the case on two grounds: first, the correct procedure was followed; second, the Civil Court of the Government has no right to interfere in such cases, or in any matter relating to religion

There has been a great deal of ecumenical cooperation throughout India. In one of the papers there is an up-to-date report on negotiations for church union. Our own Inter Mission Business Office is one of the best examples of co-operation between missions and churches. We do business for 90 mission organizations. There is also a great deal of co-operation with the Catholic Church throughout India. The Methodist Church cooperates with the Catholics in relief work, hold joint institutes for industrial evangelism and give joint Christmas and Easter programs for the non-Christian public.

One of the problems is how much control should the Board of Missions have over the money sent to the various fields. One of my good friends and I often discuss the problem of Christian giving and Christian receiving. What is the proper relationship between the donor and receiver? Can the donor recognize the man who receives as equal to him? Can those who receive do so without feeling inferior? These are ancient problems but they are very pertinent to us in India today. I find myself in very strong disagreement with most Americans when they state that the problems of the nations are due to hunger. We know that hunger causes many problems, but we cannot save the world or bring about peace by feeding the hungry. It is far more important to recognize each individual for his human worth than it is to supply his material needs.

319

Bombay vividly illustrates rapid growth and change. Almost five million people live in an area of 180 square miles. Modern multistoried apartment buildings are being constructed at a rapid rate. Even so, housing those who migrate from the villages in search of work is a very critical problem. Squatter colonies spring up like mushrooms around every construction site The construction laborer lives in the open until he is able to collect pieces of tin, bamboos, and other material to build some type of hut to protect his family from the sun and the rain. The result is that those colonies look like a dirty tattered fringe and hide the attractive buildings.

Recently our Methodist congregations have translated their concern for these slums dwellers into action. One pastor's wife resigned her job as a teacher in a government high school. She went to literacy village in Lucknow and took courses in methods of teaching adults. She returned and shared her training with two other volunteers from among the members of her church. The volunteers then opened adult literacy classes. All of the classes are held in the evening after work and the evening meal. Often the classes do not begin until nine and continue until after eleven. About 200 adults completed prescribed courses, passed examinations and received certificates at public functions.

The adult students have charge of the program during the function for awarding the certificates. They take great delight in reading in public. Often in the church service a new literate is asked to read the scripture lesson. The others follow the reading with great interest and prompt the reader when difficult words are encountered. One part of their training is learning to give puppet shows that teach lessons in health and morals. These shows are usually given in the open and attract large crowds.

Other congregations have received inspiration from that church. Some churches are adopting hutment areas — (temporary shelters made of scraps of tin, bamboo and other materials). Today in Bombay there are four well-organized social service centers and 13 adult literacy centers. These centers are led by pastors, the district superintendent and the lady district worker. They supervise the work done by the volunteers. One of the centers is Friendship Center which has been a Woman's Division project for many years. It has a government recognized nursery school and classes for young mothers or brides. It serves the women and children in one of the old textile communities of the city.

The other three centers are located in the hutment areas. In one place the residents of the hutment colony constructed their own center. It is very similar to their huts. Their classes and activities are led by a dedicated Christian volunteer who is well placed economically. She was an orphan student in one of our mission boarding schools. She now gives her service to show her appreciation for what God has given her. She has been faithful through heat and rain. She teaches reading, writing, sewing, family planning, cooking, health education and other subjects.

In another center the district superintendent bought a small room for $125. The room provides a place to store the sewing machines and other materials. Most of the teaching and other activities are carried on in the open air when the weather permits.

Activities of the centers vary according to the needs and interest of the group. It has been observed that adults who were apathetic in their villages suddenly become alert and eager for more book knowledge when they come into the cities. Literacy has been the most popular class. Next in popularity are classes in sewing and cooking. Many of the women have to adjust to new types of food and new methods of cooking them. The adults also enjoy classes in Bible and singing. The teachers have cleverly adapted the Bible stories to their village type of music. They sing the story of the life of Christ accompanied by drums and other percussion instruments. At Christmas and Easter they go around in groups singing the Bible stories to all who will listen.

Ten weeks ago I returned to Bombay after a four-month leave in South Carolina and Georgia. From the day I arrived I resumed my duties in the Treasurer's office. These weeks have been intensely busy with routine office work, travel and a number of all India committee meetings. Back in Bombay after my brief period in Atlanta, I find myself making comparisons between the two places. The day I arrived an Indian Team was playing a cricket match with a team from the West Indies. It reminded me of the Thanksgiving football games. There was no bumper to bumper traffic on freeways, but there was a twelve people deep, mile-long ticket window queue of people. There were no TV sets displaying the game, but there were hundreds of transistor radios in the offices, in the shops, and on the public transportation. There was the same feverish absorption in the game. Nothing else seemed to matter. Our office staff were caught up in the excitement. Our work was secondary. But the work got done and I have caught up with all my duties.

As soon as the games were over, Bombay entered into the Christmas festivities. Even though Christians are a small minority, the people of Bombay celebrate Christmas very pompously. Along with the American Christmas cards of bells, holly, and snow scenes, I received the Indian ones of palm trees, dancing girls, and Indian art forms. India seems to have taken everything about our Christmas, except our Christ.

Electioneering followed Christmas. The contest between Bo Callaway and Lester Maddox in Atlanta paled into insignificance as I watched the local contest between the Socialist Labor leader, George

Fernandes, and the aristocratic, veteran, all-India Congress railway minister, S.K Patil. There was far more at stake. The Congress minister was defeated. Last night the laboring class exhibited their jubilance at a mammoth public rally on the open beach. I got caught up in the throng on my way home from church. No longer will India have a one-party government. Numerous small parties have whittled down the majority of the dominant Congress party. The new parties represent a great variety of viewpoints, such as anti-cow slaughter, opposition to Hindi as the national language and anti-English. No one party is strong enough to win but united they are an effective instrument in bringing about reforms in the Congress party.

In the cricket match and in the elections it seemed to me that the desire and necessity to win were far deeper and more intense than in America. My feeling is supported by riots over disagreement with an umpire of a cricket match in Calcutta and some violence during the counting of the ballots in Bombay. The Indians are desperately trying to win the battle for existence in a democratic society that provides a comfortable life. They need to feel the elation of victory. May our charity be a means of cheering them on to victory rather than an unpleasant reminder of defeat. The intensity of the struggle is felt in every phase of our church life. Under the leadership of Harry Denman and Bishop Pickett the Indian church has had its "Venture in Faith." I am confident that she will be victorious. "But *thanks be to*

God who giveth us the victory through our Lord Jesus Christ" (I Cor 15:57)

Since October 1, 1968 I have been hostess of a guest-house which was formerly managed by the Church of the Brethren. The Brethren couple related to our office have retired. No replacement has been found. In the meantime their work has been distributed among the rest of us. The hostess work is in addition to my usual office work. It is possible because I have excellent help in the house.

The guest-house is a huge apartment on the fifth floor of an eight-story building. It is located at the point of the Bombay peninsula. My bedroom opens to the Arabian Sea. To the right of our building the construction of the new "Air-India" airline building is in progress. It will be more than 20 stories high when it is completed. It is a constant reminder that home is only a few jet hours away.

This past year has been a very full one. I have enjoyed it. The work of a Treasurer in India is never monotonous. My work is very rewarding as it brings me into concrete contact with many wonderful Christian people. During the past two months I have traveled to the other three corners of India in connection with special meetings of the church.

The election last February, the war in the Middle East, the famine in Bihar and the devaluation of the pound have all had a very noticeable effect upon India and upon the work of the church. The Government in power is facing stronger and stronger opposition because the economy is weakened. Some of the opposition forces are not friendly to mission work. This undermines our security. But what have we to fear? Our security is in God.

My most rewarding experiences are with the Christians of the local congregations. Frequently I have my Sunday evening meal with members of Taylor Church. About two weeks ago our district superintendent took us on a tour of "house churches" in some of Bombay's squalid hutment areas. We were greatly inspired by young college students teaching their illiterate relatives and neighbors. The spirit of hope shone from the eyes of men, women and children. They are awakening to the possibilities of a better and more comfortable life. I pray that they will not be disappointed.

My life revolves around the office, the guest-house, travel and local church activities. As a result of "Dialogues" with the Board of Missions in 1966 and 1967 a great deal of change has taken place in the financial planning of our churches. My colleague, Mr. Vreeland, and I have visited all the 11 conferences at least once to participate in the financial planning of the conferences. This led to new legislation at the General Conference held at the end of 1968. Now we are busy trying to implement the new legislation.

As the church has tried to discover its resources it has discovered potential that it never dreamed existed. Thousands of needy people have discovered for themselves that it is more blessed to give than to receive.

I have entertained many people in the guest-house. My travels, in connection with my appointment, have taken me throughout India. Then as an extra special bonus, I had a trip to Switzerland, Belgium and the United States as the guest of Swiss Air. I had eight days at my home in Piedmont. We, eleven brothers and sisters, had our Christmas dinner with our mother on December 21, 1969. Then I rushed back to India to attend the Central Conference.

During the past year I have attended Bowen Methodist Church which is nearer my residence and office than Taylor Church. It is a small downtown church located near the hotels where tourists stay. The church has a vital mission program with only 40 members. Their gifts have been used to support village pastors and to build two village church buildings. Transients in Bombay often drop in for a service. A troubled English girl passed the church one evening when the choir was practicing. The music attracted her and she stepped inside. The warmth and sincerity of the welcome she received led her to regular attendance and a great spiritual victory. A young student from Ghana testified to how he had faltered in his faith among his

327

Hindu classmates. His faith was restored through the ministry of the pastor.

Saturday, June 7, 1969 was a very special day for the Methodist of Bombay District. For ten years, the district superintendent, pastors and laymen have been trying to build churches in the growing suburbs of Bombay. Some Advance Special Gifts funds have been received, but the cost of land is prohibitive. One suitable plot costs $40,000. A group of laymen explored the possibility of purchasing an apartment in a cooperative housing society and making it a church. The skeptics said it would never work as no non-Christian housing society would permit a place of worship on its premises. The enthusiastic laymen were not discouraged. They negotiated with city officials and a cooperative housing society. For $6000 they purchased the upper floor of one wing of a housing unit, and on June 7 it was dedicated as the Methodist Prayer and Social Service Center. The hall 48 ft by 16 ft. was filled to capacity and many persons could not find standing room. These people who had worshipped under trees, on verandahs and in Hindu school halls were jubilant. They now had their own worship center. It is a departure from traditional church buildings but in a city of apartment buildings it is relevant!

The political climate of India remains unpredictable. The dominant party of India continues to lose strength, but there is not a strong opposition party. The reasons for demonstrations and riots seem to increase each day. It seems that the conflicts of modern man is being fought by primitive methods on the streets of our cities while world politicians build up sophisticated military power.

The battles I witness are not demarcated by military barriers. These battles rage in other lands. They are born in hearts of men. What is the struggle? Why do modern men fight like savages in the streets of our cities? For each the outward reason is different. Perhaps the inner reasons are the same. Victories cannot be won by military might. Victories cannot be purchased with dollar funds. Victories will be won through the sacrificial service and involvement of committed people who like Christ give their life for others.

In July, 1969 several changes took place in my work assignment and living arrangements. Rev. and Mr. E. M. Fasnacht took charge of the Church of the Brethern Guest House and Mr. Facnacht joined the managerial staff of the Inter-Mission Business Office. I moved to the Methodist Guest House and took up the work of the hostess until May, 1970. Our church elected Mr. C. W. Thomas as Assistant Field Treasurer. He was formerly an accountant with the Indian Railways. For many years he has given leadership in his spare time in the field of stewardship. Through his leadership Bombay Annual Conference attained full support of its pastoral ministry in 1968. Thus I have been freed from the very heavy load of work which I had carried since my furlough in 1966. Now I am part-time hostess and part-time treasurer.

The 11 annual conferences of the Methodist Church in India voted to accept the plan of church union in North India by a comfortable margin. The new church is to be inaugurated in November, 1970. I was ordained an elder at the session of the Bombay Annual Conference in November. The proposed plan for the new church does not accept ordination of women nor does it reject them. The question is left open and will be taken up by the newly formed church. In spite of this uncertainty of relationship in the new church, I felt the Spirit of God compelling me to take this step.

The year 1969 has been a stimulating one. It began with our Central Conference which epitomized the mood of change that has come into our church. Throughout this year I have been impressed and inspired by the perceptive understanding, daring courage, complete dedication, and spiritual maturity of our newly elected leaders.

The year 1970 is a challenging one. To us in India is given the task of building a NEW CHURCH. There are numerous arrangements and assignments to be made. Rev. J. N. Harris, our District Superintendent, has great zeal for evangelism, and is determined to see that our evangelistic activities are not crowded out by the multiplicity of committees. We pray for the Pentecostal outpouring of the Holy Spirit on the Church in India.

During this monsoon season in Bombay the rains have frequently upset our normal activity because of disrupted transportation, poor telephone connections, shorts in our electrical wiring, damp, moldy clothes and arthritis. When I am tempted to complain I remember the long hot summers without water in our taps and flush toilets!

Miss Maxine Coleman has returned from furlough and resumed her duties as hostess at 22 Club Back Road. I moved to the Vreeland apartment at Ishwar Bhavan, Churchgate. Mr. C. W. Thomas has been elected as Branch Treasurer of the Methodist Church in India.

The Central Conference of the Methodist Church in India met in Delhi, August 5 - 9, 1970 and reversed the decision of the Annual Conferences to unite with six other churches to form the Church of North India. The whole issue has been a hotly debated one for the last two years. Letters to the editor of our Church paper "Indian Witness" were very similar to the ones now appearing in the South Carolina United Methodist Advocate regarding the plan for the merger of the two Annual Conferences in that state. Human nature seems to be the same here even though Christians are a small minority in a huge non-Christian nation.

The other churches are going ahead with the plans for the union which will be consummated on November 29. We are now in the process of disengaging from these activities. In our Inter-Mission Business Office we sit elbow to elbow with treasury personnel of three of the groups that will be entering into union. Our negative vote on organic union will not alter the fine relationship that we enjoy with them.

During the month of May I spent my vacation at home helping in the nursing care of my 80 year old mother who fell and broke her hip and had other complications. I am looking forward to my regular furlough in 1971.

Since my arrival home from India in February, 1971 I have felt hostility on the part of some church people toward me as a representative of the established missionary enterprise. This has been expressed in various ways. Had it not been for one particular incident I would be prepared to dismiss it as a figment of my imagination. That incident took place in a class at Candler School of Theology, Emory University.

Along with about 20 other students I took a course under Dr. Justo Gonsales on the History of Christian Missions. For our class project we prepared reports to give to the class on the development of the church in various countries. I prepared a report on India. The report covered two class periods of 50 minutes. In the second period I finished my report and left about 20 minutes for questions. My classmates bombarded me with questions. The questions were not about India, or my report, but concerning the validity of foreign missions today.

During the confrontation, one student that I had come to regard as a very sensitive person and one with a unique ministry during his seminary training, made this remark: "Missionaries are the most egotistical group of people I have ever met." That remark has remained with me and has caused me to consider in much greater depth my role as a missionary.

This accusation of pride has been attributed to the missionary movement by the Hindus of India. Men like Gandhi, Vivekananda, Ambekar and others have been able to accept Christ but have been turned off by the superiority stance of the Christian church.

During furlough in our anxiety to raise funds no doubt most of us oversell ourselves and our projects, and thus appear to be boastful to our donors. In our relationships with national colleagues our expression of opinion or guidance on financial policy is sometimes interpreted as domination.

We, the missionaries of today, are caught in the trap of the cardinal sin of pride. The hope of our salvation lies in the fact that there is a greater awakening to our quilt. Michael Quoist has stated that the first stage on the road to salvation is to pray "Lord, deliver me from myself."

Christmas Decorations in Bombay

Chapter 13

I LOVE CALCUTTA

I arrived home from India February, 1971 and am planning to depart for India on February 16, 1972. From March to May, 1971 I studied at the Candler School of Theology in Atlanta, Georgia. In the middle of July I moved to New York where I worked in the planning department of the Board of Missions. In the midst of my study and work in New York I have been able to squeeze in several short vacations with my mother in South Carolina. Her health continues to decline. She requires constant care. Spending time with her and relieving my sister, who stays with her, has taken priority over extra travel and speaking engagements.

This is the first time I have had a "long" furlough since the Board of Missions adopted the "short" furlough possibility. In some ways I have found the adjustment back into American life more difficult than my first adjustment to Calcutta 26 years ago. Then, the robbery, crime, corruption, and lack of medical care were very shocking to me. It appears that the United States is rapidly catching up with Calcutta in this reverse type of development

Before leaving India I turned over my work in Bombay to others and throughout my furlough have been looking forward to returning to a new appointment. I have been invited to be the Principal at Calcutta Girls' High School by Bishop Joseph Lance and members of the Managing Committee. However since I transferred my membership to the Bombay Conference, Bishop Joshi of that Conference has tried to convince me to stay in the Bombay Conference. My personal intention has always been to return to the Bengal Conference.

Furlough is a time of reflection and evaluation of my work. I have been aided in this as I have participated in some of the meetings of a task force set up to study the role of the missionary today. Some of our methods may change but the Message is the same: Christ is the way, the truth and the life.

Ours is a missionary faith. It is time the missionary encounter is set firmly at the center of our theology, our church activity and our budget promotion. It is not a matter of wider geographical horizons as much as it is the matter of bringing the whole world into all our thinking, whether in politics, economics or theology. The rise of third world nations with their cultures and religions are forcing Americans to a new self-evaluation of our obsession with materialistic values.

I have been inspired by groups of committed people in the United States who are giving a meaningful witness to their convictions and suffering for it. There seem to be fewer people in our churches than a few years ago, but the commitment of those who remain is much greater. I believe these active Christians are a minority in our population. This realization shocks me as a missionary to a "non-Christian nation."

At the famous Riverside Church Candle Light Service, I found myself sitting by a newly arrived Indian from Bombay who described himself as a believer in Christ. A few weeks later I attended the crowded service at St. John the Divine where the Archbishop of Canterbury spoke. I found myself sitting by an American, who called herself a Christian but confessed that she was entering the Church for the first time in 25 years. That Hindu's conception of Christ was more like mine than that of the American Christian.

My heart is broken because of the war between India and Pakistan. At this writing the relationship between the land of my birth and the land of my adoption is very strained. Already both sides have said many things that will take much time to forget and forgive. As in the case of all war it is the innocent who have borne the suffering. Now the sufferers are the Bengali people. Before March, 1971 most Americans had never heard of these people. Yet it is estimated that there are almost 130 million Bengali people which is more than one half the population of the United States. Almost 72 million live in East Pakistan. The other 58 million live in the nearby Calcutta area known as the State of West Bengal which is a part of the Indian nation.

My acquaintance with the Bengali people began in 1946 just one year before the creation of East Pakistan by the politicians. As a student of the Bengali language, I learned to love the beautiful poetry, music and the classical dance of the Bengali people. The 1000 year literary heritage of Bengali literature is older than Chaucer.

The division of the land of Bengal into two parts was a severe blow to this Bengali culture. One part remains with India and every tourist to Calcutta can describe the poverty of that city. But those who have lived and worked there have been impressed by the subtle thought and profound religious insight of the Bengali people. The best known personality is Rabindranath Tagore. There are many other sensitive writers and artists.

More than half the people of the Bengali culture became a part of Pakistan. East and West Pakistan were bound together by the Muslim faith, but the Muslims from West Pakistan felt that the Bengali Muslims of the East practiced a corrupted form of the faith. First the West Pakistan Government tried to purify the faith by suppressing the Bengali language. According to the Bengali people, and supported by fact, there have been 24 years of various types of oppression. West Pakistan, which is a military government, supervised the national elections in East Pakistan. After the elections they did not turn the government over to the elected representatives. Negotiations broke down, rebellious feelings increased and chaos broke loose on March 26, 1971 in East Pakistan.

While 10 million people have fled from East Pakistan to the friendly Bengali part of India the world has been paralyzed for nine months. India's emotional, economic, and political stability has been strained beyond its endurance. The result is war. All sides will lose and that includes the United States.

It is a strange war; a war in which Muslim fights against Muslim, and brown men against brown men. It is a war in which the United States is allied with the military dictatorship of Pakistan and Communist China against the democratically elected government of India.

It is not surprising that the reaction of the average American is one of recoil. Some say let's not get involved, but when convinced that we are involved the questions becomes; How? Why? My own thinking on my call as a missionary, like that of so many missionaries, is undergoing constant scrutiny. What does it mean to preach the good news to the poor, and to proclaim release to the captives and to set at liberty those who are oppressed? For me in the midst of the India - Pakistan crisis means I must ask the United States Government why it has not protested to the Pakistan government over the imprisonment and secret trial of the elected leader of the East Pakistan people? Why the silence when they have not been silent in making condemnation of India's actions?

As a Government, the United States cannot extricate itself from Indo-Pakistan crisis because of long standing involvement. As Christians we are called to bring the Gospel of Jesus Christ to bear upon everything we do. The Holy Spirit is calling all of us to repentance of our arrogant materialistic culture to the understanding of the legitimate aspirations of all people and obedience to His call for involvement with their struggles.

The Pakistan forces surrendered in East Pakistan. I am thankful for the sense of realism on the part of Senators Kennedy and Church, and for the fair reporting of the New York Times and NBC. The missionaries meeting in Westerville, Ohio last week passed a resolution supporting India's stand. Many of us are not sending Christmas cards but donating money to UMCOR instead.

I came back to Calcutta in early 1972. I am so happy to be back in India that it frightens me. My feeling of joy is mixed with guilt. I fear I am a traitor to my country, insensitive to my family situation and irresponsible in my relationship to those of you who are struggling in the US. I probe and analyze my feelings. Why was I restless on my furlough and why the utter relaxation on being back?

340

The problems are not less here. If anything they are worse! But in the mist of the complex problems I have a wonderful sense of belonging which I never had in America during my entire furlough.

In these days of 'phasing out' and turning over to 'nationals' there must be something wrong with me because I have never felt so wanted and so needed as I do now. When I arrived in Bombay from New York I was met at the airport at 3:45 a.m. and on the drive into the city heard all the reasons why I should stay in Bombay and not go on to Calcutta. Returning to Calcutta I have the feeling that I am picking up where I left off a short time ago. In fact it has been about 13 years since I lived here.

I walked into a large food store to open a charge account. The Muslim proprietor of the shop not only recognized me as someone he had known before but remembered my name and began to ask me about the missionaries who had retired. With fear and trembling, I went to the Foreigner's Registration Office to inform them that I was transferring back to Calcutta after being in Bombay for a number of years. In less than five minutes they found my old file, dusted it off and pinned my new clean paper on top of the dirty faded ones I had from 1946 to 1958. After some discussions in Bengali, the officer in charge turned to me and said in English: "Originally, you belonged to us so you are not a transfer case." These and numerous other experiences give me a wonderful feeling of having at last arrived back home.

The correspondence between Bishop Joshi and Bishop Lance over my transfer has merely spread the word that I had a choice, and I chose Calcutta and that is how I am being introduced. The appointment and job description are secondary. I have been appointed principal of Calcutta Girls' High School. Mrs. Benedict, of Lee Memorial, has been acting principal for one year. The Bishop and others claim they have not been able to find a qualified Indian willing to serve. The School is an English medium (Cambridge System) school which is fully self-supporting. It charges about five dollars a month to about 900 girls and has about 60 girls on scholarship. There are 41 teachers and 15 other staff people: an accountant, sweepers, a driver, and other service personnel. We have a 20 minute chapel service with the girls in two sections daily.

I will work with the Calcutta Urban Service team in addition to the work in the school. I met with the team this week and am looking forward to this type of community involvement. I am hoping that through my own personal involvement, I shall be able to awaken a greater social consciousness on the part of staff, students and my fellow workers in the Methodist Church.

Morning prayers at Calcutta Girls High School.

Today is Saturday. School is closed. The citizens of Calcutta are voting in the two polling stations set up in two of our classrooms. So far the voting has been very peaceful. This is a State election. The chief contestants are the new congress and the communist party (Marxist), which is an extreme group owing allegiance to the party in China. The boundary walls of our school compound have been plastered with the posters of both parties for the last several weeks. In view of the events of the last year we await the results of the voting

343

today with more than the usual interest. Mrs. Gandhi has personally campaigned in Calcutta on two occasions this month. One day she spoke 16 times.

The Calcutta trams, running on tracks as they have for the last 30 years, are more crowded and nosier than ever. They have huge slogans in Bengali painted on them. The slogans are taken from Gandhi's writing and exhort people to eradicate violence. All but 175,000 refugees have returned to Bangladesh. As we drive about we see where the camps where and are now deserted.

Canon S. Biswas. one of the Urban Service Team, said to me: "During the refugee emergency we learned what we could do. Now we want to see if we can apply some of the same principles and tackle some of the problems of Calcutta."

On May 12, 1972 my school closes. The domestic staff lock up the place like a fortress and go away to their villages for a month. This is their earned privilege. I'm having a hard time finding anyone willing to act as chokidar (security guard) for the month. The weather is HOT. It is hotter than usual this time of the year. The temperature has hovered around 104 for days with 85% humidity. My heavy baggage has not been cleared from customs. My passport is with the clearing agent so I cannot travel until I get it back. So what to do? Do I stay and act as Chokidar or do I flee away? At this stage the path of least resistance is to stay here. There is so much paper work to be done

The school keeps me busy. I have already weathered several storms: threatening telephone calls, parents demonstration against a proposed increase in fees, an attack of dysentery and a rash of petty thievery in the school. Today is May Day. At 8 a.m. the policeman took up duty at my gate. Why? I have no idea. Last week they came by and warned me to be careful without giving any reason. I guessed that it might be because of the anti-Nixon demonstrations in the city. Other than the threatening telephone calls, which I think were done by the students, I have experienced nothing but friendliness on the part of the people of Calcutta.

School has reopened after the summer holidays. In some circles English medium schools like Calcutta Girls' High School are looked upon as catering to the elite class. We do have some from the wealthy and privileged classes but we also have from the lower classes. The great majority are from the struggling middle class. They feel a good command of the English language is essential for advancement in the world in which they find themselves.

Practical scince class

Since the school is a day school only with no boarding the buildings are locked up at 4 p.m. Recently I decided to open our facilities for a night school for nearby underprivileged children. I never advertised the opening of this school publicly but by word of mouth. Very quickly my three classes were filled with 100 students. They are ages five to sixteen. Some have never been to school and others are dropouts due to financial reasons. This night school is free. The salary of the teachers is paid by Calcutta Urban Service which is a cooperative effort of several Protestant denominations. Canon Subhir Biswas is our chairman. So far I have had a very good response from the church and the privileged children of the day school.

Young Brides take sewing lessons

It is estimated that in this city there are about 400,000 children between the ages of eight and twelve who are not in school. A recent government report states that the percentage of children not in school is much higher in urban areas than in villages. Of the children who begin school is this city 70 percent drop out before they attain functional literacy. The government is actively seeking our cooperation in their crash program to educate the children of this city. The challenges and the opportunities are tremendous. Funds and other resources are available. Many people are eager to serve and seem to be crying out: "show us how."

347

This year the meaning of JOY and Celebration has taken on a new meaning for me. I have seen this city change from a city of terror to a city of courage! A city of violent demonstrations to a city of celebrations. Long time residents, journalists and skeptics state that they have never seen anything like the spirit of celebration that has prevailed in this city during the last few weeks. Festivals that were formerly a one day affair have been extended for days, stretching to weeks. There is much feasting in spite of the rising cost of food.

Politicians, sociologists and psychologists are trying to analyze the phenomenon. To me it seems that the people of Calcutta have decided that they are going to overcome their bad situation. The exuberance of their celebrations, the courageous planning, the enthusiastic cooperation to large and small schemes and the patient endurance of hardship all point to the new "climate" in this city. Through numerous special days, such as Independence, Gandhi's birthday, Nehru's birthday, Teacher's day and Principal's birthday our school has been caught up in this spirit of celebration. Never have I seen so much joy. The children take so much delight in simple things.

One evening as I was playing with the children of our night school a boy looked up at our one big trees on the playground and said, "Memsahiba,(term of respect to a mature woman) you could

348

make a nice swing on that large branch." He proceeded to tell me what kind of rope to use, how much it would cost and where I could purchase it. Next day for an investment of about five dollars and an hour's time the swing was installed. One swing for a thousand children big and small, stout and tall all line up for their turn. It is amazing how the children settle their own quarrels and work out their own system of sharing.

Young Muslim married women in our night classes

One night when all the children of the night school were supposed to be in class I could see the movement of the swing in the darkness. Thinking that some child was swinging during class time I went out to investigate. I found some mothers of the children enjoying their turn at the swing. For a moment they, too, were carefree, young and gay.

"The lines are fallen unto me in pleasant places; yea, I have a goodly heritage I will bless the Lord who hath given me counsel." Ps 16:6-7a

I see Canon Biswas about once a month. He always inspires me. One of his main efforts now is to UNITE the hundred of Christian welfare agencies into one effective unit to work with the Government. He wishes to inspire pride in our city. He distributed "I love Calcutta" badges to our students. We proudly wear them

I haven't demonstrated yet, but I have written letters to try to get the garbage removed from our street. Today a city official came to check on it. He made many promises to clean the street immediately. Then he proceeded to ask me to admit his boss's daughter into the school!

This year of 1973 I have learned something of the beauty of God's Power. In the midst of shortages, inflation and times of turmoil

His power and presence has been real. Here for many survival is a miracle and acknowledged as such by the masses.

Through the more than 1000 girls in this English Medium School I become involved in all segments of the city. Today I listened to the heart-rending story of a bright girl in class six who is unable to pay the monthly fee of about $8 a month. A little later two fathers whose daughters are her classmates came and contributed the total amount due on her account. Three of our students are proprietors of full fledged businesses since their fathers died during the year. One could not come and take her required final high school examination because there was a strike in the business that she had to handle. But the neediest student in school seems to be the poor little wealthy girl who is over protected because her mother is afraid she will be kidnapped. The only time she is a normal child is the hours she spends in the school. Recently both mother and daughter spent a school holiday here enjoying their refuge.

I have finalized the admission of 90 four- year old girls to our nursery for the new school year which begins in January. I have not kept a record of the number turned away. For the admission the fathers usually bring their daughters as the mothers do not speak English, or, are very shy. In the midst of these interviews I have been deeply touched by the beauty of the relationships among the fathers and daughters. If I were an artist I would try to capture this beauty on a canvas to adorn my wall opposite the modern Madonna.

This year of 1974, in addition to the usual school closing and Christmas activities in schools and churches, I spent about a week in Delhi attending the meetings of the Executive Board and other committees of the Methodist Church in India. The result is that instead of catching up on my work I seem to get further behind.

I am very busy and very happy. The word that best describes my life here is MIRACLES. During 1974, along with the citizens of this great city, we faced many crises and miraculously we have survived them all. Our Thanksgiving takes on more meaning as we thank God for rice, bread, sugar, soap, petrol, kerosene, water, electricity, telephones, garbage removal service and postal service. At some period these commodities or services were not available during the year. The percentage of letters that get lost in transit is greater than before. The prices have climbed steadily but when we get time to find out what is going on in other parts of the world we realize that we are not alone.

In 1973 we decided to provide six more classrooms by adding another story to one of our buildings. I almost gave up in despair in the middle of the year when it appeared that building supplies were not available. Then the message of God came to me: "You made a good beginning last year both in the work you did and in your willingness to undertake it. Now I want you to go on and finish it: be as eager to complete the scheme as you were to adopt it." Then the cement, steel and additional money came and those rooms are taking shape. We plan to use some of them when our new school year opens the middle of January.

We have some new plans for 1975, and expect our enrolment to reach 1200. We turn away more than we take in.

I expect to be in the United States for about three months in 1975 — probably April, May, June. Most of the time will be spent in South Carolina with my family and supporting churches.

The whole city went wild when India won the cricket match they were playing against the West Indies. For five days we have heard nothing but cricket. India needed to win desperately as she had done so poorly recently. So this is a tonic like winning the war or exploding the bomb.

In 1975 the Indian Government invoked the special powers given by its own constitution to handle an emergency situation that had been developing for sometime. We are not under martial law. And, the police are less in evidence than they were before.

353

It is such a relief to wake up in the morning and to begin the day free from the fear that roving bands of strikers or political agitators would march into our school and under threat demand that we dismiss classes. In the past numerous movements often brought normal life to a standstill. Now by invoking the special powers, the police and courts have more power than they had previously to arrest and hold in jail the offenders.

I believe the masses have welcomed the action of the government. There is a change in the general attitude of the people and in all spheres we are getting better service. There is a sense of discipline that was lacking before. The government is extremely busy explaining what they are trying to do and are getting wonderful cooperation from the people.

Last Sunday afternoon I was out walking my dog in our playground. Suddenly, a man rushed through our school gate. When I tried to remind him that the school was private property and that he should not enter, he started acting like an insane man. Then I saw that a large crowd had followed him and were standing at the school gate watching me as I encountered the intruder. I asked the crowd if the man was insane and they shouted, "no, he is a clever crook." Then they told me that the police had been trying to arrest him and they were trying to help the police. They said this was the third time he had escaped by taking refuge in our school. His crime: buying movie tickets at Rs2/- and selling them at Rs 4/- to those who arrived after the "House Full" sign was put up. This is a very common type of black-marketing. It is difficult to get a movie ticket at the proper price.

Yesterday, August 15, 1975 was India's Independence day. We had a short program with the raising of the flag, saluting it and reciting some patriotic poems and songs.

For the last two weeks we have had an epidemic of "pink eyes" or conjunctivitis. Many students and teachers have been absent. I have been using eye drops as a preventive and so far the drops have worked. It is difficult to run the school with so many absent. A few schools have closed because of the epidemic. Malaria, which we thought had been wiped out completely, is back in full force. And there is plenty of it around. Three or four staff members have been ill with it. They tell us that there is a new breed of mosquito that withstands all insecticides.

Recently a Baptist lady visited me. She got my name from a retired Methodist missionary. She was on a special tour sponsored by a university. Her purpose was to study education in India. She said that she had seen many, many schools in India but that Calcutta Girls' High School was the best one she had seen. She sounded sincere but my response is: "If this is the best, Lord help the others." Our main building is 90 years old. Some of the desks are 75 years old.

We have completed the construction of six new classrooms and will open additional sections of some classes in the new term. In spite of this we turn away more students than we accept. Saying "no" to so many takes a lot of my time and drains me emotionally. A simple "no" is not accepted. One must listen as the applicants tell you their life history along with their hopes and dreams for their children. Then if the reply does not change to the affirmative, they beg, they cajole; they threaten, they offer bribes and some adults weep. With my insides churning, and my nerves tied into knots, I keep on repeating: "I cannot take any more. I have done all I can do. There is no more room."

Is this the way the innkeeper of Bethlehem felt when he turned Mary and Joseph away? Am I doing all I can do? Then I remember Peter and the other disciples after Pentecost. My mission is to be a channel for Christ's love to the world. "Such as I have I give." I pray that our efforts will help many to rise up and walk in the name of Christ our Lord and Savior. I continue to enjoy excellent health and a marvelous sense of God's Presence.

Lenin Sarani (formerly known as Dharamtala St.) is one of the main streets of the City. Thoburn Church next door to the school faces that street. Princep street is a small street lined with a number of tiny electrical shops and scrap iron dealers. To improve the traffic flow we have changed our main entrance to the Princep Street gate instead of the Church entrance gate. Our most prestigious neighbor on Princep Street is the B. C. Roy Clinic which is the former residence of the illustrious physician and politician of that name. His residence was headquarters in the city for Mahatma Gandhi and Pandit Nehru during the Independence Movement.

According to the new plan of education in India some schools will terminate at class X while others will have an intermediate stage of classes XI and XII. Those in XI and XII will take vocational training or college preparatory subjects. We will offer XI & XII.

In addition to this main school our evening Hindi Medium section named Indira (for Mrs. Gandhi) Pathshala (school) continues to grow. It meets from 3 to 7 p m and has 175 students from kindergarten to class four. At the same time in the afternoon we opened a sewing class for teen-age girls. Most of them are Muslim girls who live in purdah (behind the curtain). They have a marvelous time during their two hours of freedom. We try to make sure they learn valuable lessons in addition to sewing.

In February Mother Teresa spoke to chapel and challenged the students to share what they have with those who have less. Since her visit the student government collects from each child one potato and one teaspoon of sugar per week. We emphasize that it is important to keep on remembering the poor and that any meaningful gift must mean a sacrifice by the individual who presents it. The potato and the sugar is taken from the child's ration and presented through the school to Mother Teresa to help feed abandoned children. The senior girls volunteer at the Baby Fold. Mother encourages them to hold the babies and talk to them.

We constantly endeavor to have a vital Christian witness among the students and the public. Along with chapel attendance Moral Science and Bible classes are compulsory. However this year we decided to make the Bible Class for Class XI voluntary. A volunteer from Scotland leads the class once a week. We are pleased with the results which is evident by their attendance and earnest study.

Life in general continues to improve. Prices have been stable. Though far from perfect the supply of food, water, and electricity is better than in recent years. Our excitement during the last few months was caused by rumors of children being kidnapped from schools. We do not know how much was rumor and how much was truth, but we do know that a six year old child was kidnapped from a nearby school and later murdered. Rumor had it that this was a common occurrence.

After a couple of months of dealing with anxious parents we are coming back to normal again.

Nineteen hundred and seventy six is the centenary of the taking over of the school by Bishop J. M. Thoburn who was the first pastor and founder of the church that now bears his name. For the staff and students 1976 will be remembered as the year we began a new system of education popularly know as "plus 2." This means that our students take an All-India examination at the end of class ten in all the major subjects — 13 written papers in addition to language orals and science practical. After class ten the students will have two more years before college and in those two years they are divided into "streams" - science, arts, and vocational subjects. We have been planning, working and spending our extra money on developing our facilities further. In 1977 we shall have our first class XII. This means we have two years pre-school and twelve years of schooling. We expect our enrolment to be about 1,350 in January.

I have been sharing in the responsibilities of Thoburn Church during the furlough of the pastor. Our lay leader has taken the major responsibility of planning the services and the other activities. He is an income tax commissioner and well known for his Christian integrity and witness. I am the treasurer of the Bengal Annual Conference, and my weekends are usually spent making payments and doing those accounts.

Three things in Calcutta have recently focused the attention of the masses upon Christianity. First of all, Mother Teresa continues to receive the respect, support and praise of people from all walks of life. Her simple yet profound words regarding her faith are widely quoted by the mass media. Secondly, Cliff Richards, the India born POP singer, visited the city and gave two concerts to packed houses of people who paid plenty to get a seat. The testimony of his conversion to Christianity has been published widely, and he sincerely witnesses to being a Jesus person. The third happening is the four-night program of the Assembly of God Choirs. The radio, T. V. and newspapers also cover other Christian activities.

At our School closing exercises more than a thousand pair of eyes focused upon me as I tried to give a simple explanation of the meaning of Christmas. Jesus came to the world to show us love and to forgive our sins and give us strength and courage to live according to the way He shows us. He comes to all who open their hearts and live for Him.

On January 13, 1977 a new school year began with 1,357 students and 60 staff members in the day school. Eighty-eight four-year old girls are busy playing, singing and learning English. The others are busy with their studies as well as extra curricular activities. One of our earliest activities was "Sports Day" which was held on the playing fields of the Calcutta Boys' School. A couple of weeks later the winners of those events in our own school competed with the girls of 16 other schools and won a few first places.

One of our most popular activities is the Quiz contests. The class ten girls took part in a Radio quiz contest on general knowledge and came up to the semi-finals. A team from classes five and six competed in a Road Safety Quiz contest and lost the final round by one point. The class twelve girls took a field trip to the Himalayas visiting Kalimpong and Sikkim. The class eleven girls took a trip to the seaside. We have a special activity period each week when dramas and various contests are held. This week we are celebrating the birthday of Rabindranath Tagore, the great Bengali Nobel Laureate. The senior girls are staging one of his dance dramas during the activity period.

In the evening school from three to seven p.m. there are more than 200 boys and girls with six teachers. Their medium of instruction is Hindi and their enthusiasm and steady progress is a great inspiration to all. We have another class for 30 teenage girls. Their main subject is sewing, but 14 of them are learning to read and write. Our supervisor for this evening section has been ill for most of 1977. We have been able to get other volunteers to keep the work going.

I have excellent health and find the work here the most rewarding of my 30 years of missionary service. The major portion of my time is spent in listening to staff, students and the public. Even so it seems that too frequently I am closing the door in the face of some needy or lonely person. We had to tighten our security when we discovered that a person pretending to be a teacher was winning the confidence of the small children and then slipping away with their gold ornaments.

During the last six months of 1977 there have seen four significant events, which have influenced our life: The election of a Marxist Government in the state of West Bengal; the visit of the great Cosmos hockey team with its famous player, Pele; the Good News festival with Billy Graham and Akbar Haque and the devastating cyclone in Andhra Pradesh.

In the state elections it is generally believed that the people voted for a personality rather than for an ideology. The new Central and State Government have made very little difference in our day to day life. Prices continue to rise and there is a growing restlessness among the people. A number of good schools have had strikes by the maintenance staff that seriously disrupted normal school activities. One of the leading hospitals of Calcutta has been closed for two weeks because of the strike of the domestic employees, formerly known as "servants." I revised the overtime rates of the 12 "domestics" on our staff and they seem to be happy.

The presence of the Cosmos team with the Brazilian player, Pele, stirred up a lot of excitement that cut across all cultural and class lines. Other activities of the city seemed to be suspended for two days as everyone followed the games by T. V. or radio. And the two teams tied. Calcutta claims to be the home of hockey.

The Protestant Christians planned for the Good News Festival for a year. It was held the first week of December. The response exceeded expectations. Some criticized the large amount of money spent on the arrangements. Who can determine the best way to spend money? Many of our pastors receive less than $20 a month. The amount of money raised locally for the shamiana (tent), lighting and P. A. system would support many pastors for many months. As I sat in the meetings I noted the evidence of unity among the Christian Community. One of the Bengali pastors did the best job of translation and interpretation this city has ever seen. Because of his excellent interpretation it was possible for us to worship together in a way that I had not experienced before. On the last evening more than 25,000 attended the service. The press coverage was excellent. Many heard the gospel of Jesus Christ preached for the first time.

The recent cyclone in Andhra Pradesh has been called the worst disaster of the century in India. Our Christian Relief Organizations rushed to the spot and have been at work ever since. CASA, which receives from Church World Service, has been feeding 50,000 people and airlifting medical supplies. My staff and I have been raising funds for relief. The staff asked me to contribute our Christmas party fund to this relief work. One of our domestic employees comes from the affected area and has not yet learned the fate of his wife and children who were staying only 20 miles inland.

My mother passed away on November 9, 1977 at the age of 87. She was the mother of 11 - six of us are in full time Christian work. Through the excellent international telephone service I was able to keep in touch with the family during the final days of her illness. Because of my responsibilities here I felt I could not leave the school for the funeral. I plan to spend my short Christmas vacation at Piedmont with my sister and other members of the family. I plan to be back in India in time for the re-opening of our new school year on January 12, 1978.

I spent my Christmas vacation at home with my brothers and sisters. I returned to India on January 6, 1978. We began the school year on January 10 with an enrolment of 1,440 in our regular English medium school and 280 in our second school from three p. m. to seven p.m., the Hindi medium elementary school. Both schools are doing very well.

Calcutta has the highest density of population of any city in the world. There are 30,000 people per square mile. Sixty two per cent of the population are below the poverty level with a male-female ratio of 60/40. According to one estimate 60% of the homes are one small room and nearly 70% of the families share toilets. Yet the crime rate in Calcutta is less than in any other city of the world. Someone has said when you share the same water tap with 100 others, the same latrine with 25 others and when your bedroom is six inches away from your neighbor's bedroom, you do not break each others' head. You develop understanding.

Calcutta has produced many great people: Rabindranath Tagore, Vivekananda, Mother Teresa, Dr. B. C. Roy, Satyajit Ray. I appreciate the city's humanness, its history and culture and it's cooking! Perhaps there is dirt, squalor and poverty but even the garbage pickers smile, wear flowers in their hair and keep pet dogs.

I love the old streets and alleys with their exquisite old wrought iron facades on dilapidated houses where one finds huge joint families keeping the traditional Bengali culture alive. There is a sort of feeling in the air that induces a deep understanding of one another. Faces beam when one utters a few words of Bengali. One is accepted. There is everywhere a sweet childishness, a desire to be friendly. The culture is deep and the learning vast.

Many streets are lined with second hand bookshops where rare books may be found. There are art galleries and scores of cultural programs. The quiz contests are a pastime for children and adults. I enjoy the frequent rewarding conversations with scholars on a great variety of subjects.

Today, a public holiday, our students held a "walk for cancer" to raise money for a huge new hospital for treating cancer. The students along with their mothers and fathers and well-wishers had a great time. The students competed to see who can raise the most. One child turned in Rs1,517/- A rupee to her is the same as a dollar to the average American child. Last year I gave her a scholarship for a few months as her father was unemployed due to a factory "lock-out."

While major modern cities of the world allot 25 to 40 per cent of their total area to roads Calcutta road systems cover only about six percent of the total area. For this road area there are over 5 million daily commuters, 77,000 motor cars, 19,000 trucks, 6,000 taxies, 2,000 mini buses, 2,000 large buses, 5,000 hand pulled rickshaws, 3,000 three-wheelers and 15,000 hand carts. The sidewalks are crowded with vendors of all descriptions so the pedestrian has no choice but to walk on the roads meant for the wheels.

There are about 30 missionary English medium schools in the city. These schools are extremely popular. The scramble and competition for admission creates our most frustrating problem. We have an Association of Heads of these schools and meet frequently to discuss problems, hold seminars or just for fellowship. We enjoy an amazing amount of freedom. During the year under review the High Court of India again ruled in our favor in a significant case brought by a dismissed teacher who had the backing of powerful political forces. An eminent educationist from England brought to us by the British Council remarked that he knew of no place in the world where there was so much challenge and so much freedom in which to work.

We constantly strive to make our schools relevant to the society about us and give our students many opportunities to respond to the needs of those less fortunate than themselves. During 1978 our students have responded most generously and raised above Rs. 30,000/ - ($3,800) for a number of charitable causes.

After five months in South Carolina and New Jersey I returned to take up my duties at the school on August 1, 1979. I found that the school had gone on very well during my absence both in academic work and other activities. The one job that had been pushed aside waiting for my arrival was that of what you would call public relations or receiving enquiries, and handling the interviews for admission into our new school year which begins in January, 1980. According to my record I have interviewed over 1000 during the five months since my return and that works out to about ten per school day. Of the over 1000 applicants we have admitted 175. After the regret letters are received many come back or send others to plead their case

I am trying to say "no" with love. That takes a lot of time and a lot of listening. I have to absorb their anger, their tears and their frustrations. They come from all religions, all castes, and all economic backgrounds.

When I leave the security of my compound walls and walk the streets of this city I realize that those entering my gate are an infinitesimal fraction of the unschooled, illiterate children in this city. Calcutta is much more than Mother Teresa's starving masses and dying destitute. Out of, and perhaps because of the hardships in this city, there has developed a very healthy specimen of humanity. They know how to sacrifice, adjust and compete. Their children, less than five years old, already speak, read and write in at least one Indian language and English. They have many shortages of basic needs but they carry on a normal and fairly contented life.

During Christmas week there are many special activities. I cannot begin to accept all the invitations I receive. I attended a concert of the Indian Navy band whose program included a great variety of music. When they played a medley of Christmas carols the audience of mainly non-Christians hummed along with them. Last night I attended a wedding reception and socialized with about 300 people for three hours. The first hour was without electricity as we had our daily dose of "loadshedding" (power outage). Tonight I am attending the twelfth Christmas concert by the Assembly of God Church Choirs and with guest artist, John Hall. It is being held in the largest concert hall in the city for four nights and has a full house every night with people turned away. There are other services, teas and dinners. Several times I have already read or heard this remark: "Christmas belongs to all communities."

A Muslim man gave me a beautiful Bengali poem he had composed about Jesus and told me how he hated Khomeni and that he was fully convinced that only Jesus could save the world. A Hindu editor of a well known magazine writes that he especially admires Jesus Christ's ability to absorb suffering.

Chapter 14

THE DOUBLE LANE TRAIL

Rev. S. K. Baidya resigned from his position as Superintendent of the Lee Memorial Mission on August 23, 1980. He had not been well for sometime. This responsibility became too much for him. He has gone to stay with his daughter who lives about 20 miles from Calcutta. Rani, the wife continues to teach in a government school here in Calcutta. We are grateful for the dedicated service they have rendered during the past 30 years.

The Bishop has appointed me as Acting Superintendent until another person can be found and appointed. This appointment is in addition to being Principal of the Calcutta Girls High School.

Both the Lee Memorial and the Calcutta Girls' High School have a number of capable, loyal, and dedicated Christian staff members. The Lee Memorial High School is administered by Mrs. Juthika Mukherjee. Nihar Dutta looks after the girls in the hostel. The Calcutta Girls' High School is a day school only. We have an evening program there and that is managed by Mrs. Helen Lyall. It is a joy to work with these talented women. I have not had the opportunity to get acquainted with the 150 hostel girls most of whom are under-privileged and needy. Unlike the Calcutta Girls' High

School, which is self-supporting, this hostel depends largely upon "Advance Specials" and donations through other child support agencies.

As I have taken up this added responsibility God has filled my heart with peace and joy and given me added strength. I do not know what the future holds but I know He holds the future.

The Bengal Regional Conference of the Methodist Church in India was held from May 24 — 26 1981 in the auditorium of the Calcutta Girls' High School. The meals were served by the staff of the Lee Memorial Mission. My temporary appointment as Superintendent of the Lee Memorial Mission now seems permanent. I was given permission to employ more staff as required, but I also remain the Principal of the Calcutta Girls' High School as well. The two institutions are fairly close together; there being only an open square (park) between them.

One of my chief objectives is coordination of the work and decentralization of responsibilities. During the last ten months we have achieved some progress towards these objective and that may be the reason that the Bishop and his cabinet did not make any changes.

For a number of years the Government of India has urged educational institutions to promote integration of castes, classes and religions. Recently the Board that monitors the curriculum and issues the high school certificates in our system of English Medium Schools passed a new requirement. From 1982 on a student will not receive the high school certificate until she has completed projects in "Socially Useful Productive Work and Community Service." So in the Calcutta Girls' High School we are seeking ways and means of helping our students participate in meaningful service. My appointment to the Lee Memorial does open up some new possibilities in that field.

This summer while schools are closed we have 40 children who have no home to go to and are staying with us in the Lee Memorial. Some of them have a widowed mother who has no proper home and is struggling to keep herself alive. Others may have a father who is an invalid or unemployed. I have been updating the case histories of our hostel children. I have found that we have three families of children whose fathers are suffering from acute mental disorders. No doubt their illness has been brought about by poverty and unemployment.

During the summer holidays the children of Lee Memorial go to Calcutta Girls to play and for singing lessons in western music. My highly qualified music teacher, who has no family, is enjoying the contact as much as the children. She had all her education in England where her father worked for the Indian Embassy. Her only home is

373

the Calcutta Girls' High School since her father and mother are dead. So this sophisticated, lonely music teacher from London interacts with the children who have known only the Calcutta slums and the confining walls of the hostel.

A typical village scene

Occasionally I visit the village centers and cast my eyes upon the open green fields and swaying coconut palm trees. These centers are crying out for development, and I become exhilarated by thinking of the possibilities. The Woman's Division is giving a grant to help in one of the centers.

As I have reached a certain age people often ask me about my retirement. While outwardly I do try to plan inwardly my reaction is:

"How can I retire?" It seems that my life is just beginning! The sense of Call and the Presence of God is just as real today as it was back in 1938 in the college dormitory when I said: "Yes, Lord, your will be done. I am willing to go to India and to give my life in your service there." My life is still in His hands. I pray that He will guide me and use the staff of both schools as they lead daily Christian worship and weekly Bible studies with the children.

The Lee Memorial Mission as set up at present is composed of the following: (1) The Girls' Hostel (2) The kindergarten (3) The Primary School (4) the High School (5) the International Guest House (6) the Sonarpur School (7) The Manickpur property. The school at Nihata is a project of the Calcutta Bengali Women's work committee. Often personnel at Lee Memorial supervise the work there.

The Girls' Hostel has 127 girls in residence at Raja Subodh Mullick Square and the Mission supports one now in nurse's training and three who are in college. Of the 127 girls, 106 are Christians; 56 of the girls depend entirely upon the Mission for support. Thirty-six girls receive a small monthly amount and some clothes from their family. Only four girls are fully supported by their parents. The others get varying amounts of support from relatives, friends or some agency.

The Mennonite Central Committee sponsors 20 girls. Kinderhilsweek, Germany (KHW), sponsors 20. We receive small remittances through the D. N. Stearns Missionary Fund, Philadelphia. By far the largest amount of our support comes through the Advance Specials of the United Methodist Church, USA.

Five or six rooms are used for international guests. This continues to be very busy. We have tried to reorganize our accounting procedures, and note that there is heavy expenditure on establishment such as watchmen. electricity and telephone. In the past Mission funds has paid most of this. Now we are trying to distribute those items among the various units at headquarters. The Guest House is now making a substantial contribution towards the establishment cost.

The Sonarpur School

The school at Sonarpur with 500 students is running well. Mrs. Rose Mary Mullick is the headmistress there. We have an eviction case against the former Headmaster, Mr. Santosh Gayen, as he does not seem to be willing to negotiate a settlement. He has not taken salary and other funds which are due him.

God is very good to us and His hand of protection is evident. "According to my earnest expectation and hope, that in nothing I shall be ashamed, but that with all boldness, as always, so now also Christ shall be magnified in my body, whether it be by life, or by death." (Phil. 1:20)

As we review the past it gives us courage for the present and hope for the future. The Bishop has appointed Mrs. Margaret MacGillivray, an Indian from Shillong, Meghalaya, as the Principal of Calcutta Girls' High School from August 1, 1982. Thus he has relieved me for full time work in the Lee Memorial. While I am on short furlough Rev. C. R. Biswas will be the acting Superintendent in addition to his other responsibilities as pastor and district superintendent.

One of the most unusual strikes was a strike by doctors employed in hospitals managed and maintained by the Government. Their demand was for regular supply of life saving medicines, better food for the patients, and maintenance of the equipment such as X-ray machines and E. C. G. and other more sophisticated, expensive imported equipment. In Government hospitals, beds, medicines, and services are free for the poor. All the Government hospitals are overcrowded. It is not unusual to find two patients in one narrow bed and many other patients on the floor. For those who can afford it there are private hospitals and nursing homes.

Through the schools and other social service activities I come in contact with many dedicated doctors who have one clinic for the wealthy or middle class who can pay and then another clinic for the poor. They charge the poor a very nominal sum of about twenty five cents a visit. For routine and minor illnesses we use the government hospitals and clinics for our students. In cases of emergencies we seek out a reasonable paying clinic.

In July, 1983 Rev. Sukumar Baidya, who preceded me as superintendent here, passed away. Though he had been in poor health for a number of years, he died suddenly from a heart attack. His wife, Rani, is still working as a teacher in a city government school and all his sons are employed. Sukumar was brought up as an orphan in another Christian Mission. He started work here at the Lee Memorial soon after finishing high school. While working in the office with accounts and other matters he studied privately and took the University examination and received the Bachelor of Commerce degree. He also took the conference course of study and became an ordained minister. In addition to duties at the Lee Memorial he served as treasurer of the Bengal Conference for some years. He also served as district superintendent. He became the first Indian superintendent of the Lee Memorial Mission. His most outstanding contribution to the church was the re-opening of the boys' section at 9, Beliaghata Main Road. The Lee Memorial Boys' School and Hostel at 9 Beliaghata Main Road was closed during World War II and remained closed until it was reopened in the late fifties by Sukumar and Rani Baidya. It was renamed Lee Collins Boys' Home at that time and is administered separately as a unit in itself. It continues today as a Boys' Home and High School. Mr. Dnabandhu Ghosh now administers it.

After a gap of 20 years an old health problem of mine has recurred. The present diagnosis is "deep vein thrombosis". Since August 1, 1983 I have had three attacks of acute lymphadenitis with fever. This has forced me to slow down and rest. With each attack I have been confined to my room for two to three weeks. Essential work has been carried out but many things have had to be postponed. The loving and loyal staff have helped me in many ways. I have had the free service of four well-qualified dedicated doctors. The rest has given me time to listen to God and to His people who surround me. I have plans for expansion of Lee Memorial if health permits. But through my illness I realize afresh that one of the main methods of witnessing to our gospel is to give time and love to all categories of people. Time to listen to the unemployed father who cannot feed his children; time to listen to the doctor who recently returned from abroad as he struggles to serve people in a Government Hospital without proper medicines and equipment.; time to listen to the administrator in a large company as she struggles against corruption; time to listen to students as they discuss problems in the family, in the classrooms and their inability to understand math or science.

During this time Mrs. Margaret MacGillivary served as principal of the Calcutta Girls' High School from August 1982 through June, 1984. She resigned for family and health reasons. The Bishop has appointed me as acting Principal until another Principal is found. Again I am looking after both institutions.

The Council of Indian Certificate (English medium schools) has decided to change the academic year from June to May. This will bring us in line with the schools in other parts of India that follow the same curriculum. Unfortunately it makes us out of line with the schools under the Board of Secondary education of the West Bengal State Government.

This year just before the external examinations began we were saddened because one of the students, due to take the examination, committed suicide. She did this after she was caught stealing a page from her fellow student's economic practical work book.

The Calcutta Girls' High School students have participated in inter-school activities and won some commendable prizes. They won the quiz contest which was sponsored by the Aurobindhu Society. One student won the single badminton tournament in the Birla Inter-school Senior Division.

The students who study Hindi as a second language took part in a festival organized by the Hindi High School. Seventeen schools took part in quizzes, debates, elocution, drama and creative writing using the Hindi language. Our students won a number of prizes and were judged the second best participating school. Our students are very proud of this as most of the other participating schools have Hindi as the first language and medium of instruction. We also boast that we have a very high standard of teaching the Bengali language.

This year I have supervised the Nihata Mission School. After a gap of 25 years I again have responsibility for the work at Nihata along with many other duties. Today there are 240 children studying from kindergarten to class four. On the staff there are six trained Christian teachers and two Christian non-teaching staff. Other than the local church and the witness of the local Christians there is no other organized Christian activity at the center. The Catholics have a hostel not far from the school and they send their hostel children to our school. While the level of education and literacy is higher than twenty-five years ago there does not appear to be any economic improvement in the village. The farmers are still subject to the unpredictable weather conditions. In 1983 the monsoon was insufficient. In 1984 there has been too much rain. Many of the youth are unemployed. We have been able to find jobs for one or two who were existing near the starvation level They have to commute daily to Calcutta by train.

To help the children in the school we started a mid-day meal program. The teachers have reported that there is a marked improvement in the attendance since we started giving the mid-day snack. During December, 1983 the staff and students of the school organized a concert with a variety of items including a dance drama. A Calcutta Church volunteer helped train the dancers. They raised more than Rs. 2,000/- through the program.

The students pay Rs. 40/- per year. When the crops fail it is very difficult for some of them to pay that. It is not possible to pay the teachers adequately with funds raised locally. We are thankful for the assured income from the conference and a grant from the Mennonite Central Committee, and we are looking for other means of support. We made fresh approaches to the Government but there is not much hope of getting anything from them in the near future.

I believe there is a continuing need for our Christian witness through that school. Children walk daily for many miles to come to the school because of the good quality of teaching given by our six Christian women. We want to give greater support to the persons communicating the gospel on our behalf in Nihata and the surrounding area.

"Behold I will do a new thing: now it will bring forth." Isa 43:19. The Lord has given me the verse for the coming year 1985. In our Bengali Bible when they translated it they put — "now it is germinating." This year does hold many things for India. The election results have been announced and commented upon and there is much celebration on the part of the members of the Congress party. Mrs. Gandhi's son, Rajiv, has won an overwhelming majority. Even though the voters cast their ballots for Congress local candidates for the Lok Sabha the experts all agree that the mood was that of voting for Rajiv. He is young, handsome and with a "clean image." He promises to bring some modern management methods into the running of the Government of India. We do look forward to new things in Government.

In the city of Calcutta, the Congress party has won all the seats but in West Bengal the Communist party of India has won by a slim margin of votes. Their majority has been narrowed considerably. We hope that will cause them to be more cautious and less aggressive in pushing some of their ideas that have begun to affect us and our work. No doubt there will continue to be much political activity in this state. I feel that democracy is alive and vibrant here.

I am looking forward to new things in my work responsibilities. Along with the daily routine work we searched in earnest for a new principal. From January 1, 1985, Mrs. Mary Ann Das Gupta has been appointed the new principal of the Calcutta Girls High School. She is an American from Missouri who married a Bengali and has been living in Calcutta for the last 20 years. She has had experience as a principal in another school. She is a very active Christian and feels that God has called her to work in a Christian School. I feel that God has answered prayer by sending her to us at this time.

The work has gone on as usual in the Lee Memorial Mission. Anil Das has looked after the payment of the bills and the accounts. Mrs. Juthika Mukherjee has looked after the school. Misses Nihar and Asru Dutta have taken care of the 125 children in our home and helped in many ways. The children all seem to be happy and make joyful noises with their singing. They get invitations to sing in ecumenical services. In the Lee-Collins Boys Home, Mr. Dinabandhu Ghosh and his staff manage independently but we frequently consult each other.

I have had very good health and have given overall supervision to our various units which also includes three village centers. The International Guest House continues to be popular. Recently we had a group from Poland and a couple from East Germany. Many come seeking ways to preach the "Good News" of salvation through Christ. We have a strong autonomous Methodist Church in India. In these days of international travel and other types of communication God will find ways of getting the message to the masses.

In addition to the usual administrative responsibilities of the Lee Memorial Mission the Bishop has appointed me as the pastor of one of our village churches. This is the NEW thing for me. The services are all in Bengali. I am busy trying to improve my rusty Bengali. Twenty-five years ago I knew much more Bengali than I know now. I was out of Bengal for 13 years. I worked in that village 25 years ago. Most of the present leaders of the church were children then, and at my welcome ceremony a few days ago reminded me of many things that I had forgotten. Even though I have been ordained for many years, this is the first time I have been appointed as a pastor of a church. The work in the church and the community is challenging. How can I think of retirement when there is yet so much more to be done?

The Rev. Frances Major helps in Confirmation Service

I have not been able to find anyone to help me with correspondence and photography. I have never been much of a photographer and recently the camera that I used was stolen from my room along with some other articles like tape recorder and radio These articles are easily available here but since I have not caught the thief I hesitate to buy them.

Each year my specific responsibilities vary according to the Bishop's appointment. In 1985 I have no specific responsibility for the Calcutta Girls' High School. Recently the leading English daily newspaper in the city, "The Statesman" (dating back to William Carey, 19th century) gave a very positive write up of the "second school" or evening school that I started there showing how the resources of those who "have" are used to help the "have-nots." It is a matter of great satisfaction to me that the newly appointed persons are doing a magnificent job of carrying on the work and expanding and improving it.

The work of the Lee Memorial Mission continues with the same aims and objectives-to help women and children. The new children that we have taken in during the last six months emphasize that aim. In every case the children have been forsaken by their fathers. Social welfare agencies help the mothers by giving some training to them with a view to making them able to support themselves. We help them by providing a home for the children. The women that we employ in our hostel are widow women. We now have 130 girls here in our headquarters building. The care of the boys at Beliaghatta is in the competent hands of Dinabandhu Ghosh.

The above staff members were brought up in the Mission

During the summer holidays the children enjoyed an Inter-Church Vacation Bible School. Last weekend five girls attended a youth camp. During the last week of September a child evangelist will be holding two services daily for the children. One service will be for the day scholars as well as the boarders. The other service will be for our boarders only.

Mrs. Juthika Mukerjee retired after 16 years as the Headmistress of the school. She has gone to live with her son in Canada. We are still searching for some one to take her place

The average attendance in the Nihata Church where I am pastor is 50. Many of the members are unemployed or underemployed. The village economy does not sustain the dense rural population in this state. The density of the villages is said to be as high as any place in the world. The members of my church like others commute to Calcutta for work - that is, those lucky enough to find jobs. We are told that three million people commute to Calcutta daily for work and compete with the 10 million living here.

In the villages surrounding the church we have two schools with about 350 children enrolled in primary classes and have mid-day feeding programs for the children. I am in touch with agencies that emphasize development and am still hoping that someone will take up some schemes in that area. Our emphasis has to be on local resources and educating the people to the possibilities of self-improvement and development. The Church's Auxiliary for Social Action, which U M C O R helps to fund, employs Community Organizers who teach the people how to get and use funds available through Government. They have encouraging success stories to report but these examples only touch a few of the millions who are still in need.

My message to the village church is that if we truly surrender all that we have to Jesus Christ, He takes it, multiplies it and gives it back to us. The best example is the feeding of the 5000. Seeing the hungry people, Jesus asked the disciples "what do you have?" Getting the reply, He said, "Bring it to me." What if that boy had refused to give his loaves and fishes? Jesus requires complete surrender from all the poor and rich.

In May 1986 I plan to begin a ten month furlough. For part of that time I will be itinerating in some conferences and am already receiving requests for making engagements. For most of the time my base will be South Carolina with my sister, Mrs. Eunice Kay. She has been visiting me this month here in Calcutta and it has been a joy to have her share my experiences.

I did return to the USA in May, 1986. As soon as I reached home I had a bad case of shingles so rested for a short while. During the furlough I was officially retired with all the ceremonies. I did quite a bit of speaking and in early 1987 returned to India on my retirement income. I came back to the Lee Memorial Mission.

Last week our Annual Conference was held in Pakaur, Bihar and the bishop transferred me from the Lee Memorial Mission to the Calcutta Girls' High School effective December 1, 1987 as Miss Maryann Dasgupta resigned. Last night at 11p. m. we boarded the train in Pakaur and arrived in Calcutta at 7:30 a.m. We traveled by what is called second-class sleeper (3 tier). I slept on the lower birth which is a bench like arrangement. Two people slept on the two berths above me. In a coach, which is about the same size of coaches on US trains, there were sleeping benches for 70 people. At 2 a.m. when I got up to go to the bathroom the entire floor space was covered with sleeping bodies. When I put my foot down from my berth I stepped on a man. Somehow I did manage, with the help of my flashlight, to step around and over bodies until I reached the bathroom. This is what population explosion means. On the train there were only three first class berths which are considered more comfortable. Our Bishop and his wife and the Secretary of our Conference occupied these first class berths. The rest of the delegates traveled with me in second class. The price of the eight-hour journey was $3.10.

In many ways 1987 has been a good year for the 105 students who are resident in the Lee Memorial Hostel. There has been less sickness than in the previous year but still more cases of malaria than we like to see. The city malaria control department has been more active. The representatives visit us periodically, take blood samples from the girls with fever, and give us free medicines for treating malaria. It seems that malaria has become resistant to the older prescribed drugs so new medicines are being developed and prove more successful.

Sometime ago the Reverend C. R. Biswas was appointed the Superintendent of the Lee Memorial Mission. I assisted him with the correspondence, Guest House and Hostel. Miss Nihar Dutta who has been the mother to the girls in the hostel for many years is retiring at the end of the year. I pray that God will bring to the Lee Memorial another dedicated person to take up this responsibility.

I have committed myself to remain in Calcutta for at least another year. I do not know what tomorrow may bring but to date I am very happy with my active retired life here in the conference.

In 1988 five computers were installed in Calcutta Girls' High School and more than 500 students are using them. I had my first computer training at the local YWCA. Our computer room is always crowded. We have also added a new colored T. V. set with VCR equipment. Our next project is to buy a new car to replace our 1964 model.

One of the world's greatest magicians, P. C. Sorcar, Jr., gave a benefit show for our school in November and this has helped us to finance the new equipment.

In October I attended a seminar for principals in Lucknow. In early November I attended the Quadrennial Deaconess Assembly in Jabalpur. Both meetings were full of information and spiritual inspiration. I also met many old friends and made some new ones.

Mt. Hermon School, Darjeeling, invited me to be their guest speaker for their closing day activities on November 21, 1988. I went to Darjeeling but fell ill with my old complaint so could not enjoy their activities. The attack came on while I was on a long hike in the mountains. I was carried back down the mountain in a dandy similar to a hammock anchored on the shoulders of four men. I spent three days in a Darjeeling Hospital having treatment by a nephew to the Tibetan Dalai Lama. He had his medical training in Ireland. Darjeeling is the home for many Tibetan refugees. The Indian Airlines took special care of me as they flew me back to Calcutta where I spent another two weeks off my feet.

The selection committee is actively searching for a principal of the Calcutta Girls' High School. I pray that God will have his way in this selection and appointment. We have many opportunities for witnessing for Christ among students and staff here. My plans are to return to the United States in April or May, 1989 where I shall continue my retired life according to God's leading.

I continue to be the pastor of a Village Church about 30 kms from Calcutta. On Christmas Day I shall take the service and have my dinner there.

Sometime after last Christmas a Hindu lady doctor asked me: "What does Savior mean?" Thinking of the message of the angels I explained that Jesus Christ came into the world to save us from our sins. She stopped me and said: "Yes, I know that." And she truly did as she was a well-educated person, having received part of her education in western countries. She was outstanding in her field and I benefited from her friendship. She was generous with her time and money. She always responded whenever I approached her for medical and other help. She continued: "I want to know what the 'word' Savior means?" So at this Christmas season I ask myself, "What does the coming of the Savior really mean to me and the world?"

I left Calcutta late on April 22, 1989 and after a stopover in New Delhi, Amsterdam and Atlanta arrived at my home in Piedmont before bedtime on April 23. After a short time with family members I moved into an apartment at Brooks-Howell Home where 76 other retired missionaries and deaconesses live. I am enjoying the home situated in this beautiful part of our country. We thank the United Methodist Women for providing this place for us.

The Home is one and a half hours from Piedmont by car so I am able to keep close contact with the homefolk. After several sessions with an eye doctor and cataract surgery on one eye I decided not to invest in a car of my own with a restricted driving license. I am able to get where I need to go with the help of public transport and friends. Asheville has a good city bus system with discounts for senior citizens.

During my two years of post retirement service in Calcutta, I served seven months in the Lee Memorial Mission and then moved to the Calcutta Girls' High School when a sudden vacancy occurred. It gave Bishop K. Samuel time to recruit and appoint Miss Ruth Nirmala Gnanakan as the principal of that school. From Calcutta I receive reports that Rev. Biswas at the Lee Memorial and Miss Gnanakan at the Calcutta Girls' High School are doing well.

Chapter 15

THE FINAL ASCENT

I have been living in Brooks-Howell Home for more than 13 years. India remains the dominant interest of my life. I have been able to visit there a number of times. In 1992 I visited India with Doris Gidney. It was her first visit. She experienced India through my eyes as we visited Calcutta, the tourist spots of Benaras, Agra and New Delhi. In New Delhi we attended the all India Deaconess Assembly. For me it was a reunion with many friends.

For six months in 1995 I worked with the Southern Asia Office in the General Board of Global Missions, NY. During that time a recurring question bothered me. When we give funds to a project should we not think that we are really giving them through God. All we have belongs to Him. If we truly give the gift no longer belongs to us. Are the recipients accountable to God or the donor? I have heard many responses to that question. None of them fully satisfy me.

In May —June, 1996 the GBGM gave me an extended trip to Southern Asia, including India, Pakistan and Afghanistan. At 3:30 a. m. May 1, 1996 I reached the Methodist Center in Bombay. This new building was started in the late sixties while I was still working in the Bombay office. The Women's Division building at 22 Clubback

Road was now used as the Episcopal Residence. The International Guest House was a part of the Methodist Center. Suneela Hanchimani was the hostess. At the 8 A. M. breakfast she headed the table and introduced me to the other guests.

As it was May Day John Hanchimani, Central Treasurer, Methodist Church in India, did not go to his office. I visited with him. Susheela took me out shopping I bought three sets of Salwar — Kameez (India style pant suits) to wear on the rest of my trip in India. At the time of the noon meal I visited with Dr. and Mrs. Arole of Jamkhed.

I left for the airport at 2:30 p.m. I went to the new unfinished terminal for the private airlines. These airlines were the evidence of India's economic liberalization policy. This policy encouraged privatization of transport, communication and industries. The monitors with flight schedules were not working. Young uniformed personnel directed us. These employees carried themselves with great pride and bore an air of efficiency. Privatizing definitely made a difference

It was a 2 ½ hour flight to Calcutta. I arrived in the new clean terminal where I spotted Kalyan Das, bursar of Calcutta Girls' High School. He ushered me through the airport and to Calcutta Girls High School. I was lodged in the room I had used for a store room now converted into a small guest room. Bishop Sant Kumar and family were expected and would occupy the regular guest room. My hostess was Nirmala Gnanakan who succeeded me as principal. She was from South India. It had been a long day so I quickly went to bed and slept soundly.

I awakened to the familiar sounds of crows and trams. May 2 was the first day of the 1995-96 school term. I spoke to the senior girls who now met for chapel in the Thoburn Church. After the chapel I met Bishop Kumar and discussed with him the projects of the Lucknow Regional Conference. After about an hour with the Bishop I was ushered over to the lower flat of the Thoburn parsonage. During my active life in India this flat had been rented out. The pastor, Subodh Mondol, was ecstatic as they had been able to repossess the flat and planned to use it as office and guest rooms.

Throughout the day I met with heads of Institutions and officers of the Bengal Conference. On May 3 I I spent most of the day at Lee Memorial Mission. Karuna Lee, the current superintendent, was a high school student when I arrived in 1946. During my first term she finished Isabella Thoburn College. I found that 19 of the current staff had been children in the mission during my first term. Among them were Ada and Premi who were babies then.

I had the assurance that God is in control of this trip. I can see how He rearranged my schedule as He knew far more than I about the situations like the Bishop's schedule and the dates of the general election. The next morning in my Bible reading my attention was directed to I Peter 2: 1 - 2 "Wherefore laying aside all malice, and all guile, and all hypocrisies, and envies, and all speakings, as new born babes, desire the sincere milk of the word, that you may grow thereby."

Awake by 5 a. m. the next day I enjoyed letting my mind roam and roaming it did. Never have I felt the merging of the past, present and future as I have these four or five days in Calcutta. I awaken to the familiar sounds; the crows, the trams rattling by, voices, the clearing of throats. These same sounds were here fifty years ago. This old building is more than a 100 years old. I remember things of these 50 years as they pass through my mind faster than a fast forward on my VCR. This is not 1946 or 86, it is 1996. I am retired, traveling here from Asheville, N. C. Do I understand any of the things that have happened since my leaving eight years ago? Can I comprehend the apprehensions and fears for the future of these Indian disciples who now are responsible for the work? The missionaries are no longer here. The GBGM often misunderstands the motives and actions of the present church leaders.

What am I to do? The lectionary reading for today is full of meaning for me. (John 14: 1 — 14) With Thomas I can say:" Lord, we do not know whither thou goest; and how can we know the way?" God must have a way to carry this great church forward. Then, I remember Jesus said: "I am the way, the truth and the life." I committed the various "ways" to Him. I prayed "Lord let me be a light wherever I am. Teach me how to hear the real message I am receiving from those who seek my help. Let my life demonstrate the joy of being your child. Let my actions glorify your name."

Ecc. 3: 11 "He hath made everything beautiful in his time time; also he hath set the world in their heart, so that no man can find out the work that God maketh from the beginning to the end."

My trip to India from Nov. 3 to 21, 2001 was unique in several ways. Evelyn Strader was invited back to Methodist High School, Kanpur, where she had served for 30 years as principal to attend the dedication of a new building named for her and the 125th anniversary of the founding of the school. The invitation to her indicated that all expenses would be paid for her, and since she is handicapped they agreed to pay the expenses for some one to accompany her. I was the lucky one she chose to accompany her. The most difficult part of the trip for me was to sit back and wait for Evelyn's hosts to make all our plans, reserve the airline flights through an Indian travel agent and get them to us on time. It could not have been done in the sixties. But in this new century it was done efficiently.

On Saturday November 3rd, 2001 Janice Lyons, a former missionary to India drove us from Asheville to the Greenville/ Spartanburg Airport and we collected the tickets and boarded the flight without any difficulty. We traveled via Memphis and Amsterdam on KLM. The three flights were full. We arrived in New Delhi late on Nov. 4th.

Another unique part of the trip was that many thought two women in their eighties were very unwise to travel so far after the terrorist attack on the US on Sept. 11. They did not realize that during our active service in India we faced many dangers. Further we thought if God chose to take us to heaven during this trip to India, we were ready to go to either Heaven or India. We found the extra security precautions another interesting encounter.

In Delhi I did not have to search for a wheelchair as I did in other airports. A little man with the wheel chair met us as we got off the plane. He knew all the ropes and whizzed us through all formalities including the customs. The minute we left the custom area and started outside two or three former students of Methodist High School greeted us and took us to the Radisson Hotel. We had a very comfortable eight hours of sleep and a long bath. We had a late breakfast, exchanged some money and waited to be picked up to go to the domestic airport for the 11:15 flight to Lucknow. Our host, Anand Mishra, was held up in a traffic jam and finally arrived at 10:50. Our complimentary car with a driver from the hotel speeded along winding through the terrible traffic, occasionally using the shoulder on the road to pass other cars. Within 15 minutes we were in the airport. It was 10 minutes until take off time of the reserved flight on Sahara Airline. They had closed the check-in counter and refused to take us. This private airline had an excellent record of being on time and did not wish to spoil that record.

Anand began trying to get us on the next flight. What a change in role for me! I let Anand and his helpers pamper us with drinks, food and anything we needed while we made ourselves comfortable in the private sector waiting room. It was a very big hall. I was amazed at the number of things it contained. On one side of the hall were several airline offices, a milk bar, a post office, telegraphic office and an apple juice bar. On the opposite side of the hall were check in counters of the various private airlines and their exit gates. At one end were rest rooms for men and women, a shop and an air insurance counter. On the opposite end construction was going on to enlarge the hall. A large plastic sheet hanging from the ceiling partially hid the construction. The comfortable seats were arranged in the middle of the hall.

We used the post office and bought both internal and foreign air letters. We completed and mailed a number of letters. John Hanchimani, Central Treasurer for the Methodist Church in India, interrupted us while we were writing. He had been attending a meeting in Chandigarh and was on his way to Bombay. Since he is also diabetic he found sugar free refreshments for me and taught me what to look for.

Anand returned at 2:30 and announced that we could not get on another flight until after 4 p. m. We will never know the details of what happened but the departure was delayed in small segments and we left at 8 p.m Our new reservation was on the Government controlled Indian Airlines. We changed to the Indian Airlines waiting room. In contrast to the private sector one it was huge and empty. It had beautiful, spotless marble floors. After having a meal in the large empty dining room we were transferred to the VIP lounge area as it was felt we could rest better. Evelyn and I stretched out on couches. In the midst of our rest one of the officers came into the room, took pity on these travel weary tourists and invited us to go to the very special lounge used by heads of state. It was used by President Clinton when he visited India. From the crowded, noisy private sector waiting room we progressed upward until we reached the best most private one. Indians know how to make the rich comfortable and we had a taste of that comfort. It made up for the long delay from 11 a.m. to 8 p.m. It illustrated many of the changes in India.

For about 40 years after Independence the government controlled everything. A major change was made in Indian economic policies about the time I retired. It was called economic liberalization and was initiated by Rajiv Gandhi. With liberalization the private sector airlines, businesses and industries were developed. It permitted free trade. This has transformed India. I had glimpses of this on earlier trips. On this trip the change hit me full force. During our day in the airport we were offered drinks to quench our thirst. We had many choices, coco cola, pepsi, limca, fanta, Indian tea, coffee and other Indian drinks. Bottled cold drinking water was plentiful. Evelyn did not need the thermos she had brought along.

At about 8 pm we climbed into a vehicle that would take Evelyn to the plane in her wheel chair. On reaching the food loading side of the plane the vehicle mechanically lifted the platform on which Evelyn was sitting up to that door opposite the passenger entrance. The attendants rolled her to her front row seat. I climbed some steps and joined her. We reached Lucknow after a short flight. Three or four former students of Methodist High School welcomed us in Lucknow. One of them drove the three of us in his Mercedes to Kanpur where a bigger crowd waited with many malas (garlands) of roses and other flowers. It was 10 p.m. We visited until after midnight over cups of tea.

403

After a day of rest we went to Lucknow. We enjoyed the journey during the daytime. Though wide and well maintained the road was congested with all kinds of traffic. Most noticeable were the speeding, heavily loaded lorries (trucks). I thanked God that they were only the kind my father drove when I was a child and not the eighteen wheelers. There were efforts to have a divided highway of four lanes. The lanes were observed in some places where barriers divided them.

We visited Emma Thompson English Medium School which Evelyn had founded during her last term in India. The school has 1200 students. The students presented the drama Cinderella. At the end of the program Evelyn spoke to the students.

A group of us went to Clark Hotel for lunch. The modern Hotel caters to tourists. Since September 11 they have had very few foreigners. They lowered their prices to attract the local people. Our hostess and other Christians took advantage of the bargain prices. They remarked that we now have a global economy. We discussed the economic impact of September 11 on India's economy. Several had relatives who escaped the World Trade Center destruction.

After lunch they took us around the city. I did not recognize the place where I lived in 1960. The spacious compound I knew is filled with a couple of high rise buildings that overshadows the old bungalows. On the trip back to Kanpur it dawned upon me the improvements in the Indian made cars. They are air conditioned with electronically controlled windows, trunks and locks. There are a variety of models.

In Kanpur several new guest had arrived for the big celebrations. I enjoyed visiting with retired Bishop and Mrs. Parmar. In his retirement Bishop is writing Bible Study materials that have been translated into 18 languages. He writes in English and Mrs. Parmar translates them into Hindi. Lillain Wallace, retired missionary living in India, arrived later and she and Evelyn visited while I slept. All the buildings are illuminated. Shamianas are erected in open places. Everything is taking shape for the celebration tomorrow.

On the 8th we awoke with excitement. The first item on the celebration program was the dedication of the new building, the Evelyn Strader Block. Though the new building was a short distance from the Principal's bungalow where we were staying, the students insisted that we get in a car. They drove us around the corner of a building in sight of the playground. A large honor guard of students ran along side the car and ushered us to the dais (platform) of the stage under the Shamania (large pavilion made of canvas). All stood and applauded as Evelyn got out of the car followed by Lillian and me, and Evelyn climbed the few steps onto the stage.

There was a call to worship, scripture reading, prayer and a couple of praise hymns beautifully sung in English by the school choir. Then Evelyn spoke from the platform as the 2000 students, ex-students and guest beamed with adoration. That outside ceremony was short and sweet. Then we were ushered to the cornerstone of the building where Evelyn cut a ribbon and unveiled it. Leaning heavily on the arms of two ex-students, Evelyn climbed three flights of stairs to the large, spacious auditorium said to be the largest and most modern in the city of Kanpur. The celebrations continued with many speeches of history, thanksgiving, introductions and greetings ending with Bishop Thomas leading the liturgical dedication service. The last item was the Indian classical ballet entitled "Ten Commandment." It was composed and directed by one of the staff members. The young students depicted Moses receiving the tablets and interpreted each of the commandments. The program which began before ten ended after one with the serving of refreshments to all.

The Evelyn Strader block includes science and computer labs, six classrooms, a small conference hall, gymnasium and the large auditorium with balcony and large well-equipped stage.

In mid afternoon we had lunch followed by rest. At dusk we visited with other guests and waited for the special evening program. The evening program began with the lighting of the 125 deepas (small lights on a brass stand) This symbolized the 125th anniversary celebration of the school. During the lighting there was music and the computer projection of the Kanpur High School web page. The Secretary of the Council of Indian School Certificate was introduced with due ceremony and flowers. That Council sets the curriculum, administers final examination and issues the certificates (diplomas) to graduates of a large number of Indian English medium high schools. It took the place of the British Cambridge Examination Board after the Independence of India and is modeled on that Board.

After about three hours of entertainment we went to a garden decorated with many lights for our Indian feast. By the time we finished eating it was after 10 p.m. I went to bed and slept well until 4 am. I enjoyed lying awake and letting all the reactions to the previous day's event sweep over me. I talked to God. He felt near and helped me sort out some of my reactions. Our Methodist Church is totally Indianized. The presence of a large number of the officers of the Methodist Church in India produced conflicting emotions. They were justifiably proud of the accomplishments of Methodist High School which built this imposing new building with funds raised in India. The first time they were introduced and responded with greetings I was very happy. But the third time they were introduced I wondered if it was overdone.

I evaluated the variety of items on the program. Indian dancing has changed from classical to contemporary, lively and fast

407

moving. The choir performed in the contemporary style of some of our churches. They jazzed up "Leaning Upon the Everlasting Arms" with the Indian drums and other instruments. The students are no longer harassed by the old strict discipline of stiffness and complete silence. They yelled and screamed like American young people when pleased.

Then my mind wandered to the amazing Lillian Wallace, the only missionary who has retired in India. The Church continues to use her in crisis situations. When she was introduced she received a thunderous ovation from students, staff and guest.

Friday was filled with a great variety of programs. In the morning we sat in the new auditorium and watched the participants on stage use the modern facilities of the stage. A drama on the history of the school was outstanding. They depicted Isabella Thoburn and Clara Swain arriving in India and something of their work, Clara Swain in medicine and Isabella Thoburn in education. Isabella established the Methodist High School for girls in 1876 in addition to Lal Bagh School and Isabella Thoburn College.

The spacious playground was the venue for the afternoon session. The chief guest was the Governor of the Uttar Pradesh State. He arrived late, spoke in Hindi and left. He had a reputation of being anti-Christian. Our friend Anant Mishra received him and welcomed him with a speech about the school. The next day the local newspaper quoted him as advising the school that they should not proselytize. Those who heard his speech and understood Hindi stated that he made no such remarks at the school celebration.

A program of physical education demonstrations followed. The outstanding item was the depiction of the creation story. The evening program was a fire works display entitled STARLIGHT and professionally done. All programs of the day were long and carried out with great precision and excellence. It was all a bit overpowering. As a former principal my thoughts were how could they prepare and carry on the routine class work while practicing for the items on the programs for this celebration.

By Saturday morning a number of the guests, including Lillian and Evelyn had gone. The student seminar took the entire morning. Students from about 20 schools listened to lectures and then discussed "How to meet the Challenges of Today's World." The first lecturer was introduced as one of the leading economist in today's world. He gave a simple yet eloquent speech. He spoke about the 4 D's - diversity, democracy, development and dialogue. The second speaker, a lady, emphasized action. She stated knowledge is useless unless acted upon. A third person spoke but I could not follow his thoughts as I could not hear all of it. After the lectures the students took over and boldly discussed the subject of the day. It was a stimulus to intellectual thinking. I was glad it had been included along with all the entertainment.

The finale was on Saturday night. It was a musical extravaganza with one of Bollywood's (Bombay's movie industry) movie stars as the chief guest. The entire playground was used to accommodate the audience. There were 8000 seats available. They sold out and the demand for more was so great the police were on hand to prevent gate crashers. The excitement was volatile. As I had a train reservation to Calcutta I left the entertainment shortly after the movie star arrived

I took the Rajdhani express which runs between New Delhi and Calcutta with very few stops. I reserved a berth in the 2 tier AC coach. My berth was an upper. In the old days I loved the upper berths because it put me above the crowd. But my body has changed and I found it difficult to climb to the upper. A kind gentleman agreed to exchange with me and moved to the upper. The cost of the ticket included bedding, bottled water, morning tea and meals. I hastily made my bed, stretched out on it and pulled the curtain. Privacy! Another simple but adequate improvement! I slept well. The familiar swaying movement of the Indian train aroused the feeling of being back where I belonged at home in India. As soon as I stirred the next morning the familiar bearer with a kettle of hot tea and disposable cups was present. He even produced sugar free tea, sweetened with one of the Indian artificial sweeteners.

The train reached Howrah Station at 10 a.m. on Sunday morning. A delegation of friends welcomed me with heavy garlands of flowers. It had rained during the night making it pleasantly cool. The friends rushed me to Thoburn Church where the service was in progress. When Reverend Raj the pastor finished his sermon, my friend, Donald Kessop introduced me and I had to respond with a few words. Even though a number of visitors were present to greet me, the large sanctuary seemed empty.

After the benediction we gathered in the familiar fellowship hall for tea. The same familiar place, routine and faces were comforting. I reached the guest room of the Calcutta Girls' High School at noon and had lunch with Montu Rakhit, the principal, and Jo Wasal, a teacher of the school.

After a brief rest I walked to the Lee Memorial. It was closed for Puja holidays. A couple of the class four staff were there. One was the son of one who had been active during my time. From there I went on to Collins Institute which was also closed. I could see they had a new building and all the old buildings looked well maintained. I sauntered on down Lenin Sarani to Central Church and attended their service at 4 p.m. The district superintendent is also the full time pastor of the Church. After the Bengali service Montu and Jo along with the Janakdeo, driver during my time at CGHS, took me for a drive around the city. The highlight of the drive was seeing the new bridge over the Hooghly river which relieved much of the congestion on the old Howrah Bridge.

I was impressed with the improvement in traffic in Calcutta. They have introduced one way traffic on the main streets and restrictions on the slow moving vehicles. As a result the traffic moves. It was a contrast to standing still in the New Delhi traffic jams. The driver complained that he had to drive greater distances because of the one way streets. He did admit that traffic kept moving.

Kalyan Das, the former bursar of CGHS and his son Dr. Partha Das were waiting when we came back from the drive. While I visited with them Montu and Jo went out and bought Chinese food for our supper.

The next morning I attended the chapel service of the Senior school held in the sanctuary of Thoburn Church. Class XII girls led the service. The girls reminded me that they were the last class I had admitted before retiring. After singing a couple of hymns they requested me to speak. I spoke using the hymn, "Great is Thy Faithfulness" as my theme. I requested them to sing if for me. They sang like angels.

The enrolment of the main school which meets from 8 a. m. to 2 p.m. is 2,200. The maximum size of a class has been raised from 45 to 52. The second school, Indira Pathshala, meets from 3 to 7 p.m. Six hundred children and 50 adult women attend that School. It is primary and middle school classes for the children. For the women, literacy and sewing instruction is provided and occasionally parenting and health classes. Most of the women are young Muslim brides.

In God's planning He chose the best time for my visit. This morning the junior section celebrated "Children's Day." The Senior school will celebrate it tomorrow. The teachers performed for the students and the children love it. The Children's Day is an annual celebration of the birthday of the first Prime Minister Nehru. This year his birthday coincides with Diwali, the festival of lights and the most popular Hindu Festival.

Earlier in the year the students celebrated Teacher's Day when the students performed for the teachers. The teachers and students compete to see which group can give the best program. After the program tomorrow the school will close the rest of the week for the Diwali holiday.

Monday night I had dinner in the home of the vice principal of CGHS, Beulah Raju. While there the news came on the local BBC (British Broadcasting Corporation) TV station about the American

Airline crash in Queens, New York. The announcer said: "Just 14 minutes ago, the American Airlines crashed in Queens, New York and at least four buildings are burning." We watched the scenes of the smoke rising from the fires as it happened. That night, when it was morning in the US, I realized anew that the world has become one for those fortunate enough to own TV. The middle class in India own TVs and cars that they purchase on time payments. Some of the teachers now own their own cars. It is estimated that out of the one billion living in India, about 300 million belong to the middle class. That's more than the population of the United States. I do not forget that the percentage of those classed as poor is more than that of the middle class. But not all Indians are poor.

About 30 years ago I accepted the challenge of reaching the middle class for Christ through the Calcutta Girls' High School. The Anglican Priest, Subhir Biswas encouraged me by saying they can do more for the poor people than you can hope to do. He was right. The number embracing Christianity is very small. But I am very pleased with how the middle class Christians, Hindus and Muslims respond to the needs of their less fortunate neighbors. They give overwhelming support to the maintaining the second school in CGHS.

In 1999, THE TELEGRAPH, a large English newspaper gave the Indira Patshala, night school of Calcutta Girls' High School an award of excellence naming it "A School That Cares." In an article about the school they wrote: "Now Indira Pathshala is a household word in Dharamtolla (section ofCalcutta). After serving the locality for over 25 years, Indira Pathshalla has come of age and has now takes its place among all the Schools in Calcutta… Indira Pathshala richly deserved the public acclamation bestowed on them by winning the Telegraph Award for the "The School that Cares."

At 9 a.m the next day Mr. Das and I started on our journey to the villages, Mr. Das, retired bursar of CGHS, lives in North Calcutta with his wife and son's family. Mr. Das has bought a home in a village and spends some of his time there doing social work. During the day we visited three village projects south of Calcutta. The first was managed by a couple of pastors from the Church of North India. We had our morning tea break with them. From there we went on to the Wesley School and rural aid project. Kalyan manages this project. The number of students in the school has decreased. The government approved schools refuse to admit students from private unrecognized primary schools. This affects most of our village mission schools. Obtaining recognition is very difficult. At Wesley, Mr. Das has introduced other projects that attempt to help the villagers earn money. There are many Christians in this area. Calcutta Girls High School hired several unemployed youth from this area. It is in the area where I served a church as pastor just prior to my retirement.

Yesterday after everyone had left the children's day celebration Subhashish, from one of these villages, came to my room as I was getting ready to rest. My first reaction was that he wants something. He hastily told me that he did not want anything. With great pride he told me that he had finished his high school education, that he had bought a plot of land in his village and was making plans to build his own house. As he beamed I breathed a prayer of forgiveness for my silent reaction and thanked God for this success story. While we visited the Wesley project Subhashish and his wife prepared dinner for Mr. Das and me. After dinner he showed me the plot of land he had purchased.

From there we went on to Nihata where I once had dreams of building a village center. That dream failed. I had a visit with two of the teachers who were teaching during my tenure there. The property was very run down. At the last Conference session the Bishop appointed a young deaconess to live and work there. Later I met her at the deaconess conference in Asansol. She clung to me. She needed help. But I was helpless. On the other hand I had a good report of the Nihata Church which I had pastored.

As we drove on the village roads I saw a few bicycle rickshaws for passengers. The carts attached to the bicycles for transporting produce were more prominent. The hand pulled rickshaws have disappeared. The passengers prefer the motorized rickshaws and I saw many overcrowded ones motoring along the crowded village roads. As we sped along the new bypass to Calcutta the traffic moved in an orderly fashion with fairly good speed. I recalled the many hours spent in traffic jams in our old unairconditioned Ambassador car. Maybe I am biased but it seemed that there was far more discipline and order in the Calcutta traffic than in Delhi. A Delhi based friend agreed with me.

Late that evening Bishop and Mrs. Thomas arrived. Montu had some urgent family matters to attend to so she left the three of us to fend for ourselves. For our evening meal we decided to go to a Chinese restaurant. To get there we walked on the crowded lanes near the school. The lanes were very crowded with many pedestrians and a few of the old hand pulled rickshaws. These rickshaws are not allowed on the main streets. They seemed to have plenty of passengers in the narrow lanes.

Early the next morning we left for the Deaconess Conference at Ushagram, Asansol. Bishop and Mrs. Thomas, the Calcutta district superintend and I traveled in a fast train filled with comfortable seats. I sat next to Bishop Thomas and enjoyed my two hour conversation with him. Breakfast was included in the price of our ticket.

Evelyn and I were invited to be guests at that Assembly. I was very happy I could attend for two reasons: Ushagram is a part of the Bengal Conference of which I am a member. We were their only guests from outside India. In all their other Assemblies there have

417

been representatives from the Women's Division or Deaconess Associations. Again I marveled at the efficiency of Mrs. Helen Brown, the acting Executive Secretary, since the elected Executive Secretary, Kumudini Israel, died during the quadrennium. The success of our trip is due to Helen Brown. The well planned program for the Assembly was another evidence of her ability. Everyone participated. During the first day Bishop S. R. Thomas gave the keynote address. During two sessions the issues in the keynote address were discussed.

The theme of the Assembly was "Equipped for Excellence in Jesus Christ". Mrs. Juliet Thomas led the Bible study. She is an excellemt Indian woman preacher. Mr. Anand Pillai, a management expert, gave a condensed course in Christian management skills using the book of Nehmiah. He illustrated his lectures with computer generated slides. Six Naga young people were in charge of the music. The Nagas live in that remote area of India between Bangladesh and Myamar or Burma. Ninety five percent of their tribe are Christians. The tribe is very famous for their singing and it was a special treat to have the group present.

About 100 Deaconesses representing all the Regional Conferences attended. With great enthusiasm the delegates from Hyderabad and Madhya Pradesh Conferences reported on their visit with the Deaconesses in the Philippines. Several Bishops were present with their wives. Other than Bishop Thomas, who gave the keynote address, they took a back seat and applauded the maturity of the women.

One afternoon I visited Rev. Kamalekha Sarkar, pastor of Asansol Town Church. He grew up in the Nihata Methodist Church where I was pastor for a few years. I helped him enter the ministry. My visit with him and his family was a kairos moment. The Bishop confirmed that he is doing very well and the Asansol church, the largest one in the Bengal Conference.

After the Conference we had a wild midnight ride by car from Asansol to Calcutta. We had to flow with the traffic of thousands of heavily loaded India made lorries on the ancient Grand Trunk Road. They were only four-wheeled. We arrived at CGHS at about 2 a.m. Bishop and Mrs. Thomas caught an early flight back to Lucknow.

After a few hours of sleep and breakfast I started my day with Miss Reena Reed, Superintendent of the Lee Memorial Mission. I had not met Reena before. She grew up in Western India and graduated from Yeotmal Seminary. I attended chapel with her and met most of the staff. Several who were children during my first term are teachers there and I enjoyed visiting with them. Reena introduced me to staff and students speaking in Bengali which she learned after taking up the appointment at the Lee Memorial Mission. I had refreshments with the staff. During the refreshment Reena introduced me to about 40 girls who are supported with Lee Memorial funds received from abroad. Several are supported with funds from Germany.

Several Christian workers from North East India were in the guest house. The mission discontinued taking international guests several years before because of Government demands for detailed daily reports on guests from abroad.

Late that afternoon Evelyn and I took the plane to Delhi. Evelyn's former student, Ashrita Shalla, and her husband met us at the airport and took us to the YMCA International Guest House. We chose to stay there because it was near the Connaught Circle, a popular shopping area.

The next day Ashrita and her husband helped us with our shopping. The highlight was the hour we spent in the shop owned by them. The husband is a Kashmiri, a native of that territory which is a bone of contention between India and Pakistan. While we were celebrating in Kanpur he was in Kashmir. His shop was filled with the beautiful merchandise that he had brought back to sell to tourists like us. He gave us a discount so we bought plenty.

Our flight for USA left in the evening but we had to report four hours early. We had a wonderful Kashmiri meal with the Shallas and then departed for the airport. There we learned that the need for our early report time was because a large number of Indian passengers needed the help of airport and airline personnel in filling out the departure forms in the English language. The queues were long and moved slowly. The three planes on our return journey were full. After the long tiring trip we arrived at the Greenville/Spartanburg airport where the Lyons met us. We reached Asheville in the wee hours of Thanksgiving morning. I thanked God for providing every detail of the trip. A trip which was a fitting close to my Indian Jatra.

In putting all these experiences onto paper I have again soared to mountain tops in remembering how God led me step by step. The journey with God has been incredible thus far and continues to get better.

About the Author

Frances Major was born to Waymon P. and Etta F. Major of Route one, Piedmont S. C. She was the fourth child of eleven. Six of the eleven became full time Christian workers and the other five faithful lay witnesses.

Frances, who spent forty two years of Christian service in India, has a story to tell and here it is told very well indeed. She was a teacher, preacher, foster-mother of orphans, headmistress, evangelist, high school principal, founder of a night school, and treasurer of Methodist women's work in India. She cares for the whole person. She loves Calcutta while most visitors have seen only its sordid side.

Today she serves God in Asheville, N. C.

Printed in the United States
73571LV00009B/45